Realizing
Metaphors

PUBLICATIONS OF THE WISCONSIN

CENTER FOR PUSHKIN STUDIES

General Editors

David M. Bethea

Alexander A. Dolinin

Realizing Metaphors

Alexander Pushkin and the Life of the Poet

DAVID M. BETHEA

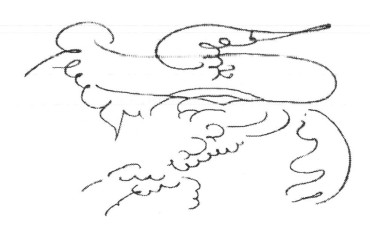

The University of
Wisconsin Press

THE UNIVERSITY OF WISCONSIN PRESS
2537 Daniels Street
Madison, Wisconsin 53718

3 Henrietta Street
London WC2E 8LU, England

1   3   5   4   2

Printed in the United States of America

All illustrations are courtesy of
the Russian Academy of Sciences,
Institute of Russian Literature (Pushkinskii Dom),
in St. Petersburg.

Library of Congress Cataloging-in-Publication Data
Bethea, David M., 1948–
Realizing metaphors: Alexander Pushkin and the life of the poet /
David M. Bethea.
262 pp.   cm.
Includes bibliographical references and index.
ISBN 0-299-15970-1 (cloth: alk. paper).
ISBN 0-299-15974-4 (pbk.: alk. paper)
1. Pushkin, Aleksandr Sergeevich, 1799–1837.   2. Poets,
Russian—19th century—Biography.   3. Derzhavin, Gavriil Romanovich,
1743–1816—Influence.   4. Metaphor.   I. Title.
PG3350.B45   1998
891.71′3—dc21
[B]   98-10320

For Kim, who knew better than the poet:

ut Hymettia sole

cera remollescit tractataque pollice multas

flectitur in facies ipsoque fit ultilis usu

CONTENTS

ILLUSTRATIONS

PREFACE

Psychologically speaking, we all live on the inhabitable parts of a land bordered by crueler climatic zones called the "literal" and the "figurative." Explain the tangle of emotion and thought that is the true "us" by reference to the one-to-one literality of system, whether it be linguistic, political, economic, social, biologic, or chemical/genetic, and something in us recoils from this landscape — barren, desertlike, exposed to the unforgiving sun of "cognition," always on the lookout for the next watering hole and slight bit of shade. Give in to the tangle and say that it is all words, and not merely words but words we freely manipulate and with whose help we refigure (one-to-another) the world and its constant reminders of loss and limitation, and the landscape becomes equally intolerable: some mountain aerie where all is secondary and tertiary abstraction, where the urge to stay clear of the fray has made one's ideas almost palpably unnecessary, and where finally there is insufficient oxygen to sustain the life of the mind. It is hard to say which of these extreme landscapes, dwelled in exclusively, is the more inhospitable to mental growth. One thing is clear, however: to speak about the "humanities" as being defined *primarily* by one or the other climatic zone, rather than by the ecosystem (what Yuri Lotman called the "semiosphere") that is their creative interplay, is a fundamental misstatement ("configuring") of the problem, with regard to not only how we write and think, but how we orient and comport ourselves in the world.

Once upon a time, *pace* Plato, poets were our most accurate explorers and mappers of this real-yet-imaginary land in between. They may still be for all we know, although who and what, properly speaking, qualify as "poet" and "poetry" in our rapidly evolving culture is contested territory. Whatever the case, the present study is entitled, not completely naively, *Realizing Metaphors,* and it is about the forward, as opposed to backward (read "Freudian"), movement of metaphorical thinking and metaphorically engaged biography. It is dedicated to a poet whose own quite specific definition of inspiration, composed for a culture that was still young, was suffused by the simultaneity of cognitive and sensory, systematic and unpredictable, historical and imaginary, figurative and literal. As I attempt to point out, Alexander Pushkin lived in and through his poetry in such a way that he "realized" — that is, he both grasped as ideas and experienced as feelings — the mythic images at the core of his oeuvre and at the pivotal junctures of his biography. At the same time, these preliminaries are a good place to remind the reader that Pushkin did not cut a broad swath in his use of figurative language: indeed, his poetry, so palpably "Gallo-Russian" in origin, is as elegant and restrained in its deployment of imagery as Shakespeare's is all colors of the palette. Hence it requires a leap of imaginative empathy on our part just to understand that this poet could be chided by a literal-minded critic for taking what in his context were liberties — say, calling a flock of noisy geese a "caravan" or describing a glass, rather than the champagne in the glass, as "fizzing." Such pedantic wrangling over the rules of poetic discourse may sound to us, caught in the strobe lights of late-twentieth-century culture, like much ado about nothing. But to Pushkin the risks, in all aspects of his life, were great. And so, to return to my central point, I know of no other figure in world literature with a comparably recorded biography in whom the creative tension, the ever-present dialogue, between literal and figurative is more robust and more alive than Pushkin. In this respect, writing about Pushkin has created its own problems, the "solutions" to which are as exhilarating as they are tentative and, yes, to a significant degree themselves metaphorical.

Which brings me to the shape of this study — its methodology, relation of parts to whole, mode of presentation. *Realizing Metaphors: Alexander Pushkin and the Life of the Poet* was originally conceived as a long "scholarly" article or short monograph on Pushkin's relations with the greatest Russian poet before him, the eighteenth-century statesman and "singer of Catherine" Gavrila Romanovich Derzhavin. Consequently, the initial title read, straightforwardly, "Pushkin, Derzhavin, and the Life of the Poet," and its wording represented in my mind something approaching equal billing or shared space. Whenever working with literary structures, and especially with the poetry of a figure as intensely organic as Pushkin, it has seemed to me wise to proceed inductively rather than deductively. However, while thinking through the problem of Derzhavin's "shade" and Pushkin's simultaneous attraction to and "swerving" from it, I became convinced that larger issues ("the life of the poet") and other methodologies (something between "psychology" and "philology") had to be engaged in order to get at this economy. This in turn pushed me to develop the first part, which is openly (but I hope not entirely uncheerfully) polemical, consciously essayistic, and committed to the, I suppose, rather quixotic attempt to realize in critical prose the very metaphors (mainly sculptural) that twirled at the center of the poet's personal mythology. And by "realize" I do not mean merely grasp or understand. Thus, to lay my methodological cards on the table, if the first part argues ("situates" amid/against Freud, Bloom, Jakobson, Lotman), the second demonstrates (already "assumes" in the context of the massive scholarly industry); if the first part deals with the poet's erotic economy (the "Pygmalion myth"), the second part focuses on his male friendships and rivalries (the "exegi monumentum" theme); if the first part attempts to vector in on, from various angles, the principles for understanding how art relates to life and vice versa for Pushkin, the second part proceeds chronologically through several "turning points" en route to demonstrating how, through his poetry, Pushkin actually "created" his life. In other words, what emerged from the first long article was a double-paneled artifact presumably unfit for any intellectual furniture store, antique or modern, Russian or western: part essay, part monograph, part dialogue between past and present, part genre experiment for a "whither the humanities?" cultural context at home, part homage to but also swerving from the noble tradition of Russian "philology," part advance publicity for Russia's greatest poet and cultural figure on the occasion of his two hundredth birthday (1999). Errors of fact, or in this case tact, are, as is meet to proclaim at this point, my own.

There have been, needless to say, countless attempts through the years to read Pushkin. Indeed, it is one of the chestnuts of the scholarly industry that everyone has his or her ("my") Pushkin. And yet, while the record shows many elegant and persuasive readings of individual works and of the relation of works to genre category within the larger oeuvre, some important aspects of the Pushkin phenomenon remain, it seems, undiscovered. Precisely how, for starters, the poet used the force field of limitation/freedom, not only in his art (its "genre consciousness") and not only in his life (its sense of "fatedness") but in their alchemical interaction, to create a biography is still very much an open issue. And one reason it has stayed open is that we have not had the proper language to penetrate it. This is of course true a fortiori for a western reading public that, to put it crudely, has habitually seen Russian literature commencing with Turgenev, Dostoevsky, and Tolstoi and can't quite understand all the fuss about the more linguistically specific phenomena of Pushkin and Gogol. Some of Russia's poets, Khodasevich and Akhmatova in the first instance, who were part-time Pushkinists, did have the language and proper angle of vision to begin to retrieve the alchemy for the noninitiated (and the initiated), but precisely because they were poets in their own right and had their own creative biographies to live, they did not not have the opportunity (or will) to finish in a systematic way what they started. The individual who has come closest to penetrating the Pushkin phenomenon in its overall "economy" is the great Lotman, who as the reader will sense in the narrative to follow is my own personal favorite: his many pathbreaking articles, exhaustively researched commentaries, and succinct but superbly reasoned biography are the standards by which any present student of the poet must judge his work. Yet even here I have, I trust not ungratefully, quibbles: Lotman's "enlightenment" orientation, his philological base, his as it were congenital unwillingness to engage the "murkier" aspects of the poet's psychological makeup on their own terms (e.g., his superstition and later in life his emerging religious sensibility), and his very structuralist/semiotic language (the "construction" of biography, the emphasis on "codes" and "grammars" of behavior, etc.) can only take us so far. It is, to be sure, very far indeed, and farther, thanks to the remarkable wealth of information and "scientific" insight, than any non-insider could hope to get. But it is still not far enough. To go that last distance for our space-time we will need to be willing to bend somewhat the rules of our "episteme," of our indwelling ways of knowing.

I have the greatest respect for the proud tradition of Pushkin studies that has come before me. It is on the knowledge base of those such as Boris Tomashevsky, Lydia Ginzburg, M. P. Alekseev, Lotman, Vadim Vatsuro, Sergei Fomichev, and in this country, my senior colleague J. Thomas Shaw, that I have built my own ideas. These individuals have, by and large, consistently operated under the principles of the "scholarly" and the "philological." To do so in Russia has not always been a simple task, but has involved sacrifice and integrity—the "deeds of honorable people" (*podvigi chestnykh liudei*), as Pushkin once characterized Karamzin's noble turn from celebrated man of letters to "monkish" historian. Those such as Lotman and Ginzburg may have had greater theoretical or conceptual concerns, those such as Alekseev and Vatsuro may have had (and still have in Vatsuro's case) more interest in textology (the tradition of "Pushkin House"), but they always constructed their arguments on the basis of what we might call Popperian "falsifiability." They also wrote in such a way that their findings always gave the appearance of being maximally "objective." For all the reasons we know, this scholarly/scientific episteme has come under scrutiny over the last generation in the western academy: facts, it is said or assumed, do not exist outside of narratives, and narratives tell many stories. What I have tried to do in *Realizing Metaphors,* though whether I have succeeded to any degree at all is not for me to say, is "open Pushkin up" to this much different episteme, for it does tell us something, without at the same time making him hopelessly postmodern (when he is premodern) and doing away with the principles of responsible demonstration/attribution thanks to which our ideas have a life (and possibly even an afterlife) in the scholarly community. In other words, I have, consciously and perhaps even a little provocatively, taken a position "in between." And to do this I have had to try out a language that my scholarly "fathers" (and "mothers") would, presumably, see no reason to use. When the (in this instance not so young) pretender enters the fray only to end by having his ashes shot from the Kremlin walls back in the direction of Poland, what could be the response of the good Pimen but "I told you so"? In any event, I have felt myself wrestling with my elders' and betters' (in some cases living) "shades" and with their *podvigi chestnykh liudei* just as my subject once wrestled, in a language that was different for his time-space, with the shade of Derzhavin, although there the parallel must end, since I am (to put it mildly) no Pushkin and our own time space (to put it equally mildly) is no early-nineteenth-century Russia.

By way of final prefatory comment, I'm pleased to say that the present volume has the privilege of inaugurating our series at the Wisconsin Center for Pushkin Studies on Pushkin and his evolving place in Russia and world culture. With the bicentennial and its great flurry of activity very much in the offing and with humanistic study in the west in need of more demanding versions of alterity, this could be an interesting time for dialogue. But precisely because the only way to catch and pin a Proteus is through a constant but purposeful movement in between, one cannot really belong to a school or come to rest within the hermetic *langue* of a single theoretical approach. As I try to show, not Freud (psychology as biology), not Bloom (poetic tradition as oedipal struggle), not Jakobson (the statue myth as structuralist binaries), not even Lotman (the code and its relation to literary biography) can provide a position of sufficient foothold and "torque." Why? Because each begins with something too narrowly stable, too systematic. To pin Proteus one needs what is left out of each of their plots and coming from multiple directions—something like the several tethers required to keep a large and powerful (and in our case semimythological) animal from overwhelming and dragging in the opposite direction the would-be tamer at the end of a single lead. Our students and future "poets," whoever they may be and whatever their "poetry" may look like, don't need to pull on this animal called "Pushkin," or "life," with single leads. Such comparisons are, of course, only metaphors, but that is, as I have tried to lay out in the pages to follow, the point.

ACKNOWLEDGMENTS

The present study was undertaken with sabbatical and research funds from the College of Letters and Science, the Graduate School, and the Vilas Trust at the University of Wisconsin–Madison. All of these bodies, which have enabled me to fulfill my various research plans over the years in more ways than I can tell, have my sincere thanks. *Realizing Metaphors* was also made possible with the generous help of a visiting fellowship at Gonville and Caius College, Cambridge, in 1994–95. It gives me particular pleasure to thank the master (then Peter Gray) and fellows of Caius for their support, goodwill, welcoming table, comfortable lodgings, and the loan of such a beautiful and historic setting at the initial stages of the project, when my mind so needed to "unplug" from pressing duties at my home institution and to roam about freely in other times and other places. Among the British colleagues who arranged talks and presentations and otherwise took me under their wing are Neil Cornwell (Bristol), A. G. Cross (Cambridge), J. A. E. Curtis (Oxford), Malcolm Jones (Nottingham), Arnold McMillin (London), and Valentina Polukhina (Keele). As the Russians say, "mir tesen," which translates into English as something close to "it's a small world": by the end of our stay in England we were feeling very much at home thanks largely to these and other new friends.

Either in part or in whole, this book has benefited immensely from challenging readings by various colleagues, many of whom are themselves distinguished Pushkinists and/or specialists in Russian literature (and in one case a practicing poet): Clare Cavanagh, Anna Lisa Crone, David Danaher, Sergei Davydov, Alexander Dolinin, Natasha Reed, Irina Reyfman, Gary Rosenshield, Stephanie Sandler, Olga Sedakova, J. Thomas Shaw, Yuri Shcheglov, William Mills Todd, Dan Ungurianu, and Michael Wachtel. Their corrections and suggestions have been quietly incorporated throughout the text; any inaccuracies still remaining are, either through stubbornness or some other more glaring weakness by now invisible to its bearer, entirely my own. Several graduate assistants, including Megan Dixon, Donald Loewen, and Clint Walker, have suffered my last-minute requests gallantly and have helped by taking an active part in the editing and proofing process—without them it is hard to imagine what state of chaotic unreadiness the manuscript would still be in. I would also like to take this opportunity to thank my good colleagues at "Pushkin House" (Pushkinskii dom) in St. Petersburg, especially Vadim Vatsuro, Sergei Fomichev, and Tatiana Krasnoborodko, as well as Vladimir Markovich (St. Petersburg University) and Galina Sergeeva ("Piligrim"), all of whom have aided me in different ways throughout the course of this project. And Allen Fitchen of the University of Wisconsin Press has been not only a source of wise counsel as acquiring editor, but more than that, a supportive and trusted friend.

Several sections of *Realizing Metaphors* have appeared, or are scheduled to appear, in modified form elsewhere: "Iurii Lotman v 1980-e gody: Kod i ego otnoshenie k literaturnoi biografii," *Novoe literaturnoe obozrenie* no. 19 (1996): 14–29 (also forthcoming as "Iurii Lotman in the 1980's: The Code and Its Relation to Literary Biography," in *Russian Literature in the 1980's,* ed. Arnold McMillin [London: Harwood Academic Publishers]); "Bakhtinian Prosaics versus Lotmanian 'Poetic Thinking,'" in forum on "prosaics," ed. Clare Cavanagh, *Slavic and East European Journal* 41.1 (1997): 1–15; "Where to Begin: Pushkin, Derzhavin, and the Poetic Use of Filiation," in *Re-Reading Russian Poetry,* ed. Stephanie Sandler (New Haven: Yale University Press, 1999); and "Why Pushkin?" in *Why Pushkin? Essays in Appreciation,* ed. A. D. P. Briggs (forthcoming under auspices of Pushkin Bicentennial Trust in Great Britain). I am grateful to Professor Briggs for the suggestion of the title "Why Pushkin?" which I have used as the heading for the first section in this book.

Last but not least, I'd like to acknowledge the real presence in these pages of my daughter Emily and, especially, my wife Kim, to whom the book is dedicated. Thanks to them metaphors and metamorphoses are, for me, not what life may be about, but what life, centrally, *is.*

A NOTE ON
TRANSLITERATION

In the text that follows, and in the expository sections of footnotes, I have endeavored to render Russian names accessible for the nonspecialist reader: thus, "Tsyavlovsky," "Yuri," "Tatiana," "Batyushkov," etc. Occasionally I have left intact a more accurate orthographic representation — "Pugachev" rather than "Pugachov," "Grinev" rather than "Grinyov" — because the cue to pronunciation would only cause confusion if the uninitiated reader were ever to look up additional information on that figure. Where I transliterate Russian, and where I provide bibliographical information in the footnotes, I employ the Library of Congress system without diacritical marks: thus, to use the same examples as above, "Tsiavlovskii," "Iurii," "Tat'iana," "Batiushkov." While this may result in some confusion for the nonspecialist audience, especially where both systems appear within one footnote, it is hoped that the added accuracy more than makes up for the, in this case unavoidable, inconsistency. Longer citations of primary text are given not in transliterated form but in Cyrillic.

ABBREVIATIONS

CPF   Alexander Pushkin, *The Complete Prose Fiction,* trans. and intro. Paul Debreczeny (Stanford: Stanford University Press, 1983)

Druz'ia   *Druz'ia Pushkina: Perepiska, vospominaniia, dnevniki,* ed. V. V. Kunina, 2 vols. (Moscow: Izd. Pravda, 1986)

"large 'Academy' "   A. S. Pushkin, *Polnoe sobranie sochinenii,* ed. V. D. Bonch-Bruevich, 17 vols. (Moscow: Akademiia Nauk SSSR, 1937–59)

Letters   *The Letters of Alexander Pushkin,* trans. and intro. J. Thomas Shaw (Madison: University of Wisconsin Press, 1967)

Pis'ma   A. S. Pushkin, *Pis'ma,* ed. B. L. Modzalevskii, 3 vols. (Moscow-Leningrad: Izd. Trudy Pushkinskogo Doma Akademii Nauk SSSR/Academia, 1926–35)

Pss   A. S. Pushkin, *Polnoe sobranie sochinenii,* ed. B. V. Tomashevskii, 10 vols. (Leningrad: Nauka, 1977–79)

Sll   A. S. Pushkin, *Stikhotvoreniia litseiskikh let, 1813–1817,* ed. V. E. Vatsuro (St. Petersburg: Nauka, 1994)

PART I

Realizing Metaphors,
Situating Pushkin

Metaphorical thought in Dante, as in all true poetry, is accomplished with the aid of a property of poetic material that I suggest we might call reversibility or recurrence. The development of a metaphor can be called development only in a provisional sense. And indeed, imagine an airplane that in full flight designs and launches another airplane (disregarding the technical impossibility of this). In just the same way, this flying machine, though absorbed in its own flight, nonetheless succeeds in assembling and launching a third. To make my comparison even more precise, let me add that the assembly and launching of these technically inconceivable new machines produced during flight is not an ancillary or secondary function of the flying machine, but is a most necessary appurtenance and part of the flight itself, and is no less a condition of its possibility than the manipulability of the steering unit or the unimpaired functioning of the motor.

  —Osip Mandelstam, *Conversation about Dante*

A survey taken in April [1997], National Poetry Month, by the Poets International Society, a publishing house specializing in poetry, has found that 97 percent of Americans can't name the poet laureate (Robert Pinsky). When asked to name contemporary poets, the average person could name between zero and one.

  — *Wisconsin State Journal*, 26 May 1997
(Pushkin's birthday [Old Style])

✄ Why Pushkin?

There are all the predictable ways our moment has at its disposal to gauge this leap—is it into the "text"? into "life"? into an "info-byte"?—but let us start with the obvious. Poetry as we know it is dying. Literally. Indeed, one doesn't have to be a Nietzsche to imagine a time when it will be dead.[1] Even with all the well-taken "yes, buts": not that there are not great poets still practicing their craft and not that there are not talented and sensitive critics and scholars still reading their works. Such caveats are, it seems to most of us, increasingly, and hopelessly, *academic*. For the fact remains that poetry, as mortal embrace of the immortal, as place where literal and figurative twirl around each other as equal partners in the dance of meaning, is no longer "real." Our intellectual life (unless one is Camille Paglia) is one of scare quotes, and poetry by its very nature is unafraid, unwilling to qualify the throb it feels at its source. To speak of something as "poetic" in a culture in which the average person can name between zero and one contemporary poet is to engage in a game from which the others have left. The dance is over. "Poetry places language in a state of emergence," as Bachelard once phrased it,[2] but apparently we are losing the tools for feeling that coming forth. Hence poetry is becoming unnecessary, a vestigial tail our eyes and ears, satisfied by other forms of im-

1. One of the most intelligent and enchantingly worded recent statements about the viability of poetry in the contemporary world is made by Olga Sedakova (herself an outstanding practicing poet), in an interview with the British Slavist Valentina Polukhina: "Chtoby rech' stala tvoei rech'iu," *Novoe literaturnoe obozrenie* no. 17 (1996): 318–54. Having recently been poet in residence at the University of Keele and having given talks/readings at a number of institutions throughout the U.K., Sedakova cites the Scottish poet Liz Lochhead's declaration of the "self-evident fact that our time has become estranged from poetry. It is apparent that the Death of Poetry is one of the cultural deaths, following Nietzsche's Death of God, that is forever being announced" (347). In the pages that follow, as I attempt to place "Pushkin" and Pushkin studies in the contemporary context, I will be carrying on a dialogue with Sedakova, who in my opinion is a remarkably eloquent—though not necessarily "heeded"—advocate for Russian "poetic culture."

2. Gaston Bachelard, *La Poétique de l'espace* (Paris: Presses Universitaires de France, 1957), 10.

mediacy, are all too willing to forget. "Is noneschatological poetry possible?" asks Milosz.[3] The answer is, at least for the vast majority of our society, no. We sense no end and no beginning, only the prosy, ad hoc middle. Yes, the corpse could revive; it's just difficult to imagine it given the current trajectory of our history. Mandelstamian flying machines need air upon which to perform their acrobatics; otherwise, they remain on the ground and become purely mechanical. The existence of a Seamus Heaney or a Robert Pinsky (or a Helen Vendler for that matter), the fact that beauty and intelligence can still be presented in a language we reflexively call "poetic," does not obviate the larger fact that history takes, and makes, its own. We are being swallowed by something, and that something is, to this particular reader of poetry, very real, very scary, and not easily namable. And a fact, as Bulgakov's murderously playful devil asserts, is the most stubborn thing in the world.

So this is where we have to start. To start anywhere else would be to hide behind a dying convention: scholarship with its scientific pretensions, criticism with its Arnoldian role of urbane post-horse, sweet appreciation with its homage to genius at a safe distance. We should refrain from taking too much pride, à la Rousseau, in the self-regarding "honesty" of our confession, beginning as we do within the bowels — dark and not particularly sweet-smelling — of our own purblind contingency. After all, how can one in good conscience initiate discussion of Russia's national poet and greatest gift to world culture with reference to the local — i.e., one's hometown newspaper? The answer is that all bets are off. One is willing (*I* am willing) now as never before to bare the device (of one's telling, of one's indwelling ways of knowing) because there is nothing to hide, neither "science" nor "poetry." Being wrong can shame the scientist, being inelegant or ridiculous can shame the aesthete, but what happens when all such categories become hopelessly attenuated and mutually contaminated? The king has lost his head, as Foucault would say, and yet we continue to hunt down, to *surveiller et punir* a headless torso (the "poetic" as

---

3. Czeslaw Milosz, *The Witness of Poetry* (Cambridge, Mass.: Harvard University Press, 1983), 37. Cf. Sedakova's remarks in the already cited interview: "Many speak — some with joy, others with anguish — about the end of Russian literature as a unique phenomenon. But the basis [for such comments] is the same: poetry cannot be joined with a well-to-do [*blagopoluchnaia*] and democratic life [the reference here is to the postglasnost era], and thus it is preferable [to live] without poets and without [concentration] camps. And the poets themselves, it seems, are not against this: Dmitry Prigov, for example, brought news of the end of Russian poetry to the Slavists of Belfast, as I was told by them there" ("Chtoby rech'," 336).

logocentrism), when what we should really be doing is taking a hard look, disciplining if you wish, our own words and our own selves.[4] We are witnessing what the philosophers of science call, rather grandly, a paradigm shift. Only this paradigm shift is apocalyptic in its very lack of high drama and right-angled pyrotechnics, in its tortured, tangled inwardness: anthropology, in Lévi-Strauss's prescient pun, as "entropology," as cultural inertia.[5] The whole world seems open, from Beowulf to bodypiercing, but that very openness and utter, what's new immediacy is an end to genuine dialogue. We feel as truly *insignificant* as any time in the history of the species—thank God? thank Satan?[6] —and this applies a fortiori to the things we "write" with the stylus of ASCII codes and the papyrus of gigabytes. The first person pronoun, once the mark of scholarly-critical bad faith, has become the site, simultaneously, of our greatest inauthenticity and greatest authenticity. Decentered indeed. Information flows over us in unprecedented tidal waves while knowledge recedes into

4. See, e.g., Mark Edmundson, *Literature against Philosophy, Plato to Derrida: A Defense of Poetry* (Cambridge: Cambridge University Press, 1995), 153–98.

5. The full citation from Lévi-Strauss reads: "Thus it is that civilization, taken as a whole, can be described as an extraordinarily complex mechanism, which we might be tempted to see as offering an opportunity for survival for the human world, if its functions were not to produce what physicists call entropy, that is inertia. Every verbal exchange, every line printed, establishes communication between people, thus creating an evenness of level, where before there was an information gap and consequently a greater degree of organization. Anthropology could with advantage be changed into 'entropology,' as the name of the discipline concerned with the study of the highest manifestations of this process of disintegration" (Claude Lévi-Strauss, *Tristes Tropiques,* trans. John and Doreen Weightman [1955; New York: Penguin, 1992], 413–14). Cf. Sedakova's insightful comments on how this notion of entropy/inertia might be framed in aesthetic terms: "I feel distinctly the inertness of this movement downwards, of this centuries-old vector of art—this 'gambling on lowering/deflation' [*spekuliatsiia na ponizhenie,* a pun on 'selling short']. It is likely that from the Renaissance on art has been concerned with broadening the sphere of the 'aesthetic,' in order to transfigure into a new—more complex, more heady—type of harmony that which, as was thought previously, does not yield itself to harmonization. And in that very movement there is a kind of truth, something akin to the conscientiousness of the artist before all that is unprepossessing and unloved: let us not bypass this with our attention either. But this path in one direction has become a vicious inertia" ("Chtoby rech'," 322).

6. One of the clearest signs that American society has entered the sort of eschatological mode one associates with the coming of a new millennium is its longing for a personified evil that has long since departed the scene. See Andrew Delbanco's persuasive and ethically challenging book *The Death of Satan: How Americans Have Lost the Sense of Evil* (New York: Farrar, Straus and Giroux, 1995).

the distance, a buoy bobbing, to no apparent purpose, on the high seas. The poetry that we love and that some have dedicated their adult lives to understanding and bringing to (cognitive if not emotional) life is dying a mythical — which for poetry is the only life there is — death. Even in Russia, that country most in need of its poets, the culture of Mandelstam, whose highest of high modernist verse mesmerized our generation with the deep breathing of its classical cadences and whose tragic, holy-foolish life seemed almost unbearably meaning-laden, can now, in the postglasnost era, be parodied in the darkly hilarious poetry of Moscow conceptualism.[7] If laughter liberates, is there a time at which it can ever imprison? What we took to be the language of gods was, alas, the same old language of man; what magically spoke to us can now *be spoken to*. Pushkin, meet your Jeffersonian homunculus.

Why Pushkin? In 1999, on the verge of a new millennium, Russians will celebrate the two hundredth anniversary of the birth of the poet who, in a sense that is not entirely metaphorical, gave them adult speech and taught them how to desire and dream in a world haunted by arbitrary rule, injustice, massive illiteracy among the general population, and the constant embarrassment of civic impotence. Pushkin gave to Russians an inner world almost as rich in promise as their outer world was rich in denial. (The wag might counter that Jefferson and Madison have given us, mutatis mutandis, an outer world

---

7. In the poetry, broadly defined, of Dmitry Prigov, Lev Rubinstein, and Timur Kibirov, and in the essays and criticism of Mikhail Epstein and Mikhail Aizenberg, Moscow conceptualism and "metarealism" (Epstein calls it "metaphysical realism," K. Kedrov "metaphorical realism") have in the 1980s and 1990s mounted a spirited assault on the "sacred" in Soviet art, in both its plastic and its verbal varieties. What this means in practical (authorial) terms is that the notion of heroic biography has been systematically undermined by placing formerly authoritative speech, including the language of the high modernist "lyrical I," in the mouths of humorously depersonalized types — the faceless "we" of Prigov's "militiaman" or "Reagan" (the Soviets' version of the "evil" American president). As Rubinstein says, "It seems to me that today we are experiencing the obvious deheroicization and eroding away [*razmyvanie*] of the avant-garde as a means of existing artistically [*khudozhestvovanie*] and of being [in the world]" (in *Lichnoe delo No __* [Moscow: v/o Soiuzteatr, 1991], 234). Aizenberg, who is perhaps conceptualism's principal spokesman now that Epstein has taken up residence in North America (Emory University), writes that "In conceptual art it is not the author who expresses himself in language, but the languages per se, always belonging to the other [*chuzhie*], that discourse among themselves" ("Vmesto predisloviia," in *Lichnoe delo No __* [Moscow: v/o Soiuzteatr, 1991], 6–7). The links between conceptualism as artistic practice and deconstruction as critical practice appear obvious.

almost as rich in promise as our inner world is rich in denial.) Almost, but
that is the point. Pushkin was keenly aware that he and his words existed in
the world, even as they constantly and everywhere *stood in relation to* an other
that hovered somewhere between heaven and earth (*mostly* earth) and that
spoke back. Like Shakespeare, Pushkin is beyond good and evil: he is the world
discovering itself, becoming self-aware, never feeling shame in his language
or in its right to fabricate.[8] His trajectory, carved out of a cruel epoch, is the
very opposite of solipsism and retreat to inwardness. His language is that force
which, like its owner, pokes about the world as though the latter is a hermaph-
rodite among naked women in a Turkish bathhouse (*Journey to Arzrum*): it is
not yet its job to feel uneasy, as Tolstoi's language would, at the sight of this
nakedness and strange otherness. First one has to find out what it is, then one
can worry about whether it is good or bad. In George Steiner's dichotomy
taken from Wittgenstein (a Tolstoyan), Shakespeare's "playful exhibitionism"
makes him a "creator of language/wordsmith" (*Sprachschöpfer*), while Tolstoi's insistence on being "true to life" makes him "one who knows ethically,
who object-knows" (*Dichter*).[9] But I would say to call Shakespeare (or Pushkin) "exhibitionist" is to pose the question in the wrong way, to place Milton
before Shakespeare (or Tolstoi before Pushkin), to see language discovering
itself and *preparing to become* thought, religion, ethics, self-conscious interiority as *already* shameful, when it hasn't yet had the luxury of its own fall.
"Plato was wrong when he banished the poets. Wittgenstein misreads Shakespeare. Surely, this must be so. And yet," concludes the brilliantly coy Steiner,

8. Two quotes here may give the reader a sense of Pushkin's clear-eyed good humor
and lack of sentimentality about the role of the "poetic" in his time and in his own life.
The first comes from his comments (c. 1826) made in the margins of an article his friend
Prince Vyazemsky was considering republishing, "Poetry is higher than morality, or at
least it is something else entirely. Good Lord! What does the poet have to do with virtue
or vice? Only their [i.e., virtue's or vice's] poetic side" (*Pss*, VII:380–81). And the second
is found in a letter to Elizaveta Khitrovo, one of the poet's more perceptive female corre-
spondents, written between early August and mid-October 1828: "Would you like me to
speak really frankly to you? Perhaps I am elegant and proper [*comme il faut*] in my writings, but I am an absolute vulgarian at heart and my inclinations are all of the third estate
[i.e., coarse]" (*Letters*, 358; *Pss*, X:196; original in French). In citing the Shaw translation
of Pushkin's letters in the pages to follow I have occasionally made stylistic adjustments
that, in my judgment, more accurately reflect the idiomatic nature of the original.

9. George Steiner, "A Reading against Shakespeare," *No Passion Spent: Essays 1978–
1995* (New Haven: Yale University Press, 1996), 116–21.

who just can't "leave alone" a world that is, for its brief moment, sufficient unto itself and makes no apologies for it.[10]

I believe that Pushkin speaks as powerfully to us today as he did to his contemporaries almost two centuries ago, and this despite the fate of poetry and the "poetic" in our obsessively demystifying world. By the end (1830s) Pushkin's world was also beginning (ours to be sure is much farther along) to outgrow poetry and to demand more prosy shades of relevance. I make this case because—and I know the arguments about bad faith and hypocrisy that can rain down on one's head in such instances—our world really is, it seems to me, approaching in its inner impoverishment and cant the legal and institutional wasteland that was in Pushkin's day (and in some ways still is) Russia. I believe as well that the task of *translatio* involved in rendering the Pushkin phenomenon in accessible language to an anglophone audience is not entirely quixotic. We do need rules for reading "Pushkin," but those rules are not based on science and can't be presented, at least not honestly, as "structure" or "grammar." Those words are, as Derrida will not let us forget, metaphors parading as system, and Pushkin lived in a world where the systematic (whether a rhyme scheme or a dueling code) was only a point of departure and was by definition arbitrary. First of all, it bears repeating that for Pushkin the literal (say, the poetic craft itself—making sonnets, constructing strophes, wielding a meter appropriate to the topic at hand, etc.) and the figurative (what the poet can and should say qua "poet," how a theme such as erotic love can and can't be "poeticized," etc.) are both *real* and (*pace* Derrida) *fully present* in his language.[11] When in his famous poem about the upas tree the word for the poison plant (*anchár*) and the word for concentrated human power on earth (*A tsár'*, "And the tsar") are symmetrically juxtaposed in the first and last stanzas, we are witness to a linguistic world in which evil is named *in its emergent form.*

10. "Reading," 128.

11. Pushkin and Shakespeare are very much alike as "creators of language," with this important exception: if Shakespeare is rich and exuberant (metaphor), Pushkin is elegant and understated (metonym). As Alexander Dolinin has recently suggested, Pushkin will learn much from the "anticlassical" formal structures and patterns of characterization in Shakespeare's plays, such as *Measure for Measure,* but the sheer metaphorical density of Shakespeare's language will (understandably) escape him: he will, by and large, project onto the Shakespearean dramatic forms his own (more classical, more understated, more metonymic) linguistic expectations. See Alexander Dolinin, "Pushkin and England," in *Alexander Pushkin: A Handbook,* ed. David M. Bethea and Alexander Dolinin (Madison: University of Wisconsin Press, forthcoming).

These are two terrifying sentinels staring each other down from atop their respective strophic hills. The link with the tsar is not, à la Freud and the entire blindness-and-insight school, the "real" or "deeper" meaning we are looking for.[12] Both meanings — nature/man, death that "happens" / death that "is caused" — must coexist; if anything, the *sound* of *anchar* is the first and crucial turn in this shamanistic dance. It is the poet's power (as opposed to the tsar's) to name in this, *deeply un-Freudian,* way, and we cannot say, mercifully, whether the words arrive at the nib of his quill consciously or unconsciously. He could just be, and probably was, doodling. Over and over again in Pushkin's work we are made aware of a poetic naming that is primary, laden with more meaning than we can ever understand,[13] and that projects a fullness of being in precise inverse proportion to the limitations and "fatedness" of its experiential counterpart.[14] In short, one cannot write as Pushkin wrote (and, as I will be suggesting, *live* as Pushkin lived) and believe that his words are fully reclaimable as a case of romantic ventriloquism and "exhibitionism." Something else is involved here. Thus it will be absolutely crucial to our placement that it be understood that Pushkin grew up in a world struggling to make sense of Napoleon and not yet aware of his poetic double, Byron. Yes, Pushkin would wrestle with the influence of Byron, but his linguistic consciousness would not be shaped by that influence.

For romanticism and its thrust toward interiority have had, with our western passion for self-making, an incalculable effect on how we read the world. Marx, Nietzsche, and Freud are all unthinkable on the near side of the romantic divide, before the exploration of human consciousness as potentially isolatable category (or space/site to be "excavated") took on a reality of its own.

---

12. See *Pss,* III:79–81, 441–42.

13. "In contrast to a likeness that we could look at from the outside, a symbol is the very movement of the primary meaning intentionally assimilating us to the symbolized, without our being able *to intellectually dominate* the likeness" (Paul Ricoeur, *Freud and Philosophy: An Essay on Interpretation,* trans. Denis Savage [New Haven: Yale University Press, 1970], 17; emphasis added).

14. "Too often it has been said that imagination is the power of forming images. This is not true if by images one means the representation of an absent or unreal thing, a process of rendering present — of presentifying — the thing over there, elsewhere, or nowhere. In no way does poetic imagination reduce itself to the power of forming a mental picture of the unreal; the imagery of sensory origin merely serves as a vehicle and as material for the verbal power whose true dimension is given to us by the oneiric and cosmic" (Ricoeur, *Freud and Philosophy,* 15).

Pushkin, while supremely sophisticated and always aware of what language promises and withholds, is decidedly "pre-" in this one important and heuristically uplifting regard: very little is actually *present* in this world and what is is unlikely to be directly cognizable. Arguments about language merely standing in for a presence that is never fully there are something our poet would have understood implicitly, but he would not have faulted language, especially poetic language, itself for it, would not have applied Derridean or Lacanian linguistic screens to the Freudian biological screen of suspicion (blindness reveals insight) lying underneath. For the mirror has its tain. What is present? Only two things. Death is present, but we don't call it Thanatos; rather we call it Captain Elagin being flayed alive, his corpulence being used for salve, by Pugachev's rebels.[15] Pushkin doesn't yet see the need to describe death as *metaphysical* abstraction, a relation to a relation, because it is too real in its own right to be absorbed in good faith into his personality, domesticated. Let it be what it is: random, often brutal, not a name but a thing. To a friend (Vyazemsky) who has lost yet another child, Pushkin retorts unsentimentally, "Fate won't cease playing games with you. Don't be angry with her, for she knoweth not what she doth. Imagine her as a huge monkey given complete freedom. Who will chain her up? Not you, not I, nobody. There's nothing to be done, just as there is nothing to be said." [16] Lear's fool could not have handled the tragic absurdity with greater deftness.

The other presence is that which is both most and least obvious: not sex per se (the mechanics), and certainly not Eros (the mythologized idea)—talk about presences that don't pay their way!—but precisely that something else our own ethically riveted historical moment is so angry with and ashamed of. If it must be named, then call it the potency (is this the same as "power"—not something necessarily realized but something existing *in potentia?*) one feels in and through the other as that other comes to life in one's hands. It is the future calling: the birth of nature, the birth of culture. No matter the rules, no matter the umpires, one knows one is in the game. But it is a stand-in-relation-to relation: having the other there as *coming-to-life* co-participant is absolutely essential. It is not about playing with oneself, it is not merely priapic. This, to name it in the specific case, is Pushkin's Pygmalion myth, which is bound to be as controversial in terms of current sexual politics (it implies difference or, if you wish, inequality) as it is crucial in terms of the poet's creative biography.

---

15. *The History of Pugachev* (Istoriia Pugacheva, 1834), *Pss*, VIII:123.
16. *Letters*, 309–10. The original is in *Pss*, X:160.

Today we might call it something banal and limply figurative like the life force or the pleasure principle (or if we are really in a demystifying mood, an erection), but my point here is that Pushkin could not imagine it as distinct from its mythopoetic armature, especially if the object of his passion, such as his Madonna-like wife, possessed a beauty equal to that of his art, but even more desirable, because not his. I will have more to say about this in due course, but for now let it simply be stated that no amount of "poetry" (gorgeous language as language) can stand in for the "natural rights" of this potency: "Aesthetics stop where sex begins," as Paglia archly informs us.[17] It may not be the only story, for there are many stories unfolding around Russia's Proteus, but in this story Pushkin was willing to break his Prospero's wand, cast his glittering gifts to the wind (metaphorically speaking), and leap back into the sea of life and, as he rightly divined, tragedy and death. This is what makes the "god" in Russia's first love human, why he can be loved.

Here Pushkin talks about that coming-to-life in a poem so private he chose not to publish it in his lifetime:

> O, how tormentingly through you am I [made] happy,
> When, bending to my insistent pleas,
> You give yourself to me sweetly, without rapture,
> Modestly cold, you barely respond
> To my ecstasy, you heed nothing,
> And then, more and more, you come to life,
> Until at last, against your will, you share my flame![18]

There are a multitude of ways one could "enter" this poem ("No, I do not prize stormy pleasure"), all drearily familiar to current critical practice: one could aestheticize the situation by describing it in structural terms—showing, for example, how the verbs in this stanza counterbalance the noun-laden impression of the first stanza (not cited), and how this picture (or nature morte) could be "semanticized" to reveal Pushkin's preference for the cool Madonna types (the *smirennitsa*, the "modest one") he can bring to life to the hot "bacchantes" (the *vakkhanka* of stanza 1) who from the start writhe in

17. Camille Paglia, *Sexual Personae: Art and Decadence from Nefertiti to Emily Dickinson* (New York: Vintage, 1991), 17.

18. *Pss*, III:356. The original reads: «О, как мучительно тобою счастлив я, / Когда, склоняяся на долгие моленья, / Ты предаешься мне нежна без упоенья, / Стыдливо-холодна, восторгу моему / Едва ответствуешь, не внемлешь ничему / И оживляешь-ся потом всё боле, боле — / И делишь наконец мой пламень поневоле!»

his embraces and hurry him to his climax; or one could smash this unbecoming mirror on the wall and, speaking to Pushkin rather than being spoken to, one could "discipline" him for stereotyping his females and not giving them equal billing in his power-play; or one could do something else altogether, such as commenting on the other discourses (social, political, economic, etc.) this discourse, in its erotic self-absorption, occludes. All are possible, but can we really *learn* any longer from them, particularly if we bear in mind that no prose discussion in English can rival in terms of sheer elegance, economy, and "moving statue" quality the original Russian?

The rules I would offer for bringing Pushkin back to life (*our* Pygmalion myth) are not "grammars," but "vectors" (direction plus force: let's not hide our metaphoricity, for in that image-making potential/potency is the only life the "humanities" will ever have). Next, let us understand as fully as possible the limitations, the "fatedness," with which this poet had to deal in his space-time.[19] This should not make us quietistic about our own (or others') problems, but truly agnostic, a word I prefer to the atheistically tinged "secular." For Pushkin himself was agnostic, in the sense that, exquisitely perched between paganism and Orthodoxy, violence and civilization, east and west, he would have loved to believe, but he felt too attached to this world, too fascinated by it, to come to rest in any stance other than the simultaneously exhilarating and wearying stand-in-relation-to. This is what he seems to be telling us, for example, in the late vignette "In vain do I flee to the heights of Zion."[20] Next, let us use, humbly and gratefully, the great monuments of Russian and Soviet Pushkin scholarship—the awesome accumulated knowledge of Annenkov, Bartenev, Gershenzon, Lerner, Shchegolev, Modzalevsky, Tsyavlovsky, Tomashevsky, Alekseev, Vatsuro, Lotman, and many others. If at times their methods of constructing meaning seem unduly hierarchical and severe, let us also understand how ideology and the darkest sorts of fable making have distorted much of their history and how the study of scientific

19. "And yet a renovating poet . . . cannot succeed merely by offering glamorous images and leaving it at that. It is the achievement of beauty within the context of authority and limit that matters, that prevents the spirit from being merely fascinated then let down on the one hand, or drawn to a sterile abstraction on the other"; and "the poets aspire to become, however temporarily, liberating gods, as Emerson called them, when they offer images of a world in which desire and limit need not be at perpetual strife, and when discipline may be a spur to creation, not merely its inhibitor" (Edmundson, *Literature against Philosophy*, 110).

20. *Pss*, III:335.

"fact" is not only a retreat to what is safe but also a defense of what is noble and untainted. As the world's greatest living expert on Russian poetry, Mikhail Gasparov, has argued, let us not ask the Pushkins questions they could not and would not have answered, calling it "dialogue."[21] For there is a kind of violence in our rhetoric: too often we are like the unchained monkey harassing poor Vyazemsky. Yes, what matters is what still speaks to us, but let us at least try to hear it with its initial stand-in-relation-to voice still intact. For in this Bakhtin was right, a fact that gives those of us who study "Pushkin" from the outside hope: only through the other, but *a genuinely constituted other*, can we come to know ourselves.

Which brings us back to Pushkin's poem about his wife and how we, in our space-time, can learn from it—learn in a way that has something to do not only with literary criticism but with "life." This is a poem that Pushkin never showed the world: it is not, for example, a case of kiss-and-tell, which the habitually prowling and territorial poet was entirely capable of, depending on his audience (male) and his genre (friendly letter).[22] But Pushkin was honest

21. See, e.g., "Filologiia kak nravstvennost'," in the forum "Filologiia: Problemy, metody, zadachi," *Literaturnoe obozrenie* no. 10 (1979): 26–27; and "Kritika kak samotsel'," *Novoe literaturnoe obozrenie* no. 6 (1993–94): 6–9. The latter has been translated as "Criticism as a Goal in Itself," in *Russian Studies in Literature* 31.4 (Fall 1995): 36–40. As Caryl Emerson encapsulates the Gasparov position in a recent article, "One of Gasparov's recurring targets has been the aggressive, self-assertive Baxtinian reader. Such readers, convinced that their opinions are valid (even indispensable) merely by virtue of being 'outside' another's in time and space, are always 'expropriating' or assimilating other people's words, thus pretending to show openness and respect for the other but in fact absorbing that other with unseemly speed into an ever inflating self. Such practice is sufficiently unwise in ordinary life, Gasparov intimates. But for the profession of philology— which above all must honor distance, recuperation of authorial context, and humility before the text—it is a disaster. . . . In Gasparov's opinion, these [Baxtinian] habits include a loose and undisciplined dialogism that often reduces to little more than the desire to make everything 'speak to me' on my present-day terms; a tendency to place exaggerated value on prosy paraphrase as 'internally persuasive discourse' (with its not-so-hidden assumption that my own awkward, groping words are always worth more than a text I might memorize or recite unaltered to someone else); the concomitant celebration of a code-free world; and thus the careless application of the word 'dialogue' to what should be the delicate tasks of scholarly reconstruction. Such practices, he insists, are narcissistic, solipsistic, and an insult to serious philology" ("Prosaics and the Problem of Form," *Slavic and East European Journal* 41.1 [Spring 1997]: 18–19).

22. It should be noted that "No, I do not prize stormy pleasure" (Net, ia ne dorozhu miatezhnym naslazhden'em) does not even exist in autograph copy. There has been

in the *ta mele* (poems to be sung/chanted) of the lyric format, and one cannot imagine him being more "open" (again, within the narrow walls of the highly conventional song) than in this confession. Here, one would like to think, he is not "constructing" himself before the eyes of the world. So we should respect this privacy, in the sense that knowing who one's addressee is always affects the meaning of one's words. Pushkin knew this, and we will not know him if we don't. Yet we can also study those words now: to the "Pushkin" who wrote them it no longer matters. And the poem *has* been found. To those of us who might tend to aestheticize/fetishize the art object and remove it from time as a verbal distillate of so-called male power and authority, and to those of us who might object that this very gesture is a denial of half the world's human potential, a making of a human being into a myth, I say let us understand the problem here in Pushkin's terms and then, and only then, make our conclusions. Let us use Pushkin and Shakespeare and Dostoevsky (especially Dostoevsky!) to "read" Freud and his creation of myths.[23] Only then, through

---

some confusion about the dating: when the poem was originally published, in 1858, its date of composition was given as 1830; however, to most later commentators that timing seems unlikely. In addition, on the now nonexistent autograph from which subsequent copies were made, the designation "19 January, S[t.] P[etersbur]g" was written in—a detail which could place the writing of the poem a month before the Pushkins' wedding on 18 February 1831, and thus make the description of its passion *imaginary.* This latter prospect—that the poet is writing in anticipation of his wedding night—of course further complicates the present discussion. In the copy of the poem that was retained among the papers of Pushkin's widow there stands the date "1831," which would rule in favor of the "19 January 1831" assumption. On the other hand, additional copies of the poem exist which bear the title "To My Wife" (K zhene) and have datings no earlier than 1832.

23. See, e.g., Harold Bloom, "Freud: A Shakespearean Reading," *The Western Canon: The Books and School of the Ages* (New York: Riverhead Books, 1994), 345–66, where Freud is discussed "as a writer, and psychoanalysis as literature," and where Bloom attempts to demonstrate that Freud's stubborn insistence on subscribing to the theory that the plays were penned by the Earl of Oxford was motivated primarily by his perhaps desperate desire "to read the great tragedies as autobiographical revelations" (348–49); and Harriet Murav, *Holy Foolishness: Dostoevsky's Novels and the Poetics of Cultural Critique* (Stanford: Stanford University Press, 1992), where various nineteenth-century trends in science (which anticipate Freud's own positivism) are shown to be encompassed by Dostoevsky's fictions (his notions of liminality and of revealing higher truths through "lower" forms of foolishness) rather than the other way around. It is interesting that Bloom himself, whose own chief precursor in *Anxiety of Influence* was undoubtedly Freud (poetic "copulation" = oedipal family romance), has taken in recent years to regretting the pervasiveness of the Freudian metaphors for the unconscious in contemporary critical thinking. As he writes in *Poetics of Influence* (ed. John Hollander [New York: Schwab, 1988], 207), "we walk about

this creative use of the other, can we begin to free ourselves from ourselves and, it follows naturally, use language in a way that is potentially agnostic.

But how, the impatient reader might ask, would this work in the present case? Well, first of all, through a creative leap backward, we would try to see Pushkin both as he was in the 1830s and as he became subsequently, in the myth of "Pushkin" as Russia's national poet, as Russia's Shakespeare. To do this one has to, as much as possible, *deromanticize* Pushkin, because it is this process of "stepping down," I would like to argue, that makes him most of all ours. Yes, we read him because he is a genius, and presumably we wouldn't be reading him at all if he hadn't been a writer, but it is his failure, or rather his pyrrhic victory, which I shall be addressing in a moment, that returns him to us. We must try then to be agnostic about the faith systems, including the notion that the poet "owns" his work (in what sense did the man Pushkin own this confession?) and that this is the source of his "power" (what power in this instance?), that have intervened since Pushkin's time. The nonmonumental, deromanticized Pushkin was, by the time he wrote this poem (let us be honest!), small, ugly, almost simian in appearance; from an old and noble blood line that had fallen on hard times and whose immediate scions (father, uncle) did some skillful dabbling in literature but were otherwise undistinguished; on cool and correct terms with parents who had not cared for him particularly as a child; politically unreliable and everywhere surrounded by the whiff of scandal; overwhelmed with debt and worried about how to raise a family and "keep up appearances" in the shadow of dunning creditors; proud of his work but rapidly becoming *démodé* as literary icon and representative of poetic culture (history marches on!); married to one of the most beautiful women in Russia, who was very young, who wanted (and deserved) a social life of her own, and on whom the tsar himself had his eye, etc. Now this man among men, gifted with words that seem in their glory to make time stop, chooses (after much inner perturbation) a woman who does not passionately love him — why should she, from her position? — but who agrees under the circumstances to marry him. Let us also repeat that, despite his "Don Juan" list, Pushkin is versts apart from Byron: he is not "beautiful" (metaphorically speaking, his clubfoot

---

now assuming we are uneasy triads of id, ego, and superego, and mingled drives of Eros and Thanatos. It takes an effort to remember that the Freudian agencies and drives are tropes, and not actual entities or real instances of human life. This is the tribute we pay to Freud, and I mean 'tribute' in more than one sense. We pay tribute to Freud involuntarily, as we do all powerful mythologies and idealisms that together constitute our historicized dungeon of facticity."

is his face); he must seek rather than be sought out; he must "plead" (*na dolgie molen'ia*) with his cool Madonna to love him back; his linguistic as well as his societal behavior cannot be, for all its literal and figurative show of long finger-nails, self-regarding—it must be *oriented toward the other*. And he knows it. That is why Pushkin is Russia's Shakespeare and not Russia's Byron: he gives his countrymen the linguistic birthright *to desire* (the seat of all poetry) in a manner that is more than pagan and less than strictly Judeo-Christian, and that is—the promised land for the educated Russian—fully *European*.

Thus, as the poet brings his Hermione to life, he also turns himself to stone—not the hardness of an erection, but the hardness, the sense of being immured, of death itself. This Desdemona, again absolutely innocent, will strangle her Othello. It is nobody's "fault"; it is a Greek tragedy, taking place somewhere in that space of the upas tree poem, between "it happens" and "it is caused."[24] That is what this poem tells us when we read it against the background of the last years and in conjunction with other works that form its shadow plot. Yet this is precisely not, as the Freudians will aver, the return of the repressed. Rather, as I would choose to reclaim it, Pushkin *knows* (nothing is hidden from him!) in his poetic bones that the statue is coming for him—that is the price of his gift (this airiness must have a weight) and that is the price of choosing over it (for the two can't peacefully coexist) a real-life beauty that cannot, and should not, be animated by it. This is not Oedipus being driven to a blindness that is insight, but something closer to the Sphinx of creativity itself. Not etiology and parapraxes replayed into cultural cure (the clank and grind of metallic-sounding abstraction rotating ever backward), but a deeply felt and *lived* shouldering of tensions—word-making, deed-making, honor-making, family-making, history-making, love-making: Ecce homo!—that pulls *our* plot into the future.[25] Both the literal (Russia's greatest poet, Russia's greatest beauty, Russia's tsar, the court and diplomatic intrigues that give a "fated" quality to the final months leading up to the duel, etc.) and the figurative (the Pygmalion myth) coexist and fight to the death (and life) of

24. For a balanced and insightful recent assessment of the myth and reality surrounding the role of Natalia Pushkina in the death of her husband, see Ia. L. Levkovich, "Zhena poeta," in *Legendy i mify o Pushkine*, ed. M. N. Virolainen (St. Petersburg: Akademicheskii proekt, 1994), 233–48.

25. "Dreams look backward, toward infancy, the past; the work of art goes ahead of the artist; it is a prospective symbol of his personal synthesis and of man's future, rather than a regressive symbol of his unresolved conflicts" (Ricoeur, *Freud and Philosophy*, 175 [see n. 13, above]).

each other. Pushkin wanted to be a poet and wanted to give his people this sense of language "in a state of emergence" that they needed to be self-aware. But he wanted even more, and for that he is "Pushkin." This, then, is one of the readings, but I believe it is a legitimate one, that I will attempt to demonstrate in the following pages.

There is no real creation of beauty without risk. Pushkin lived in a time that was rich in martial spirit and rife with the subjugation of indigenous others. He understood the full ambiguity of being both subjugator and subjugated, and his words, depending on addressee, reflect that ambiguity, constantly shimmering with what is *not* said. If he rattles his saber here, he often shows, even in the same work, how the saber can be turned on the warrior there.[26] He also, which will be another of our stories, chafes over time at being "just a poet," just a creator of words rather than a doer of deeds. In our era, one can hear fighter pilots tell stories about what it means to them to fly their planes near the speed of sound, in formation (the idea of *form*), their wingtips only a foot or two from their comrades'. No false moves allowed, everything depending on the skill, grace, and technical (*formal*) expertise of another to whom one has entrusted one's life (and vice versa). Hurtling pieces of metal and fire dancing tarantellas in the air. Anyone whose *first* reaction is to come at this martial ballet from the vantage of ethical categories *tout court* (these pilots are "children," they are simply "playing games," therefore they *should,* they *ought* to "grow up") is practicing a kind of demystification which, let us face it, has no *feeling* for poetic form. These planes are not words, but things involved in (yes) human interaction, and is it not appropriate to liken their acrobatic movements to strophes written (and then immediately erased) on the wind? Add to all this the moral ambiguity of war, a context in which risk is multiplied and socialized, and one begins to see where mythic time is born (never out of understatement) and why some pilots (those that survive, that is) feel they are living disembodied, ghostly lives once these wartime dances end. Shakespeare and Pushkin would have understood implicitly the ambiguity of flying these heartless machines, the beauty *and* the risk. We are fortunate to have Pushkin's definition of inspiration, which is also, as I imagine it, identical to Shakespeare's: "*Inspiration?* It is the disposition/orientation of the soul to the most vivid reception of impressions, and consequently, to the rapid grasp of ideas, which aids in the explanation of the former." [27] This is not ecstasy (*vos-*

---

26. See, e.g., his "Delibash," *Pss,* III:133.
27. *Pss,* VII:29.

torg in Russian), not losing oneself in feeling, but the absolute *simultaneity* of sentience and thought, with the sensory impressions coming in *from the outside* but being *grasped,* shaped, from within. Just as there is no creation of beauty without risk, there is no creation of beauty without form.

Natalia Nikolaevna Goncharova was not merely fetching but stunningly, *blindingly,* beautiful, endowed with a power that was given, not made/earned (the source of so much of our current ethical vs. aesthetic wrangling).[28] (See illustrations 2–4.) Being nearsighted, with a slight squint that gave her an otherwordly mien, she didn't fully comprehend this power, and thus it would be wrong of us from our space-time to barge into her story with words such as "manipulate" or "use." In this respect, one finds it particularly touching, and somehow also "fated," that this visionary beauty was herself vision-impaired. From all reports Natalie was mild of manner and sweet-tempered, graceful in her movements, not voluptuous but, with her long neck, almost swanlike — a societal version earlier in the century of one of those creatures out of Tchaikovsky, to be transmogrified through music and dance. Thus she herself was in no way "cruel," but the force field created by this moving, embodied form "caused" (again, the upas tree) a viciousness — toward the husband, toward the wife, toward what they represented — to come into being. Many of the myths about her projected by later poets, especially Tsvetaeva and Akhmatova, are embedded with a judgment (not entirely free of jealousy and envy) of this Helen of Troy beauty that "caused" the fall of Russia's greatest man of letters.[29] As Paglia says with her refreshingly brutal honesty, "Everywhere, the beautiful woman is scrutinized and harassed. She is the ultimate symbol of human desire. The feminine is that-which-is-sought; it recedes beyond our grasp."[30] Pushkin wanted to *serve* something commensurate with, even (or especially, in his mind) greater than, the gift that he had been given and

28. In Prince Vyazemsky's words, Natalia Pushkina was "amazingly, devastatingly, ravagingly attractive" (*udivitel'no, razrushitel'no, opustoshitel'no khorosha*), as cited in I. Obodovskaia and M. Dement'ev, *Natal'ia Nikolaevna Pushkina,* 2d ed. (Moscow: Sovetskaia Rossiia, 1987), 284; the authors in turn are quoting Vyazemsky's papers as found in the Arapova archive, which is held in IRLI (25559, CL, XXXIVb, 2, l.195).

29. Some of the "loaded" mythical categories (her beauty, her reputed roles as femme fatale, coquette, good mother, etc.) that have attached to Natalia Pushkina during the past two centuries are discussed perceptively and without parti pris in Stephanie Sandler, "Pushkin's Last Love: Natal'ya Nikolaevna in Russian Culture," in *Gender Restructuring in Russian Studies,* ed. Marianne Liljestrom, Eila Mantysaari, and Arja Rosenholm (Helsinki: Slavica Tamperensia, 1993), 209–20.

30. Paglia, *Sexual Personae,* 32 (see n. 17, above).

had nurtured.[31] There was nothing in his world more powerful and more up-lifting than this "mute" beauty that moved.[32] Natalia Nikolaevna was, for this particular moment in time, the living embodiment of the statuesque.[33] Unfair, wrong, benighted? It wouldn't have occurred to Pushkin to put it in those terms, to moralize about something this poetic, to attempt to cure such blindness with enlightenment. He wanted to be aligned with it, whatever the risk (which, to repeat, given his prior history of words and deeds, he knew). That is also why he is "Pushkin," a category equally aesthetic and ethical *at the same time*. Pushkin wrote in his "Madonna" poem about his fiancée, who he claimed in a contemporaneous letter to her was as like the Perugino pictorial representation as "two drops of water,"[34] "My desires have been fulfilled. The Maker / Has sent you down to me, you, my Madonna / The purest model of purest charm/delight [*Chisteishei prelesti chisteishii obrazets*]."[35] The mythi-

---

31. "In one of the early works of M. Bakhtin ['The Problem of Form' (1924)?] there is the idea that at the moment of aesthetic creation the author, as it were, pardons himself. From the outside, it would seem, that is indeed how one would describe it — 'he [pardons] himself.' But from within it is experienced as an action *not one's own*: the music, or the movement, or the line, or the verbal configuration [*slovesnyi riad*] with which you are occupied — this is what, it seems, pardons you, or allows you to feel that you, the concrete you, does not really matter that much and can't seriously hamper anything. I believe that such moments of 'self-pardoning' happen not merely in [the process of] artistic creation. [They can happen] in any distraction with something other than oneself, in marveling [over something], in being in love" (Sedakova, "Chtoby rech'," 334 [see n. 1, above]). Perhaps the most famous text in all Pushkin on the theme of "quixotically" serving a luminous beauty is the poem "There once lived on earth a poor knight" (Zhil na svete rytsar' bednyi) from the unfinished play *Scenes from Knightly Times* (Stseny iz rytsarskikh vremen, wr. 1835; title not Pushkin's).

32. It will be my argument, to be developed in later sections, that Pushkin was in fact trying to give his "statue" living speech: as the letters to his wife indicate, the poet was dissatisfied with mincing French as a proper form of domestic communication and had begun to write Natalie in a more robust and earthy Russian. Thus it could even be said that he was, in a way that today we might still think "patronizing," teaching her something that would be ultimately useful for her in the "real" world.

33. Pushkin of course was not the only one of his time to see his wife's extraordinary beauty in these terms. Prince V. F. Odoevsky, for example, compared her to the statue of Euterpe in the Louvre (in *Russkii arkhiv* 1 [1878]: 442; cited P. E. Shchegolev, *Duel' i smert' Pushkina*, 2 vols. [Moscow: Kniga, 1987], 1:75).

34. *Letters*, 423; *Pss*, X:234. The letter (in French) was dated 30 July 1830.

35. *Pss*, III:166. The original Russian reads: «Исполнились мои желания. Творец / Тебя мне ниспослал, тебя, моя Мадонна, / Чистейшей прелести чистейший образец.»

Figure 1. Alexander Pushkin. Watercolor by P. F. Sokolov, 1830s.

Figure 2. Natalia Nikolaevna Goncharova-Pushkina (1812–63), who became Pushkin's wife on 18 February 1831. Watercolor by A. P. Briullov, 1831–32.

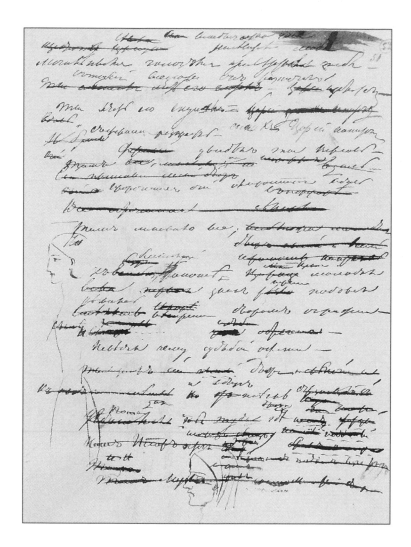

Figure 3. Page with the rough draft of the poem "To a Grandee" (K vel'mozhe), written on 23 April 1830, from the third Kishinev notebook. The poem details the life of Nikolai Borisovich Yusupov (1751–1831), a member of the court during Catherine the Great's rule. The figure to the left is Natalia Goncharova, to whom Pushkin was in the process of proposing that spring. In the poem he writes, "With rapture you appraise / Alyabeva's resplendence and Goncharova's charm."

Figure 4. Page on which Pushkin began *The Bronze Horseman* (Mednyi vsadnik) in October of 1833. Both the sketches on the upper left and on the right (in the shaded area) are considered to be Pushkin's wife, Natalia Nikolaevna.

Figure 5. Pushkin's self-caricature of 1835 or 1836 with his head enshrouded in laurels and the inscription "il gran' Padre AP." In another sketch of himself as "laureate" the poet blots out his own likeness in a gesture of self-renunciation.

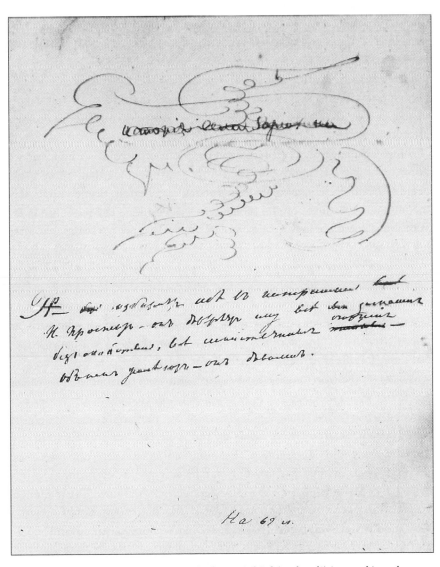

Figure 6. Pushkin's illustration of a fantastic bird (cockerel?) inserted into the manuscript of *The History of the Village Goriukhino* (Istoriia sela Goriukhino).

cal requires the already shaped other: a view (not a harsh pornographic gaze) that simultaneously looks backward (Perugino) and forward (Natalie). And metaphor becomes myth (not de Manian allegory) when the story first starts to *read us,* when it acquires its own futurity, when Natalie becomes (for Push- kin one has to assume the association was made instantaneously) enough like Perugino's Madonna (*comme deux gouttes d'eau*) that her story will shape, *no matter what,* Pushkin's. Though herself in the world and without doubt a creature of contemporary social habits (including a certain amount of seemly "flirting"), Natalie was, in the mind and heart of her husband—who for all we know was right—as innocent of the rumored wrongdoing that "caused" his death (a death *not in quotes*) as Perugino's Virgin herself. If one visits today the museum-apartment on the Moika that was Pushkin's last residence in St. Petersburg, the place to which his mortally wounded body was brought after his duel with d'Anthès, one can be told by the staff of how this distraught woman, upon learning that her husband had finally died, went into a kind of convulsive trance in which her swanlike beauty twisted itself on the floor like a ball of roiling snakes. Legend or fact? If true, had this poor woman, Russia's Leda, at last, as another poet might have said, "put on his knowledge with his power" once fate's "indifferent beak [had] let her drop"? We'll never know, but surely it is the stuff that new myths are made of.

Whatever the case, one hears in our present time of troubles new voices emerging, which is finally the only thing that will change for the better our growing sense of irrelevance as teachers of the humanities and apologists for a "poetry" that no longer needs us and is clearly deaf and dumb to our finger-wagging and "disciplining." Pushkin and Shakespeare don't need us; we need them. Camille Paglia will never be accepted as parishioner in our cathedral of learning because she is too iconoclastic, too unwilling to attenu- ate, too—if you will—mythopoetic. She is also funny, entertaining, and a very good writer. And still it moves, insists this vampy postmodern Galileo, and the church fathers (and mothers) look down on the apostate (like the angry popes in the cornices of the great Sienese duomo) and dourly insist that it doesn't. Paglia's celebration of "elegant," "eye-intense" pagan (espe- cially Egyptian) culture at the expense of "word-worshipful" Judeo-Christian culture is certainly welcome in the current atmosphere. But she too, in my opinion, gets certain important things wrong. Her bold essentialism makes nature (and nature's extension, the "female") that "chthonian" mythical other against which the "sky-cult" of Apollo (and the "male") creates its words and worlds. Nature, however, is not "ugly and violent"[36] — those are *our* terms, taken from *human* consciousness, itself hopelessly androgynous. Nature, as Kant first told us, cannot be directly cognized; it is still only *words*. Despite what the Sierra Clubbers might want to think, "wilderness" does not exist outside our conceiving of it: it too is a human construct. Thus we would do well to try to imagine a nature that is both "real" (as much "itself" as it can be) and inhabited by human beings. Neither sex, in principle, should be at a disadvantage, because all we will ever have, in our own terms, of the world "out there" is already, through *the potentiality* of words, "in here." Metaphor and metaphysics, with their similar etymologies but necessary differences, are the sum total of what is given us to lift a world that is not red in tooth and claw, but simply _____ (you fill in the blank).

Still, I would not like to make this postmodern, but to try to take it beyond, since that is where we are going whether we like it or not. Metaphor and metaphysics *are,* if not the equivalent of natural childbirth, the sperm and the egg of our always halting, always partial, always momentary pull out of the muck. And here is where Paglia, who likes cats and elegance and does not seem particularly long in "maternal" qualities, is wrong to feel pity for the always potentially ridiculous Apollos who are just trying to get back what they lost when they exited the birth canal.[37] The birth of a real idea (or a real poem) is not as simple, straightforward, and psychically "hygienic" as one might think. It *is* labor, and there are times when one senses a kind of painful dilation at work: it is bigger than you are, it is trying to get out, it hurts, it takes over everything (including the body), and *it will have its way.* (By the same token, any woman who has ever experienced natural childbirth will tell you that it is not only about the body.) One feels protective of it when it is finally out and one does not want to let it go into the harsh world until it can make it on its

36. Paglia, *Sexual Personae,* 35.

37. "Every man harbors an inner female territory ruled by his mother, from whom he can never entirely break free" (*Sexual Personae,* 18); "Men are in a constant state of sexual anxiety, living on the pins and needles of their hormones. In sex as in life they are driven *beyond* — beyond the self, beyond the body. Even in the womb this rule applies. Every fetus becomes female unless it is steeped in male hormone, produced by a signal from the testes. Before birth, therefore, a male is already beyond the female. But to be beyond is to be exiled from the center of life. Men know they are sexual exiles. They wander the earth seeking satisfaction, craving and despising, never content. There is nothing in that anguished motion for women to envy" (19); "Nature has blessed him [man/men] with obliviousness to his own absurdity" (20), etc.

own. Are these just metaphors, empty words? I think not. Who can say what is greater, the creation of words or the creation of bodies? And who can say any longer where one creation ends and the other begins?[38] That's why we need Pushkin, because he can pose the questions in the right way.

38. Building on the research of distinguished developmental psychologists (L. S. Vy-gostsky, Jean Piaget) and physiologists (A. A. Ukhtomsky), a Moscow University-based group of Russian psychologists have recently done some fascinating work on the psychology of creativity and the importance of metaphorical thinking in any notion of evolutionary development. Among the leading figures in this group are V. P. Zinchenko and A. A. Puzyrei. For Zinchenko, Mandelstam is a revealing exemplar. As Zinchenko remarks apropos *Conversation about Dante:* "Mandelstam writes that, in the thirteenth century, the Gothic cathedral was the logical development of the concept of the body. Hence one spoke about it in terms of man's 'second nature,' an organ projection, etc. Essentially these terms imply the reversibility of the external and the internal, the corporeal and the spiritual. The spiritual has 'extension, volume, receding into distant depths and latitudes.' It is the collective 'body,' as it were, of history and man, providing us with a specific environment composed of the utensils and instruments of the soul and serving as an anthropogenic space, an entire sphere. It is the environment of effort. 'To create something, anything, and that includes in the sphere of the spirit, work is necessary, but work is performed by muscles. Perhaps it would be fitting to speak of the muscles of the soul, the mind, of civic spirit, of historicity, etc. Hence, in human and historical reality, the external is also the internal, and the internal is the external'" ("Problems in the Psychology of Development," *Russian Social Science Review* 35.2 [March–April 1994]: 48–69; this passage is from p. 58). At the end of this programmatic article, after making the points that "human nature and poetry are similar . . . in Mandel'shtam" (62) and that (here *Conversation* is cited again directly) "poetic material does not have a voice" but "exists only in its execution" (63), Zinchenko notes that Ukhtomsky used Mandelstam's (*metaphorical!*) notion of "functional organ" in his own work as physiologist and psychologist: "these extracerebral functional organs [cf. *Conversation,* where the poet states that 'representations may be regarded not only as objective givens of consciousness but also as a person's organs, just like the liver or the heart'] are just as real as anatomical-morphological organs" (68). I will be returning to what Zinchenko calls the "wondrous intertwin[ing]" of "myth, metaphor, and scientific reasoning" (64) in the pages to follow.

Here I should also note the obvious links between Zinchenko's and Puzyrei's works and those of contemporary cognitive linguists and Peircean semioticians in the west, who are apt to foreground how linguistic structures are themselves enveloped by, and reflective of, larger cognitive models, which have their origins in actual bodily experience. As Mark Johnson writes, "[S]o-called linguistic meaning is treated as a specific case of meaning in a broader sense, namely, meaning as involving our grasp of structures that give definiteness, coherence, order, and connectedness in our experience of anything" (*The Body in the Mind* [Chicago: University of Chicago Press, 1987], 37; see also George Lakoff and Mark Johnson, *Metaphors We Live By* [Chicago: University of Chicago Press,

"Word-worship," writes Paglia, "has made it difficult for scholarship to deal with the radical cultural change of our era of mass media." And "behind every book is a certain person with a certain history. I can never know too much about that person and that history. Personality is western reality. It is a visible condensation of sex and psyche outside the realm of the word."[39] Here I would say the critic's "vector" is a healthy corrective and almost right, but precisely where it is wrong, where it moves backward instead of forward, is in its notion (myth?) that there is a "visible condensation of sex and psyche *outside* the realm of the word." To believe that really is to chase phantoms. Image and word for the great mind—and who wants to spend time with anything less?—cannot be separated out, for that is the seat of "charisma," inspiration: the simultaneous processing of vivid impressions and of the equally vivid ideas produced by those impressions. *Personality* is crucial and, yes, we need to learn as much about it as possible in its concrete hypostases—we need to continue our *service* as students and eager gatherers of facts. At the same time we need to accept that there is no charisma outside the word if we are dealing with matters cultural. This can be, if looked at in a certain way, tremendously liberating. It is not Pushkin the romantic genius or Natalia Nikolaevna the ultimate ice goddess we idolize, making them and their story into modern primal scenes of the golden calf. It is the energy, correctly aligned, that belongs to no one (al-

---

1980]). Likewise, the Peircean triad of symbol-index-icon, where every symbol (say, an individual word or phrase) elicits any number of indices (the tension between "literal" and "figurative"), which in turn elicit any number of icons (the possible visual representations/images of the symbol), is itself very much grounded in body-mind *interaction* rather than traditional opposition. Michael Haley, for example, in *The Semeiosis of Poetic Metaphor* (Bloomington: Indiana University Press, 1988), has extended the Peircean model in order to investigate the role of "icon" and "index" in the workings of poetic tropes. While I find the ideas of such cognitive linguists and Peircean semioticians in many ways congenial with, and complementary to, my own, my interest is more in the *simultaneity* of the idea and the emotion (i.e., poetic "inspiration"). What this latter means, however paradoxical or quixotic it may sound, is that one's language must attempt to "feel" what it is at the same time "cognizing" in order to get at the core of metaphorical thinking. My thanks to cognitive linguist and semiotician David Danaher for providing me with much of the information in this paragraph.

39. *Sexual Personae*, 34. Cf. Edmundson, *Literature against Philosophy*, 104 (see n. 4, above): "The quality Paglia tries to locate is akin to what Benjamin, a critic with more palpable religious longings, called the aura. Paglia simply refers to it as charisma, the glow that emanates from a narcissistic personality, or, presumably, from a work of art that exudes a beauty, poise, and self-possession that seem more than human."

though we give it the name of "Pushkin"), because it is still "out there," which is to say, "in here," animating us still. We have to be able to look at Pushkin the way Mandelstam, a no less fabulous *Sprachschöpfer* in his time-place, would have: Pushkin has not yet been born.[40] Metaphors become ugly and myths become fascist only when they are used, in the world, to read *others'* stories.

But we must also be honest with ourselves: most of us are not primary creators; that is our "fate." Primary creation such as Pushkin and Shakespeare were responsible for took place in a world of primary colors. Even the primary creators we do have, such as Thomas Pynchon and Cormac McCarthy, who may be, for all we know, as talented as Joyce and Faulkner, write in a way that announces unmistakably how much the world has changed, what is and is not tellable, in the space of a few short generations.[41] This is the law of compensation that Emerson enjoined us not to neglect lest our *demos* become something other than self-reliant.[42] Or, to cite the same Mandelstam whose

40. Here again I can rely on Sedakova, another poet in the Pushkin-Mandelstam tradition: "After all, tradition exists solely in order not to stop being born: to extend itself, to save itself—that is not its concern. Goethe's *stirb und werde* is one of the best formulations of the traditional. But there is another [such formulation] of which the antitraditionalists are probably not aware: the love for that *out of which* all of this was arising before it became something that has arisen [*prezhde chem sdelalos' stavshim*]—the love for the heart of this uninterrupted interruptedness [*nepreryvnaia preryvnost'*]: *stirb und werde*" (Sedakova, "Chtoby rech'," 325).

41. In Pynchon's fifth and most recent novel *Mason & Dixon* (1997), for example, the character Cherrycoke is a comic voice for the eighteenth-century point of view that feared for the mystery and magic seeping out of the ever more enlightened and mechanistically explainable world. This is a position, in his time (quite close to the imaginary Cherrycoke's), that Pushkin would have understood implicitly. Cherrycoke presents Europe's dream of an unmapped America—a dream that is "safe [only] till the next Territory to the West be seen and recorded, measur'd and tied in, back into the Net-Work of Points already known, that slowly triangulates its Way into the Continent, changing all from subjunctive to declarative, reducing Possibilities to Simplicities that serve the ends of Governments,—winning away from the realm of the Sacred, its Borderlands one by one, and assuming them unto the bare mortal World that is our home, and our Despair"—in terms that are strikingly saturated with present-day anxieties. This "settling of America," as Louis Menand has written in a review of *Mason & Dixon*, "is an allegory [typical of Pynchon] for the way getting people to think alike depletes the world" (Louis Menand, "Entropology," *New York Review of Books* 44.10 [12 June 1997]: 25).

42. See Edmundson, *Literature against Philosophy*, 67–113, esp. 95–96: "Criticism, as Emerson indicated, must be cheerfully willing to conceive the total disappearance of literature"; and "The standard [for reading and understanding literature] I want to offer is

epigrammatic force is all the more necessary to us for its coming from the outside: "The theory of progress in literature is the crudest and most repulsive form of schoolboy ignorance. Literary forms change, some yielding their place to others. But each shifting of the guard [*smena*], each such acquisition, is accompanied by loss, waste." [43] It is in this respect, that work in and around literature and culture cannot honestly internalize the notion, the framework, of *scientific* progress, that we ought to begin the arduous mind- and soul-searching task of addressing how much "Freud" is in us. As Mark Edmundson, in my view absolutely correctly, writes,

> For Freudian thinking does more to change the interpretive game than any other single development [in contemporary thought and criticism]. Deploying Freud, and particularly his theory of the unconscious, one is in a position to say things about literary works that their authors could not have said. With a stroke, the standing relations between poet and critic can be reversed. The professor no longer has to accept the role of explicator, editor, or votary. Rather she can stand as an authority, take up the role of physician to patient, finding motives for the creation-symptom that were beyond the ken of the pre-Freudian cultural world. [44]

But while all this is certainly true, I would go even farther. I would say that Freud has stolen our metaphors: he is, for the world of secondary creation, our Underground Man and our Grand Inquisitor. He clearly got a great deal right, but he *named* more than he should—he closed the circuit. He brought us "miracles" of interpretation and the "bread" of a so-called healing science, but he took away our freedom (always relative), our sense of the future (always partially occluded). His "vectors" were wrong. For the creative friction (and fiction) that pulls us up (not down), struggling and never quite in focus, through our metaphorical birth canals and into the future no human being can finally name, much less capture "scientifically." And this sort of friction—which cannot be reduced to sex, just as sex cannot be put in words—is the very epitome of psychic health and has nothing to do, in terms of its movement, with the past and "etiology." So I would suggest we begin to use our secondary

---

pragmatic and indebted to the Emerson of 'Compensation,' who knew that every gain is likely to entail some loss."

43. Osip Mandelstam [Mandel'shtam], *Sobranie sochinenii*, ed. Gleb Struve and Boris Filipoff, 3 vols. (Washington: Inter-language Literary Associates, 1964–69), II:243.

44. *Literature against Philosophy*, 22.

powers of creation, responsibly and with an appropriate sense of how "fated" is every "now" and every "then," to take back some of the ground, or rather force field of words, from the doctor.[45] To realize our metaphors against his science (even if he is, as it can be argued that the Grand Inquisitor was, right). To understand that being plot-starved for the primary colors is not necessarily a function of life "out there" (the *poète maudit,* for starters) or words "in here" (the actual poetry we love but whose life in and as genre we sense slowly atrophying). To be sure, experience *is* necessary, knowledge *can* be felt. Having said that though, there is nothing sexier, nothing less secondary, than an idea that truly lives; if we keep that out in front of us, the anxiety of genre, of high versus pop culture, will take care of itself. We live in a post-Einsteinian universe: the king has lost his head. Everything moves, but that is still not the same thing as saying everything is relative.

It is, therefore, in the spirit of Paglia — though my notion of truth must be, alas, more attenuated than hers — that I begin the present essay. Using "literature against philosophy," as Edmundson has recently done in his wise and creative book, is our best hope for a way out of the impasse in which we currently find ourselves. Rather than Freudian "descendentalism,"[46] rather than returning with new-critical nostalgia to the exclusively indwelling integrity of a poem, rather than pretending that what we do is pure scholarship/science (for is it not true that real system admits *no* deviation and anything else *is*

45. Cf. Edmundson, *Literature against Philosophy,* 195: "Criticism now often assumes that the correct procedure exclusively entails the application of various vocabularies, often social-scientific in provenance, to the works at hand. Whereas the objective ought also to involve discovering the resistances that literature offers to being encompassed by this or that generalizing terminology."

46. This is Edmundson's useful metaphor for the false bottom/transcendentalism-in-reverse at the heart of much contemporary criticism. See *Literature against Philosophy,* 22: "His [Plato's] attempt to usurp the poets occurs in broad daylight. But the critic with Freud in her arsenal can take a detour around the dialectic, and speak authoritatively about repressed context, interpreting the literary text as a dream text. She can defend herself and her readers against its power to produce fresh meanings and complicate experience by proffering fairly certain knowledge about its origins in a well-comprehended past. "This book [*Literature against Philosophy*] will argue that the theory of the unconscious, on which so much contemporary criticism bases its authority, ought to be harshly interrogated before being applied to literary texts. The theory provides access to ultimate truths. It enjoins a sort of descendentalism — not a surge to a region on high, but a quick transport to subterranean bedrock — which should be suspect for a mind bent on staying secular."

interpretation?), and rather than "disciplining" the poets of the past for their purblindness — rather than any of these "post-'s" — let us go one better and reclaim our forever sacred-cum-demystified texts as "agnostics with vectors (*not* blinders)." *Pace* Harold Bloom, the greatest poets steal "left and right" (as Akhmatova once said) and don't give it a second thought. And as Paul Ricoeur, a philosopher who was not trying to ban the poets from his republic, wrote a generation ago, in a context already sensing the street signs and stoplights of a world increasingly traveled along Freudian inroads,

> The situation in which language today finds itself comprises this double possibility, this double solicitation and urgency: on the one hand, purify discourse of its excrescences, liquidate the idols, go from drunkenness to sobriety, realize the state of poverty once and for all; on the other hand, use the most " nihilistic," destructive, iconoclastic movement so as to *let speak* what once, what each time, was *said,* when meaning appeared anew, when meaning was as its fullest. Hermeneutics seems to me to be animated by this double motivation: willingness to suspect, willingness to listen; vow of rigor, vow of obedience. In our time we have not finished doing away with *idols* and we have barely begun to listen to *symbols.* It may be that this situation, in its apparent distress, is instructive: it may be that extreme iconoclasm belongs to the restoration of meaning.[47]

A good place to start then, an even better place to start now.

---

47. *Freud and Philosophy,* 27 (see n. 13, above).

⪜ The Problem of Poetic Biography

"All happy families resemble one another, but each unhappy family is unhappy in its own way." These words belong to one of the greatest of all prose writers and—one has to imagine the connection is not fortuitous—one of the most demanding *ethical* thinkers in any tradition. Prose, ethics, verisimilitude, a stripping away of illusion, "telling it like it is"—these qualities have never existed in a vacuum. In fact, they are implicit responses to codes and conventions that came to be seen as no longer adequate to their particular time and place: poetry, aesthetics, the oneiric shape of desire, "leaving the hero his heart" (as Pushkin said), telling it like it could/should be. But neither set of expectations is, one hastens to add, right or wrong. Calling something by its right name, telling the reader that the fish Stiva Oblonsky orders is turbot and not salmon, is "correct" only if the goal is the recreation of "lifelike" three-dimensionality, or what Jakobson would term the metonymic plane in all its abutting contours and clearly glimpsed surfaces. For the eerie precision of the hologram and the reality that seems ever more virtual come at their own price. If the goal in writing and thinking is something else, say to establish a connection between one's person and certain *incompatible* orders of being (God, the devil, one's immortal soul, one's people as "chosen" or "punished"), then a shift to the metaphoric plane, to that linguistic perch where meaning is generated by asserting the likeness/identity between two *different* things separated by time and space, and to the genres associated with it cannot be far behind.

Tolstoi was not a poet not simply because his pictorial intelligence did not feel at ease rhyming one word with another. Also at work here is the fact that the convention stipulating such poetic rules for discourse formation (the "returning" sound of the rhyme partner) seemed to him artificial, and thus *false*—that is, not *true to life*.[48] Why join two words merely because, if uttered

48. As the autobiographical hero of *Childhood* remarks of his attempts to write verse following the model of his tutor Karl Ivanych, "This [poem in honor of his grandmother's name day] ought to have sounded really quite fine yet in a strange way the last line offended my ear.

" 'And to lo-ve thee li-ke our own dear mo-ther' [*I liu-bim, kak rodnu-iu mat'*], I kept

34

in close proximity, they create an acoustic *frisson* of unnecessary (i.e., not arrived at "honestly") meaning? If we were to rewrite the great opening to *Anna Karenina* from the point of view of a poet, and not just any poet but a poet who lived *before* Tolstoi and the clenched-fist quality of the latter's antiromantic precepts, then the words would go something like this: all normal (translate: nonpoetic) lives resemble one another in their internal consistency, but every extraordinary (translate: poetic) life is uniquely *unpredictable*. And these terms would be meaningful *in their own right*. Happiness or unhappiness, the domestic sphere versus the social twirl, language that gets more *authentic* the more private and elliptical it becomes,[49] would not be, one suspects, defining

---

repeating to myself. 'What other rhyme could I use instead of *mother*? [*Kakuiu by rifmu vmesto* mat'? *igrat'? krovat'?*] . . . Oh, it will do! It's better than Karl Ivanych's anyhow.'

"Accordingly I added the last line to the rest. Then in our bedroom I read the whole composition aloud with expression and gestures. There were some lines that did not scan at all but I did not dwell on them: the last line, however, struck me even more forcibly and disagreeably than before. I sat on my bed and pondered:

" 'Why did I write *like our own dear mother*? She is not here so there was no need ever to bring her in; it is true, I do love and respect grandmamma, still she is not the same as . . . Why did I put that? Why did I write a lie [*zachem ia solgal*]? Of course it's only poetry but I needn't have done *that*' " (L. N. Tolstoy, *Childhood, Boyhood, Youth*, trans. Rosemary Edmonds [Harmondsworth: Penguin, 1964], 56; original in *Sobranie sochninenii v dvenadtsati tomakh* [Moscow: Khudozhestvennaia literatura, 1972–75], I:51).

Pushkin, as I argue below, would never have imagined (*and written about*) the interior space where the very poetic function (Jakobson's term) is by definition a lie. What he says to his friend Prince Vyazemsky in a letter of 3 August 1831, on the occasion of terrible riots in the military colonies of Novgorod and Staraya Rus (it was rumored that the cholera epidemic there had actually been caused by poisoning), comes close to Tolstoi's reservations about "sincerity" (the nineteenth century's version of Adorno's famous phrase about poetry being "barbaric" after Auschwitz), but even here the horror is couched in "male" repartee and plain speaking: "But for the present we don't feel like laughing: you probably have heard about the rebellions at Novgorod and Staraya Rus. Horrible things. More than a hundred generals, colonels, and other officers were butchered in the Novgorod colonies with all the refinements of malignity. The rioters flogged them, beat them in their faces, jeered at them, plundered their houses, raped their wives. . . . The military officials [in Staraya Rus] still do not dare to show themselves on the street. One general there has been drawn and quartered, people have been buried alive, etc. The peasants participated; the regiments surrendered their commanders to them. It's bad, Your Highness [*Plokho, vashe siiatel'stvo*]. When such tragedies are before our eyes, there is not time to think about the dog show of our literature [*Kogda v glazakh takie tragedii, nekogda dumat' o sobach'ei komedii nashei literatury*]" (*Letters*, 520; *Pss*, X:289).

49. Cf. the future communications between Kitty and Levin.

categories in such an opening. The engine of plot and the shape of biography would require a different sort of fuel.

But what would happen if we went farther back still, back before the very notion of romanticism, back before the "poetic life," as something authored or "self-fashioned" (as one might say today), was yet thinkable? What would it mean to join the terms "poetic" and "life" not as literary cliché, not belatedly, through the prism of our own sensibilities, but *literally*, as though the linkage itself were primary, consanguineous, alchemical. As Shakespeare's biographer tells us, the Bard went to his grave "not knowing, and possibly not caring, whether *Macbeth* or the *Tempest* or *Anthony and Cleopatra* ever achieved the permanence of print." [50] The very thought of not taking credit for such master-pieces borders for us, with our author-centered consciousness, on secular blasphemy. How can the words of a man who was to become the national poet be in circulation and at the same time not, at least officially, legally, *belong* to him as authoring personality? But the fact of the matter is poetic immortality and the immortality of one's soul were not yet in copyright competition, and the truth of Shakespeare's own faith—was he Anglican or (secretly) "papist"?—was more important on the scales of divine judgment, and thus forever hidden from the eyes of posterity, than the publicly acknowledged authorship of some entertaining spectacles whose Renaissance genre prestige was questionable and whose ability to lure the crowds away from bearbaiting was the main thing.

To repeat, one of the central problems in writing a poetic biography, which is not at all the same thing as a *biographie romancée* or a contemporary product of the frenetic school, is to *deromanticize* the notion of poet (we have no evidence to indicate that Shakespeare ever thought of himself, or could conceive of thinking of himself, as prophet or "unacknowledged legislator") while at the same time studying the principle of poetic transference that is at work in his art and in his life. We have to think our way back to a time when products of the imagination, in this instance plays, were both closer to life and closer to death, when theaters routinely burned down, when seasons got suspended and players went hungry because of the next visit of a deadly plague, and when a wrong step on the street could land one in a midden heap. For the Shylock who says "I will have my bond" or the Mercutio who says "Ay, ay, a scratch, a scratch; marry, 't is enough" or the Hamlet who says to Ophelia "It

50. S. Schoenbaum, *William Shakespeare: A Compact Documentary Life*, rev. ed. (New York: Oxford University Press, 1987), 174.

would cost you a groaning to take off mine edge," the space between word and deed, figure of speech and impassioned act, is paper-thin. One reason Shakespeare has become "Shakespeare"/the Bard is, one could argue, that his notion of authorship, while certainly this-worldly and tied to a patronage system that had its rules and protocol, was not yet fully secularized and demystified through romantic irony. The young and epicene earl of Southampton could be, unproblematically, the dedicatee of *Venus and Adonis* and *The Rape of Lucrece,* but to say that he and he alone *is* the Fair Youth who "defeats" the speaker in sonnet 20 because he is "prick'd out" for "women's pleasure" is to tread too close to biographical literalism. The poet's words here, just like the speeches of Macbeth or Othello, are contracted with a space-time that is roiling with pagan superstitions and Christian passions. Hence, on the one hand there is the private citizen, the son of the glover, the premature groom, the legendary deer poacher, etc., and on the other the author of the sonnets and plays. But to get from the one to the other Shakespeare himself gives us no help — that help is not yet "thinkable." And this lack, I would suggest further, is strangely empowering, if not to the author as public personage and romantic hero in his own right, then to his language and its place in the tradition. The "origin without origins" and the father figure who has no *linguistic* anxiety of influence cannot, by definition, be conscious in a postromantic sense.

Alexander Pushkin is, in this respect, a tantalizing puzzle for the scholarly community. We know much more about him, Russia's national poet, than we do about Shakespeare. He is much closer to us in time, in temperament, in metalinguistic subtlety. His voluminous written traces extend over many genres and include a very active correspondence with friends and literary associates. Given the evidence, then, one would expect that not only the parallels between the life and the work but the *rules for their interaction,* as it were, would be much closer to the surface, much better known and appreciated. But that is not the case. On the one hand, Pushkin is routinely made into a romantic figure by western commentators, one who learned from Byron to "fashion" a presence for himself along the seam of narrator's voice (*outside* the action) and hero's exploits (the plot *inside* a narrative poem or novel-in-verse) and thus, in anticipation of a postmodern sensibility, to "construct" his biography in a way to attract the reading public. On the other, he has become in the context of Russian/Soviet Pushkin studies what Apollon Grigoriev first identified as "our everything" (*nashe vse*) — the father figure who borrows at will, whose likes and dislikes are taken at face value and rarely challenged, who serves the tradition as a kind of authoritative intertextual clearinghouse, and who, despite the manifest tragedy in his personal life, seems not to have registered those tensions overly much in his written work, where everything has been safely masked and objectivized. If the western tendency is to absorb Pushkin into our chronotope and to psychologize and ask him questions that are often irrevelant or "unthinkable" to him, then the Russian tendency has been, with rare exceptions, to avoid the intrusiveness of psychology, at least as a tool for literary analysis, altogether. One doesn't cavalierly psychoanalyze a culture's "origin without origins" — the *nashe vse* element is too fraught with taboo and the shame of pretendership.

The inevitable result of these opposing tendencies — either to democratize Pushkin (i.e., to make him "one of us") or to idolize him (i.e., to make him a benignly indifferent god of language) — is that we still know too little about how the psychology of creation works in his case. So much is projected onto Pushkin because there is no intimate psychological space in his writing, no moment when he appears to "let down his guard" that is not *already* conventionalized by the rules of that particular discourse — including even that of the private letter.[51] And the reason for this, I would submit, is not simply that Pushkin doesn't tend to "open up" the way subsequent generations do;[52] it is rather, and more crucially, that he *doesn't perceive the need to* — i.e., that need is not a category of cognition. Meaning comes from a different sort of friction. As Joseph Brodsky wrote shortly before his death, Pushkin doesn't leave projects "uncompleted" (a designation convenient for scholars and freighted with disinterested intentionality) but simply "abandoned" (a designation that suggests an idea either has been thought through or no longer leads anywhere but in any event is now not registered as a virtually metabolic need to write).[53]

51. This does not mean of course that Pushkin is routinely "holding back" when communicating with such close friends as Vyazemsky, Delvig, and Zhukovsky. It simply means that even in private letters to these individuals he normally maintains a kind of male banter (going back to the highly witty and conventionalized language of the Arzamas days) and — this is the main point — does not speak about his feelings, motivations, anxieties, etc., from an *inner*, psychologically intimate point of view. See note 48 above.

52. Beginning most obviously with something like Belinsky's painfully soul-baring letters to Bakunin in the 1830s, as analyzed in Lydia Ginzburg, "Belinskii and the Emergence of Realism," *On Psychological Prose*, trans. Judson Rosengrant (Princeton: Princeton University Press, 1991), 58–101. The original is found in Lidiia Ginzburg, *O psikhologicheskoi proze* (Leningrad: Sovestskii pisatel', 1971), 76–134. See below.

53. See Brodsky's 3 January 1996 letter (original in English) to Slavist James Rice in *Znamia* 6 (1996): 147–48.

From top to bottom, writing is for Pushkin a conventional affair; no words committed to paper can be conceived of as unmediated. To understand this, and yet not to postmodernize it, to make it a question not of choice or fashion but of fate or world order, is one of the great challenges of contemporary Pushkin studies. If we can begin to understand how this notion of linguistic fate dovetails with that of biography (the "life of the poet"), we will have made considerable progress.

We do know, for example, that Pushkin was, following Nikolai Karamzin, one of the first Russian writers to make the tradition conscious of itself as both European *and* other and to teach it to borrow and rework prior sources — often ones that were foreign and therefore in the reading public's eye privileged — in a way that was mature, self-confident, edged with parody, incessantly *dialogic*. Aleko (*The Gypsies*), Onegin (*Eugene Onegin*), and Silvio ("The Shot") are Byronic heroes whose predictable behavior (acting in certain situations like their darkly disenchanted model) makes them less rather than more alive, hence less rather than more genuinely "poetic." Likewise, Petr Grinev (*The Captain's Daughter*) acts like a Scott protagonist only up to a point — with regard to his peripeteias amid the warring camps, he does not in fact "waver" in his oath to the Empress Catherine. As Lydia Ginzburg pointed out more than once in her seminal studies, Pushkin was the last great Russian writer to be governed by what might be called "genre consciousness" (*myshlenie zhanrovymi kategoriiami*).[54] This means that there were certain things that could be said within the confines of certain genres, but not in others.[55] A lyric poem such as the famous "I remember a wondrous moment" (Ia pomniu chudnoe mgnoven'e) could be both absolutely sincere (this is where the poet *could* talk about himself) and absolutely conventional (i.e., these are the musings of an

54. See, e.g., discussion in *O lirike*, 2d ed. (Leningrad: Sovetskii pisatel', 1974), 183: "An abiding legacy of classicism is thinking in terms of genre categories. In those places where we find the existence of genres or at least of genre tendencies, we also find, included in the structure of every genre, the existence of the image of a lyrical subject, a carrier of lyrical nuances, a carrier of emotions that are odic, elegiac, or [full of] satiric anger."

55. Cf. "Between the author and the reader there is a defensive shield of poetic convention. The same author [Pushkin] forbids himself in his letters the expression of feelings that are not protected by an abstracting poetic form. . . . A paradoxical correlation [arises]: in a friendly letter, which would seem to be the most intimate type of verbal art [*slovesnost'*] . . . intimacy turns out to be forbidden. The intimate, in transfigured form, becomes the domain of literature designed for the public" (L. Ginzburg, *Pretvorenie opyta* [Riga-Leningrad: Avots, 1991], 209).

artificially constructed "speaker").[56] Which is to say, the lines could be addressed to Anna Petrovna Kern in one sense (the "inspiration"), but not in another (the actual woman to whom Pushkin would refer in private correspondence as the "Whore of Babylon"). If this strikes us as paradoxical or disingenuous, it didn't Pushkin. Just as Shakespeare could have his Dark Lady, so could Pushkin have his *utaennaia liubov'* (secret love). In either case, however, we are dealing with the products of "genre consciousness," whose sacred contract is shattered if the connections to the poet's life, which in any event could be tenuous or imaginary (i.e., not acted upon), are literally decoded. On the other hand, a later work such as *War and Peace* that combined, within two covers, family romance, mass troop movements and battle scenes, and philosophical arguments about causality in history would have been, one suspects, even worse than a "loose, baggy monster" to the conceptually chaste author of *The History of Pugachev* and *The Captain's Daughter*. Requiring at least three separate genres (novel, history, note) and three distinct "voice zones," it would have seemed an act virtually delusional (and profoundly *unpoetic*) in its linguistic hubris and metacognitive overreaching.

Ode, elegy, friendly letter, lyrical cycle, narrative poem, romantic tragedy, novel-in-verse, witty anecdote in ottava rima, prose tale, history, historical novel — each of these genres had rules that affected not only the formal structure of discourse (whether lines rhymed, what sort of meter was appropriate with what semantic cargo in tow, whether the topic would be exalted or "low," personal or national, whether the realia at issue could be directly described or needed to be paraphrased or mythologized, etc.), but the *consciousness* that could be presented in those terms. These rules could be challenged and played upon, but they could not be ignored or dispensed with. For Pushkin

56. As Pushkin wrote in a November 1825 letter to Prince Vyazemsky, "Why do you regret the loss of Byron's notes? The hell with them! Thank God they are lost. He made his confession in his verses, in spite of himself, carried away with the rapture of poetry. In cool prose he would have lied and acted crafty, now trying to sparkle with sincerity, now bedaubing his enemies. . . . To write one's *mémoires* is tempting and pleasant. There is no one you love, no one you know, so well as your own self. It's an inexhaustible subject. But it's difficult. Not to lie is possible, but to be sincere is a physical impossibility" (*Letters*, 263–64; original in *Pss*, X:148). But then later, probably in 1835, Pushkin began to write an article on Byron's biography based in part on Thomas Moore's life of his friend, published in 1830 in Paris (Byron left his memoirs to Moore, who cited them in his work, but then destroyed the originals). This unfinished piece by Pushkin is itself quite autobiographical, since Pushkin, typically, uses aspects of his former idol's life and background as a way to *speak about himself.*

this was as much a fact of life as any aspect of his biography, including his six-hundred-year-old genealogy. At the same time, this was not, as has often been stated, any simple or straightforward "classical" inheritance (the "Pushkin as belonging to the eighteenth century" argument), for the poet who created *Boris Godunov* was subtly challenging his own rule-bound French beginnings (the "unities"[57]) as inappropriate for the expression of a uniquely Russian historical consciousness.[58] What Pushkin wanted to become was not a Slavic Voltaire or Racine but precisely *the Shakespeare of Russian culture* — the *dikar'* (barbarian) and "northern genius" whom Voltaire and La Harpe had, in their Gallic pride, dismissed.

Thus when, as Ginzburg describes, the concept of "lyrical hero" (*liricheskii geroi*) arises in Lermontov (*not* Pushkin) because the younger poet is moved to speak about himself in language that seems less constrained by genre conventions, hence more "unmediated," more authentically *self-conscious*, we have entered on new terrain. This is in some sense now *the personality (lichnost')* of Lermontov speaking, and not Pushkin uttering words into a role, donning the buskins of genre. Moreover, what the lyrical voice says about itself makes it, to use Douglas Bush's still astute distinction, suddenly *alienated* (the domain of the modern or postromantic hero) as opposed to *isolated* (the domain of the Renaissance or preromantic hero): which is to say, living the demoralizing lies of Nicholaevan Russia was not only the acid that burned through the vessels of genre thinking, but the impetus for turning the poet against the existing world

57. See, e.g., Pushkin's draft letter of July 1825 to N. Raevsky *fils*, where he speaks about classical versus romantic drama, verisimilitude (*vraisemblance*), the unities (*le temps, le lieu etc. etc.*), and the greater sense of truthfulness in Shakespearean plot and character-ization ("Voyez Schakespeare. Lisez Schakespeare, il ne craint jamais de compromettre son personnage, il le fait parler avec tout l'abandon de la vie, car il est sûr en temps et lieu de lui faire trouver le langage de son caractère" (*Pss*, X:126–27; English translation in *Letters*, 236–38).

58. Here one would have to agree with Boris Gasparov's astute formulation that "Pushkin's position with regard to classical and romantic poetics manifests itself rather in a negative fashion — in his ironic attitude toward any literary party, any onesidedly polemical program. Pushkin's 'genuine romanticism' strives for a synthesis of all mutu-ally contradictory positions, both the 'old' and the 'new,' yet at the same time it does not endorse any one of these positions without a certain dose of irony. It is for this reason that the given phenomenon [Pushkinian 'romanticism'] has not been subjected to any kind of programmatic definition" (B. M. Gasparov, *Poeticheskii iazyk Pushkina kak fakt istorii russkogo literaturnogo iazyka* [Vienna: Wiener Slawistischer Almanach/Sonderband 27, 1992], 73).

order per se, with its social, governmental and religious structures.⁵⁹ This is, as I commented, new linguistic territory, one that will eventually produce the notion of "psychological realism," the searing correspondence of Belinsky and Bakunin (ethical "honesty" vs. aesthetic "self-grinning" [*samoosklablenie*]), the emphasis on consistency between "outer" and "inner" man, the phenomenon of Herzen and of a work (*My Past and Thoughts*) conceived as both theoretical and noninvented (i.e., "nonartistic"), the novelized heroes of Tolstoi and Dostoevsky, and words that have, in Bakhtinian terminology, developed "backward glances" (*slovo s ogliadkoi*) and "loopholes" (*slovo s lazeikoi*).⁶⁰ It is not simply poetry and prose *as genres* that are at stake as the watershed (circa 1840) is passed—this indeed is one of the misconceptions of prior thinking on the topic. No, it is poetry as convention/genre consciousness that yields to prose as the illusion of *consciousness per se*, that is, consciousness that imagines itself either existing outside of formal constraints altogether or being housed in a "genre" (say, *War and Peace*) so fluid and all-encompassing as to remove "poetry" as a legitimate (*literal* as opposed to figurative) partner in the dialogue. For as Bakhtin⁶¹ has taught us, the convention of the novel, beginning with such protogenres as the Menippean satire, is to have no convention, but to absorb what has come before into an ever open site where two equally living and changing consciousnesses enter into dialogue. But this is itself a linguistically, if not psychologically, utopian pretense. Seen with Bakhtinian eyes, poetic codes become "monologic," with one partner in the utterance being shackled to something fixed and mechanical (a rhyme scheme, for example). What is *lost* by looking at language, plot, and biography this way is one of the principal topics of the present study.⁶²

Pushkin was a man in whom coexisted verbal elegance and hot passion, the

59. "The Isolation of the Renaissance Hero," *Prefaces to Renaissance Literature* (New York: Norton, 1965), 91–106.

60. I take the lines of development here, again, primarily from Ginzburg's *On Psychological Prose*.

61. One of the least aesthetically sensitive thinkers in any tradition, by the way—a point that is perhaps not made enough of when Bakhtin's notions of the "monologic" nature of poetic structure are invoked as established fact.

62. See David M. Bethea, "Iurii Lotman v 1980-e gody: Kod i ego otnoshenie k biografii," *Novoe literaturnoe obozrenie* no. 19 (1996): 14–29; and "Bakhtinian Prosaics versus Lotmanian Poetic Thinking," *Slavic and East European Journal* 41.1 (Spring 1997): 1–15, for more on the creative potential of using poetic codes. These ideas (and texts) will be developed further below ("Lotman: The Code and Its Relation to Literary Biography").

sophistication of the salon and popular superstitions, Voltairean "freethinking" (*vol'noliubie*) in his youth and a predilection for biblical texts and for human exemplars of Christian grace and humble service in maturity. All of this, as I have suggested above, we have been too willing to "secularize" and to relegate to the categories of the conscious, the rational, the deliberately "constructed." Pushkin was also a man who, despite the limitations imposed on him by his historical context, was keenly interested in how a life can be determined by *actions* and how those actions are interpreted by those coming after.[63] Here too we tend to forget or neglect how restless and fidgety Pushkin was as a person (and writer), how he loved to bathe in icy water in the morning, how he craved movement and exercise, how he traveled the roads of Russia by choice as well as by necessity, and how physically resilient he was despite the very trying circumstances of his exiles. The only occasions in *The History of Pugachev* when the normally restrained and objective narrator actually steps a pace or two on stage and utters phrases indicating that his pulse is quickening is when he describes simple individuals, ones unexceptional and otherwise fated to be forgotten by history, who are meeting their end in the violence of the uprising and who know that death/execution is imminent — individuals, for example, whom the "peasant tsar" has captured and is in the process of deciding what to do with. Pushkin does not care, or does not see it as his business to care, what these individuals are thinking about as they prepare to die — whether they are "good" or "bad" people, whether they have accomplished much in times of peace or not. It is the *gesture* registered on the surface, the officer who cravenly begs Pugachev for mercy or the Moslem convert who crosses himself and voluntarily puts his head in the noose, that counts — that creates *plot in life*.[64] As with Shakespeare, there is a direct, irreversible, life-and-death link between verbal gesture and deed with Pushkin that places him at the front end of a tradition and that makes his interest — nay, obsession — with "honor"[65] and with how one comports oneself at the

63. See below, "Bloom: The Critic as Romantic Poet."

64. "Not one of the victims [being led to the gallows] betrayed a faint heart. Bikbai, a Muhammadan, crossed himself as he mounted the scaffold, and put his neck in the noose himself." By the same token, toward the end of the same chapter (2) of the *History of Pugachev*, when reporting how the Prichistenkaya fortress voluntarily surrendered (i.e., both the officers and the soldiers) to Pugachev, Pushkin writes that this was the first time that the rebel leader "disgraced the officers by sparing them" (*v pervyi raz okazal pozornuiu milost' ofitseram*) (*CPF*, 376, 378; original in *Pss*, VIII:122, 125).

65. See, e.g., Lawrence Weschler's fascinating recreation of Shakespeare's troubled

moment of death all-important and not yet tainted with the sentimentality (the replaying of feeling) of decadence.

In the four framing sections to follow, I would like to suggest to my reader why certain prominent schools of thought now available to us for interpreting the relationship between a poet's biography and his words are insufficient for "getting at" a phenomenon such as Pushkin or Shakespeare. It will be my argument that inherent in these approaches is a secularizing impulse, or "scientific episteme," that asks the poet the wrong questions. In this respect, the poet's interlocutor is *not* the straw man of some closed faith system. It is not my intention to explain Pushkin by making his path "Christian." But I do think that the least we can do is try to understand Pushkin by leaving the relationship between aesthetics and theology/superstition *open* and, to the extent that this is even imaginable, *not yet romantic.* I will begin with Freud and what I call the "curse of the literally figurative," and from there I will proceed to Harold Bloom (family romance as a postromantic concept and as author-centered poetic language *tout court*), Roman Jakobson (poetic language as descriptive linguistic science and the latter's inability to penetrate Pushkin's "sculptural myth"), and Yuri Lotman (the semiotic approach and its tendency to "construct" a biography by means of poetic codes). Then, in the second part of my study, I will attempt to show how Pushkin's relationship to the great eighteenth-century poet and statesman Gavrila Derzhavin requires a new sort of terminology and thinking—"ontological rhyme," a phrase that is itself a metaphor and that joins the literal and the figurative, the verbal and the biographically/historically situational—in order to get at a creative anxiety that is not strictly familial or "biological" (Freud), not strictly "linguistic" (Bloom and Jakobson), but deeply embedded in Pushkin's dark and superstitious premonition that the *acts* in his life, including ones involving his words, came at a cost and that what he *did* in the beginning of his career created a fatal expectation (one presupposing a "rhyme" later in life) that was not to be, as a matter of honor, avoided.

---

thoughts on the demise of chivalric codes when he has his Henry V order the English troops to kill their French prisoners on the fields of Agincourt, thereby winning the famous battle of 1415 but losing their "honor": "Take No Prisoners: How Would Henry V Have Fared at the War-Crimes Tribunal in the Hague?" *New Yorker* (17 June 1996): 50–59.

✌ Freud

The Curse of the Literally Figurative

One of the hallmarks of a "primitive" as opposed to modern (or postmodern) approach to language is that deity speaks *through* the poet or priest: the metacognitive assumption is that there is a "transcendental signifier" (note our era's paralinguistic phrasing) *out there* and that the speaker is not the source but rather the occasion for the message.[66] The undeniable exteriority of the god-term is everything. Even if the message is itself (e.g., YHWH's answer to Moses in Exodus 3:14–15 that "I am that I am" and that "I am" has sent Moses to lead his people out of Egypt), even if what we are speaking about is the very circularity of the poetic function, that message still carries a *divine* revelation. The burning-bush metaphor and the play with language surrounding the voice of YHWH do not, to put it mildly, solve the mystery or decode the poetry. "I am that I am" is, in J. P. Fokkelman's formulation, a being whose self-chosen role is to *stand-in-relation-to:* "God is the only one who can entirely develop the fullness of his being. But he cannot be happy if his creation and his creatures . . . do not get the chance to do so as well, within their appointed limits."[67] At the same time, these words are both a statement of fact ("I am") *and* a statement of intentionality/implied futurity ("that I am"), which

66. Discussing Plato's well-known suspicions about poets in *The Republic* as well as the dangers of poetry (e.g., its "*unthought* charm") as expressed in various formulations by Socrates in *Ion* and *Theaetetus,* Susan Stewart sums up the case for and against "lyric possession" as follows: "Socrates is interested in critiquing the claims to knowledge of rhapsodists such as Ion, but he relegates the poet to a similar position by viewing the poet as a conduit to the power of the muse or God. The meaning of *possession* here does not reside simply in the idea that the poet's utterances are not original or reasoned. Rather, such utterances pass through the speaker by means of an external force. One is 'beside oneself,' and the distinction Socrates draws in the *Theaetetus* between having and possessing knowledge has thereby complex implications for both the situation of the muse who *possesses* the poet and the situation of the poet who merely *has* what the muse endows to him" (Susan Stewart, "Lyric Possession," *Critical Inquiry* 22.1 [Autumn 1995]: 34–63; this passage is cited from p. 35).

67. "Exodus," in *The Literary Guide to the Bible,* ed. Robert Alter and Frank Kermode (Cambridge: Harvard University Press, 1987), 56–65; this passage is taken from p. 63.

is to say they are the expression of riddling simultaneity and of meaning more than one thing at once that lies at the heart of poetry.[68] To call the self-naming of this originary Other merely linguistic (verbal play without fear or awe) or to locate the need to speak in Moses (or his narrator) rather than in God is to tear both the meaning and the poetry out of this confrontation, which is the same thing. In fact, the curse of the modern-day reader is, one might opine, the same curse facing the initially doubting Moses, only in reverse, from hyper-literalism (the rod metamorphosing into the serpent) to hyperfiguralism (the serpent always meaning/being something *other* than itself): "But behold, they will not believe me or listen to my voice, for they will say, 'The Lord did not appear to you'" (Exodus 4:1). The *stand-in-relation-to* becomes a thing in itself, an occasion for idolatry. To a modern sensibility, rods don't literally turn into serpents, and so the text can't *mean what it says*. Instead, what we must be talking about is language's ability to transform itself, to make metaphors.

It is later in Exodus, after the successful liberation of Israel from the yoke of Egypt, that we come upon a scene that is crucial for our story—both Freud's and, as it turns out, Pushkin's and Derzhavin's. This is, significantly, the first instance in the Bible of a community's attempt at *literal* interpretation. First, let us look at it in the words of the Revised Standard Version:

> And Aaron said to them, "Take off the rings of gold which are in the ears of your wives, your sons, and your daughters, and bring them to me." So all the people took off the rings of gold which were in their ears, and brought them to Aaron. And he received the gold at their hand, and fashioned it with a graving tool, and made a molten calf; and they said, "Those are your gods, O Israel, who brought you up out of the land of Egypt!" When Aaron saw this, he built up an altar before it; and Aaron made proclamation and said, "Tomorrow shall be a feast to the Lord." And they rose up

---

68. For more on the paradoxical nature of that most essential of poetic genres, the lyric, including its incorporation of such conceptual antinomies as spontaneity/madeness, singularity/universality, and depersonalization/intimacy, see Iu. I. Levin, "Zametki o lirike," *Novoe literaturnoe obozrenie* no. 8 (1994): 62–72. For example, at the core of most lyrics is the assumption of "spontaneity, sincerity, an unconscious yielding of the self"; at the same time, however, this same text may be (and in the Russian tradition almost certainly is) "organized according to strict rules affecting all levels, from phonetics to semantics [e.g., meter, rhyme, devices such as assonance and alliteration]." So, how can this be, how can "God's truth and hocus-pocus" coexist in one verbal structure? That very paradox lies at the center of that which we call poetic meaning.

early on the morrow, and offered burnt offerings and brought peace offerings; and the people sat down to eat and drink, and rose up to play.[69]

This is an incredibly powerful scene for the mythic imagination. An entire people has been wondrously delivered and is trying to explain to itself how the deliverance came about. A precious metal (a symbol of wealth) is used to *fashion a graven image* — that is, an image that exists, fixed, *three-dimensional,* in the world of the worshipers. Things are brought together to make some*thing* else. Without Moses and his monotheism the people revert to their prior pagan ways; the molten calf represents one of many gods ("Those are your gods, O Israel"), and the fact that it stands *in place of* rather than as a movement-between ("stand-in-relation-to") is all-important. The calf also happens to foreground the quintessential relationship of every poet to his medium: can the divine be "finger fashioned," as Yeats would say, crafted by human hand into a beauty that is lifelike or statuesque, or does the crafting begin with the invisible — the relationship between words on Moses' tablets?[70]

Freud's attitudes toward Moses and monotheism, statuary and pagan concepts of beauty, the relationship between psychoanalysis and a creative individual's biography, and the tensions inherent in a religious as opposed to scientific worldview have been exhaustively documented. Yet even here there are numerous gaps and blank spots that suggest that, in the case of the father of psychoanalysis, these terms are intricately (even "uncannily") interrelated. Let us begin with an anecdote as narrated by James Fenton,

> To erect a statue is to make a bid for immortality, or for the immortality of the subject. When Freud's admirers wished to honor him on his fiftieth birthday, [Ernest] Jones tells us that they presented him with a medallion with his portrait on the obverse, and on the reverse a Greek design of Oedipus answering the Sphinx, around which was inscribed a line from Sophocles:
>
> ʹΟΕ ΤΑ ΚΛΕΙΝʹ ΑΙΝΙΓΜΑΤʹΗΙΔΗ ΚΑΙ ΚΡΑΤΙΣΤΟΣ
> ʹΗΝ ΑΝΗΡ

---

69. Exodus 32:2–6, in *The New Oxford Bible,* revised standard version, ed. Herbert G. May and Bruce M. Metzger (New York: Oxford University Press, 1977), 109.

70. Or, to use Paglia's binary in *Sexual Personae,* (see n. 17, above), is it to be "eye-worship" (the pagan tradition) or "word-worship" (the Judeo-Christian tradition)?

(Who divined the famed riddle and was a man most mighty)

"At the presentation of the medallion," says Jones, "there was a curious incident. When Freud read the inscription he became pale and agitated and in a strangled voice demanded to know who had thought of it. He behaved as if he had encountered a *revenant,* and so he had. After [Paul] Federn told him that it was he who had chosen the inscription, Freud disclosed that as a young student at the University of Vienna he used to stroll around the great arcaded court inspecting the busts of the former famous professors of the institution. He then had the phantasy, not merely of seeing his own bust there in the future, which would not have been anything remarkable in an ambitious student, but of it actually being inscribed with the *identical words* he saw on the medallion." And among Jones's posthumous kindnesses to Freud was his presentation, in 1955, of a bust of Freud to be erected in the court, to which the line from Sophocles had been added. Jones says of this that "It is a very rare example of such a day-dream of adolescence coming true in every detail, even if it took eighty years to do so."[71]

I take this story to be marvelously revealing, and not just of Freud but of his teller. The only way that the urbane Fenton can accept Jones's recollection as "true" is if the "ambition to live forever [i.e., as a bust in his university's courtyard] . . . grafted its burning memory onto this new desire [i.e., that the line from Sophocles should be his memorial], so that Freud himself could not distinguish the memory from the will, and he was permitted to fib."[72] "Permitted to fib" is altogether too glib for the impression generated by this massive instance of "coincidence" or the "return of the repressed." Freud feels on his shoulder the hand of something larger and *external* but doesn't know what to make of it. He is "pale and agitated" until he can explain away the secret of how the *identical words* appeared on the medallion. We recall how superstitious the doctor could be about venturing to Rome and encroaching on the territory of the sacred city's graven images (beginning with Michelangelo's *Moses*). We also recall how doggedly determined the great man was to decode, with the help of archaeological metaphors some have termed medieval and of forever-to-be-disputed "scientific" investigation, his own phobias. Here Freud

71. "On Statues," *New York Review of Books* 43.2 (1 February 1996): 35–40; this passage is taken from p. 38. The reference to Jones's biography of Freud is: Ernest Jones, *Sigmund Freud: Life and Work,* 3 vols. (London: Hogarth Press, 1953–57), II:15.

72. "On Statues," 38.

suddenly recognizes all his favorite themes — the graven image (his face in bas-relief), the ghost returning from the past (*revenant*), the plots from pagan antiquity, the challenge to authority that is always fraught with risk (let us not forget what happened to the riddle-solving "man most mighty") — and from out of that nexus *he is selected* (but by whom?) to be his tradition's new mono-theistic Moses. Coming face to face with the literal representation of one's im-mortality can be an uncanny experience. Pushkin's response to the Sphinx of ambition and future calling, as unscientifically poetic as Freud's is poetically scientific, is, as shall be shown, the flip side of the doctor's coin. The Russian poet must also confront a literal and a literalizing father figure (Derzhavin), one whose place in history seriously obstructs the son's movement and one whose view of his own immortality involves actual busts and colonnades of glory. But the response will be, in a dodge exquisitely characteristic, to erect a monument "not built by hand" (*nerukotvornyi*). More important, Pushkin will never question the *right* of that figure to be *his* starting point.

There are in essence two ways to approach the Freudian episteme: either you "believe" or you don't. Either it is *science* (as Freud himself asserted over and over), and therefore a priori true, or it is the application of *mythical think-ing* in the guise of science, and therefore false.[73] *Tertium non datur.*[74] And this

---

73. E.g., Freudianism's "self-authenticating approach to knowledge constitutes not an exemplification of the rational-empirical ethos to which . . . Freud himself had professed allegiance, but a seductively mythic alternative to it" (Frederick Crews, *The Memory Wars: Freud's Legacy in Dispute* [New York: New York Review Book, 1995], 8). Or as Alan Stone, former president of the American Psychiatric Association, recently remarked in a keynote address to the American Academy of Psychoanalysis, "What is it about Freud's vision that has made his monumental work a limiting factor rather than a scaffolding on which others can stand? Put less metaphorically, why has psychoanalysis not become a cumulative discipline? . . . The answer is that psychoanalysis, both as theory and as practice, is an art form that belongs to the humanities and not to the natural sciences. It is closer to literature than to science and therefore — although it may be a hermeneu-tic discipline — is not a cumulative discipline. When one human being analyzes another, the result is not an objective scientific explanation that can be separated from the subjec-tivity of the analyst. . . . Freud was more an artist/subjectivist/philosopher than a physi-cian/objectivist/scientist" (Alan A. Stone, "Where Will Psychoanalysis Survive?" *Harvard Magazine* [January–February 1997], 35–39; this passage is taken from p. 36).

74. Until recently, that is. In a historian of science such as John Forrester there does seem to be some accommodation, some attempt not to cast aspersions on Freud's findings for their play with aesthetic categories and their emphasis on the "hermeneutic circle." Now, in his recent book *Dispatches from the Freud Wars: Psychoanalysis and Its Passions* (Cambridge: Harvard University Press, 1997), Forrester enjoins his reader to "take seri-

applies not only to Freud's work on himself (i.e., *The Interpretation of Dreams*)
and with individual patients (the famous cases of Dora, Wolf Man, Rat Man,
Anna O, etc.), on the basis of which he thereafter theorized and generalized,
but to his substantial oeuvre as cultural critic and bedside doctor to national
or pan-human neuroses—the essays on Leonardo, parricide in Dostoevsky,
Michelangelo's *Moses,* the choice among the different caskets in *Merchant of
Venice,* etc., as well as such extended studies as *Totem and Taboo, The Future
of an Illusion, Civilization and Its Discontents,* and perhaps most important,
his swan song *Moses and Monotheism.* On the one hand are those who attack
Freud's clinical findings as "pseudoscience" because they are nonreplicable
and hence, in the words of psychoanalysis's most outspoken recent critic, "not
a probative tool."[75] How can posterity salvage what *is correct* (if anything)
in the Freudian method if independent sources cannot verify its validity or
agree on a nonnegotiable core of its principles? Here, as those such as Henri
Ellenberger, Frank Sulloway, Malcolm Macmillan, Adolf Grünbaum, Frank
Cioffi, and Frederick Crews have argued,[76] any conclusions based on "free association" suggested by analyst to analysand tend to be vitiated by their own
inherent circularity: "What psychoanalytic explanation tells us," says Cioffi
mordantly, "is itself."[77] Add to this the growing evidence that certain dra-

---

ously the suggestion that debates about psychoanalysis should not be couched in the
form: is it an art or a science? But rather: what changes in our general categories are required by recognizing that psychoanalysis is both an art *and* a science?" (5). The public
needs to recognize, argues Forrester further, that "psychoanalysis has produced in the
analyst a cultural figure whose work is aesthetic as much as it is investigative (in the style
of the research scientist or the private detective) and has made available to the patient the
opportunity to render his or her life a work of art, a narrative of chance and destiny as
well as a thriller, whether psychological or otherwise" (5). For Forrester, Freud should be
considered not so much in juxtaposition with Darwin, but as "a combination of Darwin
with Proust" (5).

75. Crews, *Memory Wars,* 7.

76. For a stimulating (as well as aggressively polemical) summation of Freudianism
and its currents offshoots, see Crews, *Memory Wars,* 3–29. A more balanced account of
the enormous Freudian "climate of opinion" (the phrase is Auden's) is found in the last
two chapters of Forrester, *Dispatches from the Freud Wars,* 184–248.

77. "Freud's Wittgenstein," in *Studies in the Philosophy of Wittgenstein,* ed. Peter Winch
(London: Routledge and Kegan Paul, 1969), 184–210; this passage is taken from p. 194.
See also, e.g., Frank J. Sulloway, *Freud, Biologist of the Mind: Beyond the Psychoanalytic
Legend,* rev. ed. (Cambridge: Harvard University Press, 1992), xiv, where he describes
"the whole process" of Freudian interpretation as "essentially circular"; or Malcolm Mac-

matic conclusions ("hysteria") have been shown to be contaminated by, if not wholly based on, crude clinical blunders (e.g., the notorious case of Emma Eckstein, who was diagnosed as "bleeding from love" but in whose nose a half meter of gauze had been left inadvertently following a botched operation by Fliess), and we begin to see how beleaguered of late has become the "classic" Freudian position.[78]

On the other hand are those who believe that Freud has truly named the heretofore unnamable,[79] that his discoveries do for the human psyche what Newton's did for physics and Darwin's did for evolutionary biology, and that the attacks on him are themselves "overdetermined," that is, defensive, "protesting too much,"[80] and in some cases crudely ad hominem (or even anti-Semitic). In other words, the issue of Popperian falsifiability is to the Freudians a red herring, one of which the doctor was himself very much aware. The position here is that, like it or not, "psychoanalysis has moved forward over the graves of bad ideas."[81] Just because the human psyche cannot be opened up and dissected like the leg of a frog does not necessarily mean, goes this counterlogic, that it cannot be studied in this way. "Science" has always moved forward by trial and error and cannot be held to the standards of the laboratory. Those who reject the Freudian model do so because they are unaccountably "afraid" of it, not because the very core of it, the tale of the return

---

millan, *Freud Evaluated: The Completed Arc* (Amsterdam: North-Holland, 1991), 610–12: "In every one of the later key developmental theses, Freud assumed what had to be explained. . . . None of his followers, including his revisionist critics who are themselves psycho-analysts, have probed any deeper than did Freud into the assumptions underlying their practise, particularly the assumptions underlying 'the basic method'—free association." Cited Crews, *Memory Wars*, 10–11.

78. See discussion in Crews, *Memory Wars*, 36–38. The famous "Dora" case, where recent revisionist studies have stressed Freud's abuse of his position of power over the patient (what Crews calls "one of the worst instances on record of sexist hectoring by a reputed healer" [53]), is treated in a feminist perspective in Robin Tolmach Lakoff and James C. Coyne, *Father Knows Best: The Use and Abuse of Power in Freud's Case of Dora* (Colchester: Teacher's College Press, 1993).

79. See, e.g., Forrester, *Dispatches from the Freud Wars,* 245: "Freud's writings are a resource for the democratization of the soul."

80. See, e.g., executive director of the Sigmund Freud Archive Harold Blum's response to Crews's attack on the Freudian position: "methinks Dr. Crews doth protest too much" (*Memory Wars*, 105).

81. Letter of Associate Clinical Professor of Psychiatry (Columbia) David D. Olds, in Crews, *Memory Wars*, 93.

of the repressed, is itself flawed. Perhaps Freud's most sensitive and insightful critic, the historian Yosef Hayim Yerushalmi, says it best: ". . . the return of the repressed is the Freudian counterpart to biblical revelation, both equally momentous and unfathomable, each intimately dependent, not on historical evidence, but on a certain kind of faith, in order to be credible."[82] It is Freud's story (no exteriority) versus YHWH's (exteriority). And the twain shall apparently not meet.

But I have not introduced Freud into this discussion of how to "get at" the workings of a poet's life-in-art in order to prove the great man right or wrong. I have done so because, whether right or wrong, whether the father of a new science or our century's self-appointed witch doctor of "animistic shamanism" (Crews), Freud has done the psychic equivalent of entering into our bloodstream, and this *is* a fact of considerable importance in our attempts to return to the Pushkinian chronotope. For more than Nietzsche or even Marx, Freud is, in ways we are only just realizing, the namer of our modern (and, what is more, *postmodern*) consciousness.[83] Terms such as the unconscious, infantile sexuality, dream symbolism, repression, parapraxis, sublimation, denial, transference, Freudian slips, etc., *have* become a part (again, whether *useful* or not is another issue) of our vocabulary and thinking. This is especially true, one could add, with regard to the parameters of biography — to how we imagine a life lived in post-Freudian time. As Derrida remarks in his recent "Freudian impression,"

> In any given discipline, one can no longer, one should no longer be able to, thus one no longer has the right or the means to claim or speak of this without having been marked in advance, in one way or other, by this Freudian impression. It is impossible and illegitimate to do so without having integrated, well or badly, in an important way or not, recognizing it, what is here called the *Freudian impression*. If one is under the impression that it is possible not to take this into account, forgetting it, effacing it,

82. *Freud's Moses: Judaism Terminable and Interminable* (New Haven: Yale University Press, 1991), 35.

83. "There is something irreversible about what Freud has done to twentieth century culture" (Forrester, *Dispatches from the Freud Wars*, 2; see also 184–85); and "Freud transformed western consciousness more surely than the atomic bomb or the welfare state" (Ian Hacking, "Memoro-politics, Trauma, and the Soul," *History of the Human Sciences* 7 [1994]: 40; cited in Forrester, *Dispatches from the Freud Wars*, 225).

crossing it out, or objecting to it, one has already confirmed, we could even say countersigned (thus archived), a "repression" or a "suppression."[84]

This typical Derridean tour de force is extraordinary in one important respect: it shows a (the?) practicing father of postmodernism returning to the authority of Freud to tell, in language that is much more intentionally obscure (i.e., willfully nondescriptive, "nonscientific") than anything Freud ever dreamed of writing, that his own experience of "archive fever" (*mal d'archive*) makes him an orthodox son of this secular religion. By "archive fever" Derrida means his and postmodern mankind's neurotic urge for an authentic word (i.e., something preserved and set apart in time and space by "archiving" and by "archivists"/*archons*) that is constantly being undone by the death drive; we desire intensely, but do so in such a way that the object of that desire (authenticity) exists *only* in the present and *only* in a condition of such radical interiority that our naming "destroys in advance its own archive."[85] But even more than that. The very ability to speak in biblical metaphors and link them to Freudian thinking has, in Derrida's sesquipedalian manoeuverings (and constant practice heretofore), forever *effaced* the distinction between literal and figurative: the philosopher/critic can now say, and mean it somehow literally (*or figuratively — it no longer matters!*), that "we have all been circumcised" by Freud, which is what Derrida does in the preceding pages.[86] The ritual that bonded (and physically, literally bound) the Jewish people to their monotheistic God and that was the outward sign of their chosenness can now be imagined as something that happens to us *through language alone.* "Where does the outside commence?" asks Derrida, the question so rhetorical as to make one's head spin.[87] Even if we try to object to this state of affairs, even if we spend our energy proving Freud's basic method wrong, we will have already, suggests Derrida, confirmed its strength and power, "countersigned" it, felt its incision and circumcision on *the body of our mind* (the latter being felt to be in

---

84. Jacques Derrida, *Archive Fever: A Freudian Impression*, trans. Eric Prenowitz (Chicago: University of Chicago Press, 1996), 30–31. Originally published as *Mal d'Archive: une impression freudienne* (1995).

85. *Archive Fever*, 10.

86. Elsewhere Derrida has toyed with the idea (from a first-person point of view) that the pervasive power of Freud's writing could be a case of mass hypnosis. See Jacques Derrida, "Télépathie," *Cahiers Confrontation* 10 (Autumn 1983): 201–30, esp. 219.

87. *Archive Fever*, 8.

equal measure real and unreal). It would be hard to imagine a more powerful logical extension of Freudian thought into the present than Derrida's sophisticated dance of clauses and his constant rhetorical extending and withholding (cf. the trademark "on the one hand . . . on the other hand"), all in an essay whose central theme is this most basic and most physically indelible of Old Testament rituals.[88]

Exodus is called the Book of Names in the Jewish tradition, thanks presumably to its opening line. But perhaps a better title for it would be the Book of *the Name*—the occasion on which, under the influence of revelation, Moses and his followers meet "I am that I am" and, after certain tribulations, ultimately accept the commandments of monotheism.[89] Circumcision is of course here literal, its cleansing cut going from the outside in. Freudian thought is based on the assumption (which cannot be proven but which we are asked to raise to the ontological status of fact) that a return to origins will reveal to the persistent researcher not a true beginning and genuine exteriority but a displaced naming inevitably endowed with its own suppressed shadow history. In the present case (*Moses and Monotheism*) it will also reveal that YHWH is the creation of the son Moses (not the other way around), that Moses is in fact an Egyptian of noble birth who absorbed his monotheism from an enlightened but soon to be deposed pharaoh (Ikhnaton), that this powerful new authority figure could not be countenanced by his own childlike followers, who in turn rose up and murdered him (the Sellin theory), and that over time this crime returned in the repressive codes of the Jewish religion. The name for exteriority ("I am that I am") and literalism (the rod turning into the snake) becomes the name for interiority (the closed circle of Moses' psychic relations to his chosen sons and daughters) and figuralism (the dream logic of phallic snake-rods).

Just to read certain passages in *Moses and Monotheism* brings to mind the now famous February 1900 letter to Fliess in which Freud describes himself as "not really a man of science, not an observer, not an experimenter, and not a thinker . . . but by temperament a conquistador . . . with the curiosity, the bold-

---

88. But for the New Testament play between literal and figurative that Derrida takes to its limit, see Romans 2:28–29: "For he is not a real Jew who is one outwardly, nor is true circumcision something external and physical. He is a Jew who is one inwardly, and real circumcision is a matter of the heart, spiritual and not literal" (*New Oxford Bible*, 1363).

89. Again, see the useful discussion in Fokkelman, "Exodus," 56–65, esp. 64–65 (see n. 67, above).

ness, and the tenacity that belongs to this type of being."[90] After launching his own ultimate book of names with a "scientific" reconstruction of how his hero came to be called Moses (the word is traced back through "theophorous" lists to such Egyptian kings as Ah-mose, Thut-mose, and Ra-mose[91]), and after traducing an article of faith central to the Jewish religion ("Moses is an Egyptian . . . whom the myth undertakes to transform into a Jew"[92]), Freud tells his *histoire* (both "story" and "history"). And this (hi)story, considering the author's failing health and the Exodus-suffused status of his last months in England, is not meant to be taken as belletristic "cultural criticism," but, one assumes, as countertheology, as something real and foundational. He is doing the unthinkable—*looking at God.* This more than anything else is what makes his work, as Yerushalmi perceptively reminds us, a "historical novel,"[93] one in which the very truculence of the author's assault on the reality of a

90. *The Complete Letters of Sigmund Freud to Wilhelm Fliess, 1887–1904,* ed. J. M. Masson (Cambridge: Harvard University Press, 1985), 398.

91. *Moses and Monotheism,* trans. Katherine Jones (New York: Vintage, 1939), 5. The original title was *Der Mann Moses und die monotheistische Religion.* Freud's philological work with ancient sources has long been disputed by biblical scholars. For a recapitulation of some of the historical weaknesses in his argument, including his adoption of Ernst Sellin's controversial thesis that Moses had been slain by the Jews, see Yerushalmi, *Freud's Moses,* 2, 5, 25–27, 82–86, 113n6.

92. *Moses,* 13. As Yerushalmi puts it in connection with this central thesis of the Moses book, "To offend was, after all, nothing new to Freud. Indeed, one senses that the degree of offense (translate: resistance) had long become for him one of the criteria for truth itself" (*Freud's Moses,* 6). Yerushalmi then goes on to suggest that Freud was, in essence, a "Psychological Jew," which is a category that is itself *pre-Freudian:* "If, for all secular Jews, Judaism has become 'Jewishness' of one kind or another, the Jewishness of the Psychological Jew seems, at least to the outsider, devoid of all but the most vestigial content; it has become almost pure subjectivity" (10). Peter Gay, Freud's biographer, describes his subject as someone who could be, on the one hand, "completely estranged from the religion of his fathers—as well as from every other religion" (a quote from the preface to the 1930 Hebrew translation of *Totem and Taboo*), and on the other, still "proud of his Jewish identity," but in a way that was "purely, aggressively, secular"; and " 'Every scientific investigation of religion has unbelief as its presupposition' [Freud to Charles Singer, 31 October 1938]. . . . Freud's unbelief, then, was more than indifference; it was an active, persistent, bellicose aversion to any religious belief or ritual whatever and the *precondition for his investigation*" (*The Freud Reader,* ed. Peter Gay [New York: Norton, 1989], xvi, xix, my emphasis; see also xv, 429; the text of the letter is found in *The Letters of Sigmund Freud,* ed. Ernst L. Freud, trans. Tania and James Stern [New York: Dover, 1992], 453).

93. *Freud's Moses,* 16.

faith-based Otherness draws in its wake all the predictable issues of biography and autobiography (Freud's relations with his father Jakob and the episode of the latter's bestowal of the family Bible, which had earlier recorded Sigismund's birth and circumcision and is now, on the occasion of the son's thirty-fifth birthday, duly reinscribed in Hebrew with lines of patriarchal love and pride[94]), Jewish identity, creative versus scientific authorship. The definition of a hero becomes for the sake of this new story the "man who stands up manfully against his father and in the end victoriously overcomes him."[95] But why, one would like to know, is this the *sole* possible naming for heroism we can, under this "Freudian impression," imagine?

My point, which is also in his arch way Derrida's, is that with the final erasure of legitimate exteriority comes the *destruction of genre consciousness,* of the dialogic balance (or "stand-in-relation-to") between the literal and the figurative, that protects the subject (and others) from that subject's self. It is a vis-à-vis that cannot be ventriloquized. Pushkin, for example, could not imagine an event that was purely symbolic: every instance in his creative work where we find a possible figurative or allegorical meaning we also find, sticking out like the ears beyond the fool's cap in the oft-quoted letter to Vyazemsky, another meaning that can be literal, tangible, palpable. Both meanings coexist as equal partners in what Yuri Tynianov has termed Pushkin's "semantic two-dimensionality" (*semantichestkaia dvuplannost'*).[96] But now not only do

94. See Yerushalmi, *Freud's Moses,* 104–6. The translation of the Hebrew inscription, which is filled with reminiscences from the Bible (Genesis, Judges, Exodus, Numbers, etc.), reads: "Son who is dear to me, Shelomoh, / In the seventh in the days of the years of your life the Spirit of the Lord began to move you / and spoke within you: Go, read in my Book that I have written / and there will burst open for you the wellsprings of understanding, knowledge, and wisdom. / Behold, it is the Book of Books, from which sages have excavated / and lawmakers learned knowledge and justice. / A vision of the Almighty did you see; you heard and strove to do, / and you soared upon the wings of the Spirit. / Since then the Book has been stored like the fragments of the Tablets in an ark with me. / For the day on which your years were filled to five and thirty / I have put upon it a cover of new skin / and have called it: 'Spring up, O well, sing ye unto it!' / and I have presented it to you in memorial / and as a reminder of love from your father, / who loves you with everlasting love." It is a fact of some importance, duly noted by scholars, that Freud's passion for collecting *pagan and Gentile antiquities* (esp. statuettes) dates to the death of his father in 1896.

95. Freud, *Moses,* 9.

96. *Arkhaisty i novatory* (Leningrad: Priboi, 1929), 269. A good example of this (to be discussed at greater length in the second part of this study) is Pushkin's use, going back

Bakunin, Speshnev, Nechaev, Stirner (not to mention Marx and Nietzsche) become thinkable, but, more important, the internal logic of their discourse, the believability of their words in their subject-object relations, do too. Why is this? Because there is no way, formally, "poetically" speaking, to separate out their personal ambitions from the truth-value of their statements. Because the founder of psychoanalysis can write *privately* to Jung, in reference to his Leonardo study, that "Biography, too, *must become ours* . . . the riddle of Leonardo da Vinci's character has suddenly become transparent to me. That, then, would be the first step in biography," but *publicly*, as in the case of his famous disclaimer about the "Dostoevsky and Parricide" essay, hedge his bets by stating that "Before the problem of the creative artist analysis must, alas, lay down its arms." [97] He can have it both ways.

The same holds true, a fortiori, of Freud in his last and most provocative book. Here too the new Moses is a master rhetorician who anticipates objections [98] and "regrets" that he will be forced to "restrict [himself] to hints." [99]

---

to Arzamas days, of the equation of "parody" with a "burying of the dead" and of a coffin (*grob*) with the outmoded work of art of a precursor. In *The Tales of Belkin* (Povesti Belkina, 1830) the central, most metaliterary story in the cycle involves a coffinmaker, with the same initials as Pushkin, who buries the "Orthodox dead" in coffins that can be "rented out for hire." This notion works perfectly for the metaliterary concept of parody: Pushkin says a mocking prayer over the graves of the dead by playing with the structures (themes, storylines, epigraphs taken from prior works, puns on famous characters, etc.) of their works, but at the same time he "brings them back to life" and "marries" them (thus the opposing image of Cupid) to their western European brotherhood (Byron, Bürger, Scott, etc.). What is striking, however, is the fact that even here the "renting out for hire" of coffins is not simply a figure of speech, as we might be apt to imagine it in our own time-space: in Pushkin's epoch there were indeed decorative caskets (in effect, "shells") that the undertaker placed over the cheap deal coffins of his clients in order to add solemnity to the occasion—but these were returned and used over again. Hence Pushkin's very metaliterary story still has a genuine factual, literal base. See David M. Bethea and Sergei Davydov, "Pushkin's Saturnine Cupid: The Poetics of Parody in *The Tales of Belkin*," *PMLA* 96.1 (January 1981): 8–21; and Sergei Davydov, "Pushkin's Merry Undertaking and 'The Coffinmaker,'" *Slavic Review* 44.1 (1985): 30–48.

97. Cited in Gay, *Freud Reader*, 443–44. The quote from the "Dostoevsky and Parricide" essay is found in Sigmund Freud, *The Standard Edition of the Complete Psychological Works*, ed. James Strachey in collaboration with Anna Freud, 24 vols. (London: Hogarth Press and the Institute of Psycho-analysis, 1953–74), XXI:177.

98. E.g., "The circumstances of the origin and the transformation of legends are too obscure to allow of such a conclusion [i.e., that Moses was an Egyptian]" (Freud, *Moses*, 14); "At this point I expect to hear the reproach . . . that I have built up this edifice of con-

But is this because the author has truly entered the promised land of science or because the first Moses, confronted with a similarly "stiff-necked" audience, also feared his followers might suddenly rise up against his authority, the literal meaning of his words: "So Moses cried to the Lord, 'What shall I do with this people? They are almost ready to stone me'" (Exodus 17:4–5)? Over and over again Freud proceeds by using *poetic* means (rhetoric) to insinuate a scientific/nonpoetic content he cannot prove empirically. He claims his conclusions are potentially far-reaching *if* we accept the "suggestion that Moses was an Egyptian."[100] Then in the next breath he pulls back and agrees that such notions cannot be "up[held] publicly, since they [are] based only on psychological probabilities and [lack] objective proof."[101] He does not, he professes, want to erect an "iron *monument* with feet of clay," for it is "unattractive to be classed with the scholastics and Talmudists who are satisfied to exercise their ingenuity, unconcerned how far removed their conclusions may be from the truth."[102] Just a few lines further on, however, he is off again on the chase: "If, then, Moses was an Egyptian, the first gain from this suggestion is. . . ."[103] This is precisely the "talmudic *terminus technicus* . . . the Aramaic word *le-didakh*, which means 'according to you,'" with which Yerushalmi begins his imaginary dialogue with Freud.[104] Everything follows not from facts all can agree upon, but from the "according to you."

The poet who operates within a system of genre consciousness and whose speaker urges us, within the expectations of a lyric poem, to leave the hero [105]

---

jectures with too great a certainty, for which no adequate grounds are to be found in the material itself. I think this reproach would be unjustified" (35).

99. *Moses*, 14. For recent studies of Freud by literary critics who are interested in isolating his rhetorical strategies, see, e.g., Robert Wilcocks, *Maelzel's Chess Player: Sigmund Freud and the Rhetoric of Deceit* (1994); Alexander Welsh, *Freud's Wishful Dream Book* (1994); and John Farrell, *Freud's Paranoid Quest: Psychoanalysis and Modern Suspicion* (1996). Forrester, in *Dispatches from the Freud Wars*, 138–83 (see n. 74, above), is particularly astute on Freud's manipulation of the reader—i.e., making him into a "Freudian" *before* he can understand the text—in *The Interpretation of Dreams*.

100. *Moses*, 16.

101. *Moses*, 16.

102. *Moses*, 17.

103. *Moses*, 17.

104. *Freud's Moses*, 83.

105. Both Napoleon and Nicholas, *simultaneously;* the poem is "The Hero" (Geroi, 1830). To be sure, in his "dialogic" poems, such as "The Hero," where there are different speakers (here the "poet" and his "friend"), it is true that Pushkin (i.e., the consciousness

his heart would not, to put it mildly, feel any solidarity with what Ricoeur famously dubbed the "hermeneutics of suspicion." His project is the very opposite of Freud's in *Moses and Monotheism*. That is because he is a poet both literally and figuratively, both formally and, as it were, "spiritually." It has been suggested, most recently by psychoanalysts and literary critics trying to save their hero (is it his heart or mind they are trying to save?), that it is the "artist" in Freud to whom we respond—hence the presence of his name in scores of humanities courses (the so-called hermeneutic disciplines) but its near total absence in departments of psychology and medical schools.[106] To which one might answer, yes and no (but mostly the latter). Pushkin does not question or decode the story behind mythic origins, although depending on the given voice zone, say that of the skeptical historian, he is fully capable of showing, through the juxtaposition of *formal* boundaries (epigraph, text proper, footnote, etc.), where "fact" ends and "myth" begins, and he is never naive or sentimental. Nor does he ever feel compelled to rearrange a prior mythos with an entirely new set of names, for his genius is not driven to place its mark on the point of origin—to look into the countenance of the Lord. Instead, just as he uses the possibilities and limitations of each genre to explore the consciousness housed therein, he comes to a myth as something potentially real and multiperspectival, to himself and his readers, and for that reason *we never know*—a life lived poetically is *never meant to know*—whether the bronze statue of Russia's most patriarchal tsar ever really comes to life and leaps from its pedestal or whether it is just the hallucination of the wretched ex-clerk. *The myth,* as it were, *reads him.*

But *Moses and Monotheism* cannot be defined in terms of genre—what is it really, essay, scientific treatise, veiled autobiographical "family romance," history, novel?—because it has no rules that are not already capable of being traduced and reversed.[107] To repeat, no evidence is falsifiable. If Robertson

---

behind the poem) plays all roles and shows over and over again, both structurally and semantically, how "truth" does not exist in isolation but is contigent on its rival arguments.

106. Stone, "Where Will Psychoanalysis Survive," 38 (see n. 73, above).

107. Likewise, Freud's "dream book," perhaps the key text for all of psychoanalysis, possesses an autobiographical element that the author (studying himself) not only does not conceal but pushes out into the sunlight of his preface to the second edition of 1909 as necessary *in the interest of science,* thereby coopting the reader in his own detective work. The issue of genre, what can be said within what "voice zone," is deliberately, self-consciously, obviated. As Derrida has rightly remarked, "How can an autobiographical writing, in the abyss of an unterminated self-analysis, give birth to a world-wide institu-

Smith's totemic theories can be repudiated by scholars or if Ernst Sellin himself can abandon his theory about the murder of Moses by the Jews, then the
psychoanalytic critic still somehow retains the last word and his access to the
"larger" truth: "Above all . . . I am not an ethnologist but a psychoanalyst.
I had a right to take out of ethnological literature what I might need for the
work of analysis."[108] Like the vulture (which it turns out is really a kite) whose
flapping wings are supposed to symbolize homoerotic content (fellatio) in
Leonardo's dream, or like the index finger holding the beard which is supposed to symbolize that the *Moses* of Michelangelo has successfully sublimated
his angry feelings rather than given vent to them, Freud's "discoveries" suf-
fer from their own *mal d'archive*. They feed themselves on the ghostly morsels
of their "if /then." Their stories spin brilliantly but sterilely in place because,
even if somehow true, their enclosing message cannot *explain* creativity as
it functions in the present, cannot "get at" a form of psychic health (which
is not the same as happiness or contentment) that acknowledges the necessity of alterity[109] and that welcomes the *arbitrary* (i.e., not controlled by us)
other/Other from which our own stories begin. They cannot satisfy—hence
the "fever"—because, being overdetermined, they end by denying the existence of this other, and this despite all the sly disclaimers.

   Proud, quick to take offense, and eager—especially in youth—to challenge
authority, in his own way intensely ambitious, Pushkin never questioned the
a priori need for rules, nor would he have understood the superego as a kind
of separate moral Académie Française of the mind. His notorious tweakings of
authority's nose, such as *The Gabrieliad* (Gavriiliada), were born not of atheism (a denial of God's existence) but rather, as Khodasevich first suggested, of
a "renaissance" affirmation, new for Orthodox Russia, of a world where nubile
Jewesses had real bodies and real desires in the absence of which it seemed almost "un-Christian" to imagine a virgin birth. Much can be grasped simply
by comparing Pushkin's scabrously lighthearted parody of the Annunciation
with Freud's relentless demystification of the Exodus story. Both contain secret
personal elements, but it is the way those elements are "packaged" that is all. A

---

tion?" (Jacques Derrida, *The Post Card: From Socrates to Freud and Beyond,* trans. Alan
Bass [Chicago: University of Chicago Press, 1987], 305). See discussion in Forrester, *Dispatches from the Freud Wars,* 138–83, esp. 140ff.

   108. Cited Yerushalmi, *Freud's Moses,* 83.

   109. What Forrester must term, in the wry tones of the self-conscious Freudian, "that
pathology we call love" (*Dispatches from the Freud Wars,* 6).

little later I will be discussing what Freud would call the compulsively returning "death drive" in Pushkin and why such a naming is inherently inadequate
both to the psychology of creation and to the notion of a "poetically" lived
life. But for now I would like to keep the focus on Freud and his *Moses*:

1) Towards the end of the Babylonian exile the hope arose among the Jewish people that the man they had so callously murdered would return from
the realm of the dead and lead his contrite people—and perhaps not only
his people—into the land of eternal bliss. . . . Let us adopt from Sellin the
surmise that the Egyptian Moses was killed by the Jews, and the religion
he instituted abandoned. It allows us to spin our thread further without
contradicting the trustworthy results of historical research. But we venture to be independent of the historians in other respects and to blaze
our own trail. The Exodus from Egypt remains our starting-point. It must
have been a considerable number that left the country with Moses; a small
crowd would not have been worth the while of that ambitious man, with
his great schemes.

2) Moses met with the same fate as Ikhnaton, that fate that awaits all enlightened despots.

3) If our research leads us to a result that reduces religion to the status of
a neurosis of mankind and explains its grandiose powers in the same way
we should a neurotic obsession in our individual patients, then we may be
sure we shall incur in this country [Austria] the greatest resentment of the
powers that be. . . . I do not only think so, I know that this external danger
[i.e., suppression by the Catholic Church] will deter me from publishing
the last part of my treatise on Moses. I have tried to remove this obstacle
by telling myself that my fear is based on an overestimation of my personal
importance . . . yet I do not feel sure that my judgment is correct. . . . So
I shall not publish this essay. But that need not hinder me from writing
it. . . . Thus it may lie hid until the time comes when it may safely venture
into the light of day, or until someone else who reaches the same opinions and conclusions can be told: "In darker days there lived a man who
thought as you did."

4) [Ikhnaton] raised the Aton religion to the official religion and thereby
the universal God became the *Only* God; all that was said of other gods became deceit and guile. With superb implacability he resisted all the temp-
tations of magical thought and discarded the illusion, dear particularly to
the Egyptians, of a life after death. With an astonishing premonition of

later scientific knowledge he recognized in the energy of the sun's radiation the source of all life on earth and worshipped the sun as the symbol of his God's power. He gloried in his joy in the Creation and in his life in Maat (truth and justice).

It is the first case in the history of mankind, and perhaps the purest, of a monotheistic religion. A deeper knowledge of the historical and psychological conditions of its origin would be of inestimable value. Care was taken, however, that not much information concerning the Aton religion has come down to us. Already under the reign of Ikhnaton's weak successors everything he had created broke down. The priesthood he had suppressed vented their fury on his memory. The Aton religion was abolished; the capital of the heretic Pharaoh demolished and pillaged. . . .

This is what has been established historically, and at this point our work of hypothesis begins.

5) We shall consider in a later chapter how the special peculiarities of a monotheistic religion borrowed from Egypt must have worked on the Jewish people, how it formed their character for good through the disdaining of magic and mysticism and encouraging them to progress in spirituality and sublimations. The people, happy in their conviction of possessing truth, overcome by the consciousness of being chosen, came to value highly all intellectual and ethical achievements.[110]

I have cited Freud's text at such length in order to give the reader a taste for both the ironclad predictability and the potentially glaring *self-referentiality* of the oedipal allegory: everything that refers to Ikhnaton and Moses could refer, mutatis mutandis, to Freud the "godless Jew"[111]—all that is necessary is to replace a monotheism of exteriority with a monotheism of interiority. Moses could not have been followed by small crowds because he was "ambitious"[112] and possessed of "great schemes"; all "enlightened despots" share

---

110. *Moses:* (1) 42–43, Part II; (2) 57, Part II; (3) 68–69, Freud's prefatory notes to Part III, written before March 1938, in Vienna; (4) 72–73, Part III; (5) 108–9, Part III.

111. The reference is to a now famous self-description in a 1918 letter to a friend (the Swiss clergyman and psychoanalyst Oskar Pfister): *einen ganz gottlosen Juden* (cited Yerushalmi, *Freud's Moses,* 8; English translation in Sigmund Freud and Oskar Pfister, *Psychoanalysis and Faith: The Letters of Sigmund Freud and Oskar Pfister,* ed. Heinrich Meng and Ernst L. Freud, trans. Eric Mosbacher [London: Hogarth Press and the Institute for Psycho-analysis, 1963], 63). See below.

112. References to Freud's ambitiousness are of course legion. Gay refers to the "thirst for grandeur" that was an essential aspect of his temperament from the early years on as

the same fate—murder at the hands of a jealous/resisting priesthood; like the truth about the murder of Moses, the next section (III) of Freud's treatise will lie hidden (i.e., repressed) until those of similar faith come to uncover its truth; the Aton religion already had, with the abstract reasoning of its monotheism, a "premonition of later scientific knowledge," while the explanation for our lack of information about it is the active suppression of the psychological truth at its core; the monotheistic essence of Judaism has helped to forge a people that scorns "magic and mysticism" and that embraces "spirituality," "sublimations," and "intellectual and ethical achievements," etc. How could Freud be uttering such vast generalizations and *not* be speaking about himself and his Jewish identity? Of course he was and of course he knew it. But the main point is that the manner in which the father of psychoanalysis has implicated himself in this story of the return of the repressed makes it impossible, by its own internal logic, to refute its arguments, for to do so is to play the despicable role of an "unenlightened" priesthood in denial. And it is, finally, this Trojan horse maneuver that caused the eloquent and otherwise sympathetic Yerushalmi to lay his own cards on the table. "So I will risk saying it. I think that in your [Freud's] innermost heart you believed psychoanalysis is itself a further, if not final, metamorphosed extension of Judaism, divested of its illusory religious forms but retaining its essential monotheistic characteristics, at least as you understood and described them. In short, I think you believed that just as you are a godless Jew, psychoanalysis is a godless Judaism. But I don't think you intended us to know this."[113]

My argument, the upshot of which is by now obvious, is that Freud's analogic/allegorical thinking explains *too much*. Creative types (Shakespeare, Michelangelo, Leonardo, Dostoevsky) and entire peoples (the Jews) remember and forget at different times and not always for the same reasons. Individual and collective lives have a positive need to discover more/other than the road

---

well as Freud's "claim that he had indeed founded a new branch of science" (*Freud Reader,* xiv, xxi). And Forrester, who sees no impediment to Freud's scientism in the fact that he "was unquestionably an ambitious man," describes how the doctor did not scruple to smuggle private information from friends (e.g., the *non vixit* dream) into his most famous book in order to "mak[e] *public* his own ambition in the form of a successful interpretation of his dreams." Thus, "by publishing the dream Freud let it be known that he cared more for readers than for friends: his wish was for immortality, no matter what the consequences" (*Dispatches from the Freud Wars,* 175). Once again, one wonders how a Dostoevsky come back to life today would interpret the truth value of such scientific findings.

113. *Freud's Moses,* 99.

back to the literal and metaphorical implications of infantile sexuality. Traditions may develop "gaps" over time, but at any one time it is highly unlikely that all those affected by that tradition will be in a simultaneous state of either total recall/anamnesis or, conversely, total forgetting/amnesia. As Yerushalmi powerfully concludes,

> One cannot explain the transmission of a tradition at any time as a totally unconscious process. Though much of the process of transmission may be nonverbal, that is not tantamount to its being unconscious. The basic modalities in the continuity of a religious tradition are precept and example, narrative, gesture, ritual, and certainly all of these act upon, and are interpreted by, not only consciousness but the unconscious. The true challenge for psychoanalysis is not to plunge the entire history of tradition into a hypothetical group unconscious, but to help clarify, in a nonreductive way, what unconscious needs are being satisfied at any given time by living within a given religious tradition, by believing its myths and performing its rites. And that task, which would also help us to understand the changes in the evolution of tradition, has hardly begun.[114]

To this I would add only that for individual "poetic" thinking (Pushkin), which in the Russian context is intimately bound up with religious (not necessarily doctrinal) experience and tradition, the rhymes for one's verses and the "rhymes" (the returning coincidences/coincidences) for one's life come from a source outside and beyond. One may be the author of one's words, but one is not the author of this source. What begins the process of creating a poem or creating a life is the *givenness* of the first rhyme partner—the *dolia* (lot, fate) that some higher intelligence hands down in the form of one's family, class, gender, nation, the sworn oaths one must take, etc. This lot is not to be questioned as some repressed primal scene containing yet another murder/overthrow of power behind it. And simply to live *within this tradition,* and within the voice zone governed by it, becomes itself potentially liberating, since the answering rhyme partner is *volia* (liberty), that which it is possible to imagine *given the ending of the first word.*[115] This rule applies in Pushkin's

114. *Freud's Moses,* 89.

115. I take my understanding of Pushkin's play with the rhyme pair *dolia* (lot)/*volia* (liberty) from Abram Tertz [Andrei Sinyavsky], *Progulki s Pushkinym* (London: Overseas Publications Interchange/Collins, 1975), 48. Virtually every occasion in his work when Pushkin has recourse to the *dolia/volia* rhyme pair illustrates Sinyavsky's point of "freedom within constraint": see, e.g., *Pss,* III:258 ("It's time, my friend, it's time" [Pora, moi

case whether he is contemplating his maneuverability within a certain rhyme scheme or within the confines of the empire he often spoke deprecatingly of to friends but refused to abandon or renounce. In *The Bronze Horseman,* for example, Pushkin's narrative poem about the costs of empire building, it is absolutely clear both that there is a masked personal element (the *déclassé* Evgeny and his Parasha are at some level standing in for the beleaguered poet and his notion of "family") and that the speaker is demonstrating how his "wonder-working genius" compares/competes with that of the greatest of tsars. On the other hand, the *givenness* of this world, including Peter's creation (the city), that the poet is said to love, is never questioned. The tragedy, the mystery, the potential for a "poetry" closer to life come with the coincidence of the two stories, Peter's and Evgeny's. So, to return to our opening remarks, the difference between the Freudian and Pushkinian epistemes, and the reason that the former cannot be applied to the latter without significant distortion, is that when Freud sees the graven medallion commemorating his fiftieth birthday and his successful solving of the riddle of the Sphinx, he takes pride in this moment of "idolatry" (even as he wills away the sensations of uncanniness

---

drug, pora, wr. 1834]); IV:135 (*The Fountain of Bakhchisaray* [Bakhchisaraiskii fontan, 1823]); IV:152, 168 (*The Gypsies* [Tsygany, 1824]); V:60 (*Eugene Onegin* [Evgenii Onegin, 1823–31]). Characteristically, Pushkin creates his own story of the birth of poetic expectation through sound in his lyric "Rhyme" (Rifma, 1830): there he invokes personas from Greek mythology (Echo, Phoebus, Mnemosyne, etc.) and the form (*unrhymed* hexameters) typical of ancient verse to engender, as it were, the lovely maiden (*nimfa*/"nymph" and *rifma*/"rhyme" are close to anagrams of each other) whose ultimate naming causes an *internal rhyme* (*milá* [sweet]/*oná* [she]) to be born in the poem's final line. See *Pss,* III:173.

Sedakova expresses (beautifully I think) this Pushkinian notion of the "givenness" of form when she writes, borrowing an image from Rilke: "it is a dance in which one must guess where one's partner is leading one; it is playing with a ball that you don't throw" ("Chtoby rech," 324 [see n. 1, above]). Elsewhere Sedakova comments on the absence of a "memory" of form as being a cause for the ad hoc and the trivial quality of much European poetry: "Perhaps, in the final analysis, this deep level [of meaning] is not engaged due to the arbitrariness of form — the well-established domination in European poetry of free, too free, verse. After all, a tight/severe [*zhestkaia*] form mobilizes the consciousness: it is a wonderful heuristic instrument" (348). This idea of the liberating quality of working with/against an inflexible formal pattern is likewise taken up by the cognitive scientist and expert on artificial intelligence Douglas Hofstadter in his recent book on poetic translation: "Paradoxical though it surely sounds, I feel at my freest, my most exuberant, and my most creative when operating under a set of heavy, self-imposed constraints. I suspect that the welcoming of constraints is, at bottom, the deepest secret of creativity" (*Le Ton Beau de Marot: In Praise of the Music of Language* [New York: Basic Books, 1997], xix).

and superstitious dread—isn't this the new Moses allowing himself to accept rather than to destroy the golden calf?). Pushkin, on the other hand, avoids any and all attempts to materialize the genius/spirit of his poetry, and ends by creating a monument that is, following the words of another son, "not made by hand," and by bidding his Muse to "obey the will of God."

❧ Bloom

The Critic as Romantic Poet

As I tried to argue in the previous section, there is a literalism (which at the same time can be completely reversible and hence a pure figuralism) about the Freudian mythos that makes it difficult to accept as continuously operative *in the present* of a creative personality and of his or her evolving biography. In the case of a poet such as Pushkin, classical Freudian logic would dictate that we look at the individual's own family romance — here his strained relations with a frivolous, penny-wise and pound-foolish father (Sergei Lvovich) and a willful, self-centered mother (Nadezhda Osipovna) — and that we project some childhood trauma (or primal scene) onto his situation that he was "destined" to overcome through the magical, "uncanny" sublimations of his art.[116] The child who was small, ugly, and unloved in the family circle becomes the protean creative individual adored in the

---

116. Among Slavists, several recent scholar-critics have used Freudian or psychoanalytic approaches in their studies both of Pushkin and of Russian literature and culture in general. Of these perhaps the most widely published are Daniel Rancour-Laferriere, Brett Cooke, Igor Smirnov, and Aleksandr Etkind. The following is intended merely to give a sampling of their (often prolific) works: Rancour-Laferriere, "The Couvade of Peter the Great: A Psychoanalytic Aspect of 'The Bronze Horseman,'" in *Puškin Today*, ed. David M. Bethea (Bloomington: Indiana University Press, 1993), 59–85; Cooke, "Puškin and the Pleasure of the Text: Erotic and Anal Images of Creativity," in *Russian Literature and Psychoanalysis*, ed. Daniel Rancour-Laferriere (Amsterdam/Philadelphia: John Benjamins, 1989), 193–224; Smirnov, "Kastratsionnyi kompleks v lirike Pushkina (metodologicheskie zametki)," *Russian Literature* 29 (1991): 205–28; and Etkind, *Eros nevozmozhnogo: Istoriia psikhoanaliza v Rossii* (St. Petersburg: Meduza, 1993). Freud's own interest in and fears about Russia are treated in James L. Rice, *Freud's Russia: National Identity in the Evolution of Psychoanalysis* (New Brunswick: Transaction, 1993). Some of the first psychoanalytic studies of Russian literature and its major figures, including Pushkin, were done earlier in the century by I. Ermakov and A. Bem. I should stress here, however, that in the aggregate Slavists have not been particularly welcoming of the "orthodox" Freudian episteme: whether "young" or "old," western or Soviet/Russian, "textually oriented" or "philological," they have tended to be antideterministic and literalist — a fact that may be explained, at least in part, by the way politicized "theory" (Marxism, socialist realism, etc.) has contaminated the study of literature in this century.

wider (culture over biology) circle of his poetry. The father who kept his son on a very short financial leash and who did not scruple to spy on his politically unreliable offspring during the latter's exile in Mikhailovskoe becomes, by this logic, a major source for the "covetous knight" (*skupoi rytsar'*) in the famous little tragedy of the same name. That is to say, first and foremost it is Pushkin's own flawed family relations that he is working through in his art, just as Leonardo was supposedly answering the homoerotic implications of his vulture dream in his unfinished projects[117] and Dostoevsky the traumatized epileptic was supposedly responding to childhood memories of a brutal father in his fiction. And to the extent — very real, to be sure — that Pushkin was scarred by his difficult childhood, these relations cannot be overlooked or placed hygienically beyond the pale. But the problem with this logic is that it "front loads" the issue and makes the deciding factor too narrowly personal and even biological. Although at some level Pushkin, like anyone (although that is precisely the point, for to call Pushkin anyone is already to make a crucial distortion), wanted love, recognition, atonement for past wrongs, he also wanted more, *much* more, than that, and he knew he wanted more — indeed, he was supremely *conscious* of it. To call such consciousness the return of the repressed and to explain Pushkin's challenging of authority with reference to the ultimately craven and rather pathetic Sergei Lvovich is to embrace the overdetermined in a way that impoverishes the notion of creative biography. So much more is at stake, beginning with one's part in the creation of a tradition, a process that involves *more remembering than forgetting*. Pushkin would not have become *nashe vse* without a significant dose of fortuitous *givenness* — the ancestors one could view as historically significant, the friends and teachers at the Lyceum who became his extended family, his nanny, his precocious verbal talent that was virtually from the beginning much more than that possessed by uncle Vasily Lvovich and father Sergei Lvovich, the benign attentions of such older sibling and avuncular figures as Zhukovsky and Karamzin, the received memories of Catherine's Golden Age coupled with the great recent triumph over Napoleon, etc. — all of which the young poet was well aware of and for which he could not take credit.

It is at this point in our preliminaries that Harold Bloom's most famous formulation, the anxiety of influence, enters the picture.[118] Bloom was the first lit-

---

117. I.e., the homoerotic implications "screen" his inability to commit or be "territorial" either in his work or in his private life.

118. "Although I can write, and probably will write, my dear — if I live — another thirty-

erary critic to shift the post-Freudian center of gravity away from biology and actual phalluses to the issues of priority in tradition and primacy of the poetic word. The internalization of the quest romance, the subject of an important early essay in *The Ringers in the Tower* (1971), became the critic's recurring master plot: not only did it explain the phases of struggle/identity formation (Promethean, Purgatorial, Imagination/Real Man) through which his favorite romantic poets did (or, as the case may be, did not) pass, it also, as de Man suggested, provided the basis for *creating himself* as romantic critic a few years later, in the book that would become his *Interpretation of [Poetic] Dreams*.[119] To him, the arch-oedipal warrior, belong such oracular thunderings as

> But what is the Primal Scene, for a poet *as poet*? It is his Poetic Father's coitus with the Muse. There he was begotten? No—there they failed to beget him. He must be self-begotten, he must engender himself upon the Muse his mother.

And

> True poetic history is the story of how poets as poets have suffered other poets, just as any true biography is the story of how anyone suffered his own family—or his displacement of family into lovers and friends.[120]

The key to Bloom's theory is its purported ability to tell us how poets think, desire, and especially resent *as poets*. Like Freud and Lacan, both of whom he uses liberally, Bloom begins by establishing his own authority through *naming*;[121] the now familiar "revisionary ratios" (*clinamen, tessera, kenosis,*

---

five books," as Bloom once told an interviewer (Imre Salusinszky), "I am reconciled to the fact that to my dying day and beyond I will be regarded as the author of one book: *The Anxiety of Influence*" (*Criticism in Society* [New York: Methuen, 1987], 49).

119. Paul de Man, *Blindness and Insight: Essays in the Rhetoric of Contemporary Criticism* (Minneapolis: University of Minnesota Press, 1983), 275. See the fine discussion in Edmundson, *Literature against Philosophy,* 199–208, esp. 205: " 'The Internalization of the Quest Romance' is one of those Romantic works that attempts to perform what it describes. . . . 'The Internalization,' fixing as it does on the Purgatorial stage of the quest, is itself something of a purgatorial essay. It submits its myth of Romantic myth to trial; it begins to defend the poetry it has both found and made."

120. Harold Bloom, *The Anxiety of Influence: A Theory of Poetry* (London: Oxford University Press, 1973), 36–37, 94.

121. "What Bloom does . . . is to take Freud as his Covering Cherub, or Figure of Identity. As Satan to Milton/Blake in Blake's brief epic [*Milton*], so Freud to Bloom. And the choice is a brilliant one. . . . [A]s Frost puts it, 'Great is he who imposes the metaphor.'

daemonization, askesis, apophrades), an arresting blend of Hebrew and Greek gnosticism, have become a critical shorthand for describing how a poet turns adversity—belatedness—into advantage. Needless to say, such prefigurings of a poet's stance toward those coming before him have no historical basis in any reality that can be identified and reliably documented—they are as free-floating and primordial as Freud's shadowy accounts of the panhuman psyche. In this Bloomian world, poets "swerve" from or "empty themselves out" before a precursor in order to position themselves to get, for a moment they need to imagine as permanent, the last word. And to the extent that Bloom (again like Lacan) has been successful in luring our attention away from actual biography and history to the competition *over words* among poets of different generations (something the Russian Formalists had been angling toward with their sophisticated treatment of parody), this development has been stimulating and salutary. Bloom too has entered our—more "high" than "low" to be sure—cultural bloodstream.[122]

Still, our incorporation of the Bloomian/Lacanian model, behind which stands the Nietzschean will to power (as it did behind Freud), has come at a considerable (unavoidable?) cost to understanding, at least when the subject is not a poet suffering from the critic-doctor's rather particularized diagnosis of "influenza." And such poets do, as I have been suggesting, exist. Bloom and Lacan have written over the cruder aspects of Freudian biologism with mesmerizing vocabularies lifted from the realms of poetry (e.g., the visionary tactics of a William Blake) and linguistics (e.g., the crucial Saussurean distinction

---

And no one has imposed more of them, Bloom observes, than Sigmund Freud" (Edmundson, *Literature against Philosophy,* 207 [see n. 4, above]).

122. The "our" I'm referring to here is by no means narrowly "Slavic," where Bloomian thinking (i.e., the intergenerational competition over poetic words qua words) may have been absorbed by some scholar-critics, beginning with those trained at Yale, but is not necessarily cited by them as conceptual point of departure. My focus rather is on how Bloom, through the power of his personality and the brilliance of his writings, has himself become a serious influence in the American academy, especially in the way that academy views the task of reading poetry in the modern, or better postmodern, world. He has succeeded in making himself into the "romantic poet" among contemporary critics; that he is perceived by American academic culture as being a kind of latter-day prophetic offshoot of the "Yale School" has only added to his status. As David Fite correctly poses the Bloomian orientation, "one reads Bloom not so much for what he says as for what he hopes to accomplish in saying it, both for himself and for his fitful fellowship of readers of poetry in a 'belated' time" (*Harold Bloom: The Rhetoric of Romantic Vision* [Amherst: University of Massachusetts Press, 1985], xi).

between signified and signifier), respectively. Practitioners of the "hermeneutic disciplines" now use *clinamen, tessera,* misprision, *objet a, jouissance,* the Name-of-the-Father, the Borromean knot, etc., *as though* these terms actually describe situations poised to yield up genuinely new information. Yet this too is a kind of idolatry, a replacing of this-for-that rather than the establishment of a true stand-in-relation-to. And these vocabularies, with their special claim to nominating authority and their ability to commingle, have not so much built upon (again, the privilege of the scientific episteme) as momentarily supplanted the Freudian "book of names." [123] In this section I propose to focus on three interrelated concepts: (1) the logic inherent in the Bloomian language of the critic and why its claims are inadequate to a poet such as Pushkin, (2) aspects of a biography that are not strictly "poetic" or verbal but which the poet takes seriously in the formation of a tradition, and (3) how Bloom's notion of influence/influenza *changes* when the precursor is from a tradition that is perceived as genuinely alien to begin with. The hope in generating such correctives is to situate Pushkin's life of the poet in a pre-Bloomian world, one where there was still competition but of a different sort, and to find some alternative ways to treat instances of the otherwise unspeakable — poetic *generosity.*

The Bloomian speaker in *The Anxiety of Influence, A Map of Misreading, Ruin the Sacred Truths,* and other works is not only unabashedly romantic. More important, he presents himself *as a poet,* and he interprets the western canon, now demystified (though never completely so) with the aid of his Freudian truth serum, *as his Muse.* "All criticism is prose poetry," [124] he tells us in one of the programmatic "interchapters" (i.e., prose poems) that purfle his larger postmodern dream vision. Clearly, this sort of historicomythical brinksmanship requires lots of upper-case verities (Counter-Sublime, Covering Cherub, Antithetical Criticism, etc.) and much leaping and falling, à la Shelley:

> Let us make then the dialectical leap: most so-called "accurate" interpretations of poetry are worse than mistakes; perhaps there are only more

---

123. As Mark Edmundson writes in *Literature against Philosophy,* 209, "Bloom never actually stages a dialectical encounter between Freud and the poets. . . . Rather Bloom seems to assume that Freud is right and applies his Oedipal terminology at every possible point. The poets receive no chance for rebuttal. It seems that Bloom has switched allegiances and that suddenly Freud, with a dose of Nietzsche added, has taken over the intellectual and spiritual allegiances not long ago reserved for the visionary company."

124. *Anxiety of Influence,* 95.

or less creative mis-readings, for is not every reading necessarily a *clinamen?* Should we not therefore, in this spirit, attempt to renew the study of poetry by returning yet again to fundamentals? No poem has sources, and no poem merely alludes to another. Poems are written by men, and not by anonymous Splendors. The stronger the man, the larger his resentments and the more brazen his *clinamen*. But at what price, as readers, are we to forfeit our own *clinamen?* [125]

What we are leaping into here is nothing less than the black hole of the poetic imagination, which Bloom, whom we can recognize by the Promethean brazenness of his own swerving from prior, more disinterested forms of reading and by the closed circuitry of his arguments (creativity = *misreading*), has offered to illumine and map for us. The term *clinamen,* uttered no fewer than three times, becomes a kind of mysterious god-term in its own right, taking on a life of its own and sucking the reader into the reality of its newfound "I am that I am." [126] Little does it seem to matter that many poets would not choose to live in the poetically essentialized histories the critic devises for them — i.e., they precisely want to be real men and women *as well as poets,* want to live in real nations or be banished from them as well as belong to the "un-real estate" (Nabokov) of art, want to possess real families and real lovers that cause them pain and joy as well as "perform coitus upon the Muse," etc. This is their essential biographical paradox and their simultaneous agony and ecstasy. [127]

125. Bloom, *Anxiety of Influence*, 43.

126. As de Man was one of the first to point out, "from the moment we begin to deal with substitutive systems, we are governed by linguistic rather than by natural or psychological models: one can always substitute one word for another, but one cannot, by a mere act of will, substitute night for day or bliss for gloom" (*Blindness and Insight*, 274).

127. I should note that nothing I say here is not known perfectly well to Bloom himself (the poet in the critic) and to the authors of works on his anxiety theory. For example, Graham Allen writes that "What Bloom begins to develop in *The Anxiety of Influence* is a psychopoetic theory, a wholly 'poetic' rather than 'experiential' psychology of creation. . . . The centre of this psychopoetics lies in Bloom's figuration of the 'poet-in-a-poet' or 'poet-as-poet,' a figure which immediately illustrates the error of interpreting Bloom's representations as referring to the autobiographies of *real* historical men and women" (*Harold Bloom: A Poetics of Conflict* [London: Harvester/Wheatsheaf, 1994], 23). Likewise, while Bloom freely uses Freudian vocabulary to describe the *agon* in a poet's "family romance," critics such as Allen maintain that their subject, even in an early work such as *Anxiety,* is actually rising up against the father of psychoanalysis: "What is at stake in Bloom's rejection of Freudian sublimation is his vision of the essentially conflictual

But just as Freud masterfully plied a rhetorical strategy in order to insinuate a scientific episteme, Bloom here does something similar, only in reverse: the episteme being ventriloquized is *poetic* in name, but, I submit, radically unpoetic in practice, since all the features that make a verbal construct poetry—issues of form and "madeness," complexities of tradition, the ambiguities of a lyrical moment that is both singular and representative, etc.—have been melted down and cast into the category of the nonessential. Or as Bloom himself puts it:

> Rhetorical, Aristotelian, phenomenological, structuralist criticisms all reduce, whether to images, ideas, given things, or phonemes. Moral and other blatant philosophical or psychological criticisms all reduce to rival conceptualizations. We reduce—if at all—to another poem. The meaning of a poem can only be another poem.[128]

It is this last move of associative logic—that which is alike/analogous in the critic's and the poet's language is now an identity, is the poem itself—which ought to give one pause. On the one hand, Bloom is saying the same thing as the poet (i.e., Mandelstam's "poetry exists only in its execution") when he argues that the meaning of a poem can only be another (in this case prose) poem. On the other hand, that Freud is clearly underwriting the metaphors—i.e., it is he rather than Blake who is the critic's Covering Cherub—gives this strong intervention that circular, "internal combustion engine" quality against which Bloom himself has recently read (misread?) Freud's own texts.[129] Pushkin, for example, our subject, could not have imagined himself in a Bloomian universe, where *ore profundo* and *poetry as poetry* stood in for risk in the "real

---

or agonistic nature of poetry itself: his sense of poetry as a drive against all constraining contexts" (22). In short, the pro and contra critical discussion that has grown up around Bloom has made it difficult to take him even at his romantic word, which seems to be the point. Pushkin, as I will continue to stress in this study, was a poet who was inspired to seek *freedom within restraint* (cf. the notion of "genre consciousness") and who could not imagine life outside its historical, experiential forms. To speak of the poet-in-a-poet or to describe poetic influence as that struggle for self-begetting that takes place not on the specific level of stylistic repetition or parody but on some deeper, more invisible level of psychological "defenses" would be, to him, unthinkable. In this respect, Pushkin is both preromantic and decidedly pre-Bloomian.

128. *Anxiety of Influence*, 94.

129. *The Western Canon: The Books and School of the Ages* (New York: Riverhead Books, 1994), 345.

world." Such thinking would have been, as he once recalled his friend Delvig saying, too cold, too abstract, too "close to the stars."

In what ways might we amend the energies of Freudian biologism and Bloomian romantic-cum-oedipal criticism in order to vector in more accurately on a target as elusive as Alexander Pushkin? First of all, the family romance (or, more accurately, struggle for authenticity) we are concerned with in Pushkin's case does not have its point of origin in his parents' intimate relations or in his own insecurities about language: in the first instance, Pushkin's ambition, to become a truly *historical* figure and to rival on Russian soil Shakespeare's impact among the English, is ludicrous to pose in terms of competing with a biological father he didn't finally much respect; and in the second, Pushkin was always, virtually from the beginning, supremely confident of his ability to work within the medium of language, to make Russian adequate to the task of saying whatever it needed to—in a word, he knew no *linguistic* anxiety and could not have felt uneasy about what was *said* before he entered the scene. Although there were without a doubt some fine Russian poets and writers prior to Pushkin, including Lomonosov, Derzhavin, Karamzin, Zhukovsky, and Batyushkov, there was no Shakespeare or Milton athwart his path.

So where does this leave us? In order to appreciate accurately the challenge posed to Pushkin by his country's past we need to understand what it meant to be "historical" to preceding generations, and to the eighteenth century in particular, for these are precisely the values with which the poet wrestled and to which he returned, with an obsessiveness Freud would no doubt gloss as compulsive, at the end of his career.[130] If Pushkin was not a product of the century whose closing saw his birth (ultimately he wasn't), it was that century's *givenness* (especially its personalities: Voltaire, Catherine, Pugachev, Derzhavin, Bibikov) by which he measured his and Russia's current options. In the first place, for the eighteenth century poetic words were not yet deeds: they could be enlightening, eulogistic, sublime, satiric, sentimental, but they did not have the full ontological status of something actually *done* on the stage of

130. Perhaps Pushkin's greatest paean to the values of the eighteenth century is found in his recreation of the eventful life and urbane tastes of the supreme Catherine-era nobleman Nikolai Yusupov (1751–1831) in "To a Grandee" (K vel'mozhe, 1830). This world traveler, diplomat and adviser to tsars, man of immense wealth and patron of the arts, interlocutor of Voltaire and admirer of the "charm of Goncharova," understood the goal of life—"you live for life"—and "sought the possible" in a way that was distinctly preromantic. See *Pss*, III:160–62.

history. Or, as a contemporary cultural critic (say Paglia) might say, they did not yet have the "glow" of a unified, historically meaningful *personality* behind them. Being a poet or man of letters was either a useful avocation (Derzhavin) or an expression of learning and science (Lomonosov) or a court indulgence that potentially opened one to ridicule as the tsar's jester (Trediakovsky) or a way to expose one's countrymen to European mores and intellectual life (Karamzin), but it was not necessarily perceived by those in power, beginning with high-placed patrons, as a calling that made one, in and of itself, historically significant. To put it crudely, the perception was that one's poetic words served another's worthy to be poeticized deeds: it was up to the poet to try to find a dignified position (he often didn't[131]) in this hierarchical vis-à-vis. Likewise, being a poet was no way to "construct a life" in the interstices between poetic text and romantically lived biography, just as the noncivic subjectivity of the elegy was not yet thinkable (all that would come later). Add to this the awesome fact that Russia would gain its first legitimate comprehensive history and Russians their first mature view of their past with the arrival of Karamzin's monumental work in the second and third decades of Pushkin's life and one begins to realize how problematic, how potentially mythological and legend saturated (i.e., poetically shaped), was the status of any major event or epochal turning point. It goes without saying that such considerations had a profound impact on what it meant to be an author—a role, for example, to which Catherine herself may have aspired in her enlightening fervor but which she was more than willing to downplay or discard entirely when it came to making difficult decisions with broad social and political ramifications. Corresponding with Voltaire was one thing, ruling an illiterate, long-suffering, and sometimes dangerously seething peasantry that had little in common with the projections of Rousseau was quite another. In short, this, the second half of the eighteenth century, was a world full of high drama, expansionist ambi-

---

131. As Lomonosov wrote in a famous letter to I. I. Shuvalov (19 January 1761), "Not only do I not want to be a fool at the table of high-born lords or earthly sovereigns, but [I don't want to be a fool] even for the Lord God Himself, Who gave me reason, until He takes it away" (*Polnoe sobranie sochinenii* [Moscow-Leningrad: Izd. Akademii Nauk SSSR, 1950–59], X:546). This letter would later be rephrased by Pushkin, when, upon learning that his own correspondence with his wife was being opened and inspected by tsarist censors, he wrote in his diary (10 May 1834), " I can be a subject [*poddannyi*], even a slave [*rab*], but a lackey [*kholop*] and jester [*shut*] I will not be even at the feet of the King of Heaven" ("large 'Academy,' " XII:329).

tions, successful wars and violent revolts (the Turkish wars, the partitions of Poland, the Pugachev rebellion), personified chance,[132] and charismatic generals and meteoritelike favorites (Suvorov, Rumyantsev, Potemkin, Panin). It was a period that Pushkin would look back upon from his youth, in the first flush of the Russia-led victory over Napoleon, as a Golden Age of heroism and noble sacrifice. Only later, upon sober reflection in maturity, would he realize some of the demoralizing aspects and cynical abuses of power lurking below the surface sheen of Catherine's gold.

I recast this context in broad outline because its very limitation and sense of "fatedness," its underlying principles of random selection, sudden rise and sudden fall (Prince Potemkin), its energy and its attendant lack of the laws and institutions we normally associate with western civil society—all this is the flip side of Pushkin's coming verbal achievement, a "content" worthy of his "form." It is a potential field of action, in which chance can take you and cast you on the crest of a human tidal wave and make you (if you have the appropriate mettle) significant (*historical*) in the eyes of posterity, that *will be denied* to our poet. For Pushkin and his world (not that different in kind from Shakespeare's, one imagines), history judges a person by the outward "beauty" of his deeds—by their nobility, their spiritual generosity, their sense of being larger than life. This, for example, is what Pushkin writes toward the end of his life about Bibikov, the hero-martyr of the Pugachev uprising (1773–74):

> Bibikov did not have the opportunity to complete what he had begun [the total defeat and actual capture of Pugachev]: tired out by work, worry, and trouble, taking little care of his already failing health, he developed a fever in Bugulma. Sensing that the end was approaching, he gave some last minute instructions. He sealed all his confidential papers, with instruc-

132. The notion of chance (*sluchai*) will be one of the salient leitmotifs of Pushkin's writings in the 1830s, particularly those having to do with the eighteenth century and with the meaning/interpretation of Russian history. Pushkin believed, for example, that no historiography coming from the outside (e.g., the French romantic school of Guizot, Thierry, etc.) could get at the essence of Russian history if it ignored this nonsystematizable notion of chance. For more on how "chance" affected the psychology (deeply superstitious despite "enlightenment" values) of the Russian eighteenth century, see Iu. M. Lotman, " 'Pikovaia dama' i tema kart i kartochnoi igry v russkoi literature XIX veka," in *Izbrannye stat'i,* 3 vols. (Tallinn: Alexandra, 1992–93), II:392–400. A lively satiric description of the vagaries of chance, replete with the gambling motif, is found in a poem by one of Pushkin's chief foils in the 1830s, Derzhavin ("On Fortune/Chance" [Na schastie, 1789]).

tions to have them delivered to the Empress, and handed the commander-ship over to the highest-ranking officer, Lieutenant General Shcherbatov. He still had time to send a report to the Empress about the liberation of Ufa, of which he had just received some oral reports, but soon after, on April 9 at 11 A.M., he died. He was in his forty-fifth year. His body was to remain on the bank of the Kama for several days, because it was impossible to cross the river at the time. The citizens of Kazan wanted to inter their deliverer in their cathedral, erecting a monument to him, but Bibikov's family wished to have his body brought to his village. A ribbon of the Order of St. Andrew, the title of senator, and the rank of Colonel of the Guards were too late to reach him alive. On his deathbed he said: "I do not feel sorry to leave my wife and children, for the Empress will look after them; I feel sorry to part with my fatherland." A rumor attributed his death to poisoning, supposedly by a Confederate. Derzhavin wrote a poem about his demise. Catherine wept over him and showered his family with favors. Petersburg and Moscow were seized with fear [or horror, *uzhas*]. Soon the whole of Russia was to realize what an irreparable loss had befallen her.[133]

The reader who knows Pushkin can sense the crescendo of emotion, more powerful *because of its restraint*, bursting through these lines: the genre is history, and thus one is not allowed to fabricate or embellish (*vydumyvat'*); Bibikov had been in Catherine's disfavor (a distinguished military man, he had been too honest and not sufficiently obsequious), and yet he sacrificed his personal feelings for the good of the country and of the monarch whose station (a *givenness* larger than the person) he could still respect; he entered a desperate situation that had been badly mishandled by predecessors and was now threatening to explode into a full-scale conflagration potentially engulf-ing Moscow and St. Petersburg; immediately comprehending the crisis and working against the odds (of which he was also aware, as his correspondence with family indicates), he managed through various symbolic gestures of a religious or patriotic nature and through powerful, coolheaded leadership to rally the frightened citizenry and turn the tide against the rebel forces; and so by the time of his death, a decisive blow had been dealt to Pugachev, crucial victories had been achieved at Ufa and Iaitskii Gorodok, and the end of the "peasant tsar's" reign of terror was at last in sight. Pushkin returns to this dra-matic situation and to the epoch that allowed it to come into being because

133. Pushkin, *CPF*, 411; original in *Pss*, VIII.162–63.

(1) in his mind it is *historical* and actually happened (i.e., there are no documents relating to Bibikov, including, most important, those that have to do with his own state of mind during the crisis, that suggest a more "suspicious" or self-serving interpretation of his role); (2) it insists upon a *nonreversibility* (or risk) at the heart of any genuinely historical activity (Bibikov's words and deeds mattered and, once placed into motion, *could not be taken back*); and (3) there was an implicit understanding of service here (one's oath, one's *word of honor* [*chestnoe slovo*] to the empress) that was "noble" in a way that could not be duplicated or artificially brought to life by Peter's "meritorious" aristocracy or by Catherine's extravagant oriental-style favoritism. It seems Pushkin truly yearned, especially in the 1830s when he felt himself more and more controlled by social (mainly "salon") conventions that had little ability to make history and (except for the ultimate trump card, the dueling code) considerable ability to attenuate risk, for the *chance* to test himself publicly, presumably on the field of battle, as Bibikov and others like him (including the poet's own forebears) had done in the previous century, just a "lifetime" ago. But he also knew, given the context of Nicholaevan Russia (cynical, nonheroic) and of his own highly circumscribed role as poet/man of letters, that the life of a Bibikov was not one he could emulate. In this respect, that is, for the Shakespeare of Russian culture whose role it was to give his country a modern language and modern linguistic consciousness, the "Satan" in his Miltonic path (as Blake might say) was not another writer qua writer (Derzhavin as poet), but the hero of a previous age who had had the opportunity to enter history *for his deeds* (possibly the Derzhavin who *had had the chance* to participate as a young officer in the campaign against Pugachev).

This, then, is the primary shortcoming in the Bloomian model ("revisionary ratios") as applied to Pushkin: in the urge to place poets in a critical narrative in which they struggle with one another over the primacy, which is the same as the authenticity, of their words, it neglects to imagine a time in which authorship was not romantic, oedipal, exclusively *word-worshiping*. Its postmodern Shelleyesque Prometheanism, full of angels and devils with Freudian masks, obviates the necessity of a life lived *in history* and of a death concretely imagined, outside the reversibility (I can take my words back and make myself into something else) of romantic self-fashioning. The Pushkin who described Bibikov's death had passed through the Byronic personality and the Shakespearean sense of history/tragedy (*Boris Godunov* truly is the first Russian dramatic presentation of the principle that, in history, words become deeds and deeds words) to arrive at a new and deeper understanding of self, one that was coterminous both with his own fate (including his marriage) and with the fate of his country.[134] But the tension between deed and word, and the consciousness (colored inevitably with some guilt and shame) that it is one thing to live history and another to write about it, carry through all of Pushkin's writings, from his very first poems to his last. To give just a few examples:

1. And you [the Moscow region] saw them [Napoleon's troops],
    the enemies of my fatherland!
And blood turned you crimson and flame consumed you!
And I did not avenge you with the sacrifice of my life;
    It was only in vain that my spirit burned with rage! (1814)

2. Battle is familiar to me — I love the sound of swords;
From earliest years I have been an admirer of martial glory,
I love the bloody amusements of war,
And the thought of death is dear to my soul.
He who in the prime of life is freedom's faithful warrior,
[And yet] has not seen death before him,
That one has not tasted full merriment
And is not worthy of the kisses of pretty women. (1820)

3. Will you be born in me, blind passion of fame/glory,
You, the thirst for destruction, the fierce heat of heroes?
Will it be my fate to be given a double wreath,
Has battle's lot ordained for me a dark end?
    . . . [Or] can it be true that neither the noise of battle,
Nor military labors, nor the rumble of proud fame,
Nothing will muffle my habitual thoughts? (1821)

4. You [Pimen] are happy! But I [Grigory], a poor monk,
Have from youthful years wandered among cells!
So why can't I amuse myself in battle
Or feast at the tsar's table? (1825)

134. All we need do to measure the distance Pushkin had traveled in his quest for the authentically or "poetically" lived life is to compare the pretender, nimble, discourse-juggling, as malleable and complaisant as a salon performer, of *Boris Godunov*, and the pretender, dark, drenched in blood, the collective "author" of inhuman crimes, a "doer" without restraint, of *The Captain's Daughter*. See David M. Bethea, "Pushkin's Pretenders: From the Poet in Society to the Poet in History," in *And Meaning for a Life Entire* (Festschrift for Charles A. Moser on the Occasion of His Sixtieth Birthday), ed. Peter Rollberg (Columbus: Slavica, 1997), 61–74.

5. To you, a singer, and to you, a hero [do I sing/send these verses]!
I have not managed, to the thunder of cannon
And in the fire [of battle], to gallop
After you on furious steed.
A rider of meek Pegasus,
I have worn till it's gone out of style
The uniform of old Parnassus. (1836) [135]

Whether acting out the role of lyric speaker or draping himself in the monk's robes of the rogue who would become pretender, Pushkin knew the precise cost (Emerson's "compensation") of creating verbal worlds so splendid in their

---

135. (1) «И вы их видели, врагов моей отчизны! / И вас багрила кровь и пламень пожирал! / И в жертву не принес я мщенья вам и жизни; / Вотще лишь гневом дух пылал!..» (*Pss*, I:73); (2) «Мне бой знаком — люблю я звук мечей; / От первых лет поклонник бранной славы, / Люблю войну кровавые забавы, / И смерти мысль мила душе моей. / Во цвете лет свободы верный воин, / Перед собой кто смерти не видал, / Тот полного веселья не вкушал / И милых жен лобзаний не достоин» (*Pss*, I:354); (3) «Родишься ль ты во мне, слепая славы страсть, / Ты, жажда гибели, свирепый жар героев? / Венок ли мне двойной достанется на часть, / Кончину ль темную судил мне жребий боев? / . . . Ужель ни бранный шум, / Ни ратные труды, ни ропот гордой Славы, / Ничто не заглушит моих привычных дум?» (*Pss*, II:31); (4) «Счастлив! А я от отроческих лет / По келиям скитаюсь, бедный инок!/ Зачем и мне не тешиться в боях, / не пировать за царскою трапезой?» (*Pss*, V:201); (5) «Тебе певцу, тебе герою! / Не удалось мне за тобою / При громе пушечном, в огне / Скакать на бешеном коне. / Наездник смирного Пегаса, / Носил я старого Парнаса / Из моды вышедший мундир» (*Pss*, III:331).

The autobiographical elements in these various excerpts are obvious to the student of Pushkin: e.g., in the first example, from the Lyceum-period piece "Recollections at Tsarskoe Selo" (Vospominaniia v Tsarskom Sele), the young poet is exclaiming his regret at not being able to defend Moscow from the French invasion with something more than words; in the fourth example, taken from *Boris Godunov*, Grigory uses the same image of confinement (the monkish "cell"/*kel'ia*) that the schoolboy Pushkin and his classmates earlier developed as a shorthand for the walls and close supervision of teachers at the Lyceum; and in the fifth example, the now aging Pushkin is speaking to his old friend and hero of the Napoleonic wars D. V. Davydov about how his (Pushkin's) poet's life has not provided him opportunity to follow in the other's footsteps — the play on cannon fire may involve a wry pun on Pushkin's part, since the root for his name is *pushka* (cannon). In this last respect, and keeping in mind that Pushkin was always exquisitely sensitive to sound- and root-play (paronomasia), one can imagine that the poet was engaging the whole phenomenon of Derzhavin's role during Catherine's Golden Age, to be discussed in Part II of this study, on this level (*derzhava* means "power," "orb") as well.

life-modeling capabilities that they, if one didn't keep score, ran the risk of standing in for the real thing. His fate was not to be Bibikov but to tell others about Bibikov's heroic achievement in such a way that it would continue to have a life in words. Here too Pushkin, not a romantic in the Byronic sense, had *to serve something he could not have.*

One of the hallmarks of the post-1830 Pushkin is the more modest, intentionally less sophisticated notion of hero and heroism that enters his work. Ivan Petrovich Belkin, Evgeny and Parasha, Dubrovsky, Petr Grinev and Masha Mironova — these are "prosaic" figures that not only project forward to the Russian novel but project backward to an eighteenth-century world that was more direct, more in touch with the irreversibility of word and deed, less polite, refined, "Gallicized." Which brings us to the issue of Pushkin's principal foreign precursor and linguistic authority figure, Voltaire, the "giant of this epoch" (*velikan sei epokhi*). Space does not allow us to address in depth the very large presence that Voltaire had in Pushkin's thinking during his formative years, but understanding at least the outlines of that presence could be particularly useful in adjusting the Bloomian model, with its Freudian based excesses. Bloom's concept of belatedness turns largely on the engagement with figures in one's own tradition, *in one's own language,* who have "gotten there first." But what happens to this notion of struggle for authenticity when the precursor belongs to a tradition that cannot in honesty be claimed as one's own? Voltaire is such a figure: he represents an otherness that Pushkin, in maturity, will come to see as confining, enslaving, undignified. On the other hand, Shakespeare will rightly come to represent an otherness that is liberating, inspiring, capable of conferring dignity.[136] Why these competing alterities, neither of which is linguistically Russian, can be imagined and used by Pushkin in these ways is fascinating and telling. First of all, the French language of which Voltaire was the eighteenth-century undisputed king was also the language of Russian polite society in Pushkin's formative years: it was the language (and culture) his uncle, father, and the young poet himself (dubbed "the Frenchman" at the Lyceum) idolized; it was the language whose civilizing locutions and complaisant paraphrasis Karamzin had imitated to make Russian more European, less "barbaric"; it was the language of lovemaking,

---

136. As early as 1822 Pushkin had written to Nikolai Gnedich, "English literature is beginning to have an influence on the Russian. I think it will be more advantageous than the influence of timid, affected French poetry" (letter of 27 June 1822 in *Letters,* 94; *Pss,* X:33).

diplomacy, and court intrigue; it was the language of Voltaire's own history of Peter[137] (the first on the continent), just as during Pushkin's lifetime it became the language of a historiographic tradition (Guizot, Thierry, Barante, etc.) that explained the rise of Europe itself and, in the hands of Russian epigones, the rise of Russia as well. French was also, of course, the language of Napoleon, who in Pushkin's childhood years became the greatest single symbol of Gallic pride and will-to-conquer. In other words, Voltaire's otherness placed Pushkin and the Russian linguistic culture he was attempting to bring to consciousness in a position where they were continually being defined by a set of values (philosophical, skeptical, systematizing, etc.) that could not do justice to their historical uniqueness and could not, because of their implicit status as "barbarians" and second-class citizens, accord them dignity.

But as always in Pushkin's case it was not the general but the specific, that which related to his own biography and personality, that motivated his rise against the weight of a confining "givenness." Pushkin started out as a poet who borrowed the mask of Voltaire's skepticism and atheism: in "The Monk" (Monakh, 1813) and in "Bova" (1814),[138] for example, poems that were not published in his lifetime, the great Frenchman serves as his muse and reverential point of departure. The schoolboy poet takes impish pleasure in tweaking the nose of religious authority (the hapless monk's uncontrollable lust) and desires nothing so much as to mimic, on Russian soil, the challenging stance of his idol: "O Voltaire! O one and only man/hero! / You who in France / Are considered a kind of god, / [And] in Rome a devil, an antichrist, / [And] in Saxony a monkey! . . . Be now my muse!"[139] But the mask didn't fit; the young Russian poet's ears still stuck out. Voltaire's atheism had a French philosophical stability to it (analysis in control of feeling) that didn't sufficiently wrap around

137. Pushkin did not agree with Voltaire's assessment of the reign of Peter I, and it can be argued, for example, that one of the chief reasons Pushkin turned in his last years to the historical study of the great tsar and his epoch was to recast and "Russianize" what Voltaire had too neatly enveloped in his Gallic worldview. See Iu. V. Stennik, *Pushkin i russkaia literatura XVIII veka* (St. Petersburg: Nauka, 1995), 283–84.

138. Voltaire is very much in the background of all of Pushkin's Lyceum-period poetry. See also, e.g., "Stanzas (from Voltaire)" ([1817] *Pss*, I:220–21). As the young poet says in the poetic spoof of his library, "The Little Town" (Gorodok, 1815), "Shall I say it? . . . the father of Candide — / He is everything; everywhere is great / The one and only old man" (Скажу ль? . . . отец Кандида — / Он всё; везде велик/ Единственный старик!) (*Pss*, I:85).

139. *Pss*, I:57. The original reads: «О Вольтер! о муж единственный! / Ты, которого во Франции / Почитали богом некиим, / В Риме дьяволом, антихристом, / Обезьяною в Саксонии! . . . Будь теперь моею Музою!»

the Lyceum Pushkin's joie de vivre and sense of play that *had no answers*.[140] The Voltairean influence[141] (along with a strong dose of Parny as well) reached its height in *The Gabrieliad* (1821), which mocked the sacredness of the Annunciation in the name of a real-life desire (i.e., the opportunity to chase the young Jewish wives of Kishinev) that couldn't be "spiritualized" away. Voltaire's *La Pucelle*, about another sacred-cum-potentially compromised female, had set in motion in Pushkin's mind a series of challenges to authority for which he, *Pushkin, would have to pay*. And pay he did, not only with the difficult history of *The Gabrieliad*, whose authorship he was eventually forced to acknowledge in private audience with the tsar himself,[142] but, equally important, *in his per-*

---

140. For more on the potentially "blasphemous" texts in Pushkin's oeuvre, see Vladislav Khodasevich, "Koshchunstva" (orig. 1924), *Sobranie sochinenii v chetyrekh tomakh* (Moscow: Soglasie, 1996–97), III:455–63.

141. Perhaps the most powerful and succinct statement that Pushkin made on the (as he experienced it) destructive essence of the Voltairean influence is found in his essay (wr. 1834, pub. [in excerpted form] 1835) "On the Insignificance of Russian Literature" (O nichtozhestve literatury russkoi): "Nothing is more opposed to poetry than the philosophy to which the eighteenth century gave its name. It was directed against the prevailing religion, the eternal source of poetry among all peoples, and its favorite weapon was an irony that was cold and cautious and a sneer that was devilish [or furious, *beshenaia*] and merciless. Voltaire, the giant of this epoch, also mastered verse as [one of the] important branch[es] of the mental activity of man. He wrote an epic [*La Henriade*] with the intent of blackening the name of Catholicism. For sixty years he filled the theaters with tragedies in which, not caring in the least about the verisimilitude of his characters or about the legitimacy of his [theatrical] means, he forced his dramatis personae to express the rules of his philosophy whether it was appropriate or not. He flooded Paris with charming trifles, in which philosophy spoke in a universally understood and joking language, one distinct from prose only because of its rhyme and meter, and this lightness seemed to be the very height of poetry. Finally he too, once in his life, becomes a poet: it was when all his destructive genius in all its license [lit. 'freedom,' *svoboda*] poured forth in a cynical [narrative] poem [*La Pucelle*], in which every sublime feeling that is dear to humanity is sacrificed to the demon of laughter and irony, Greek antiquity is mocked, [and] the holy of holies of both Testaments is defiled . . ." (*Pss*, VII:214). That Pushkin was using this background essay in order to make his way to an evaluation of *Russian* literature (the last line of "On the Insignificance" is "Let us turn to Russia") should not be lost on the reader. As the poet wrote in the "plan"/outline on Russian literature that he didn't have the time (or inclination) to expand into the piece's concluding section but that was supposed to address the current scene: "Voltaire and the giants do not have a single follower in Russia, but [his] talentless pygmies, [like] mushrooms that grow at the roots of oaks . . . possess [*ovladevaiut*] Russian literature" (*Pss*, VII:494).

142. Pushkin experienced no end of troubles as a result of his blasphemous poem. Not

sonal life, about which we will have more to say in the next section.[143] Like many Russians, Pushkin was an intensely superstitious man, and the apostrophe to peacefully sleeping cuckolds at the end of the poem about Mary's multiple erotic trysts, all concocted under the aegis of the cynical French philosopher, was a challenge that Pushkin *sensed in advance* would come back to haunt him. He was playing at being Voltaire, without being first himself (a Russian who can't afford such "enlightenment" tricks), and so it was natural that at the end of his career this highly magnetized episode would resurface in a manner that was, to our age, potentially "Freudian" or "Bloomian."

In the last year of his life, hounded by rumors of his wife's attachment to a handsome young guardsman of French descent,[144] Pushkin wrote two pieces

---

only was the work admired by the Decembrists, so that during their confinement and trial in the winter and spring of 1826 it was denounced as "incendiary verse" (*buntovskie stikhi*) by a general of the gendarmes, but two years later it became embroiled in another denunciation, this one brought by Metropolitan Serafim against a retired captain Mitkov, who was charged with reading the poem to his peasants and in that way leading them to their moral dissolution. This 1828 episode was very dangerous to Pushkin, and he hinted in a letter to Vyazemsky (1 September 1828) that he might possibly be exiled to the "east" (i.e., Siberia). After denying authorship earlier, he took this opportunity (the letter to Vyazemsky was sent by normal mail and Pushkin could assume it would be perused by tsarist authorities) to attribute the poem to his old school friend D. P. Gorchakov, who had been dead for several years (*Pss,* X:195). But when the poet was finally called before the tsar and forced to declare his true role before a private investigatory commission, he at last (we assume) accepted responsibility. According to the notes of Bartenev, who copied down the words of one of the members of the commission (A. N. Golitsyn), "Pushkin's Gabrieliad. Disavowal. Acknowledgment. Treatment of him by the Emperor" (cited A. S. Pushkin, *Izbrannye sochineniia v dvukh tomakh* [Moscow: Khudozhestvennaia literatura, 1978], I:720; see also *Pss,* IV:414).

143. It will be my argument, to be pursued in the next section ("Jakobson: Why the Statue Won't Come to Life, or Will It?"), that the superstitious Pushkin "knew" that the following lines of mock prayer at the end of *The Gabrieliad* would come back to haunt him some day: "Wonderful comforter of Joseph! / I beseech you, on bended knee, / O defender and protector of cuckolds, / I beseech—so bless me, / Grant me lack of care and humility, / Grant me patience again and again, / Tranquil sleep, and confidence in my spouse, / In my family peace and love for my neighbor" (Иосифа прекрасный утешитель! / Молю тебя, колена преклоня, / О рогачей заступник и хранитель, / Молю—тогда благослови меня, / Даруй ты мне беспечность и смиренье, / Даруй ты мне терпенье вновь и вновь, / Спокойный сон, в супруге уверенье, / В семействе мир и к ближнему любовь!) (*Pss,* IV:119).

144. Several of the memoirs of Pushkin's friends and relatives (i.e., those of A. Vulf, P. Nashchokin, L. Pushkin) confirm that the famous Petersburg fortune-teller Kirkhgof

on Voltaire for his journal *The Contemporary*: "Voltaire" and "The Last Relative of Jeanne d'Arc."[145] These articles, the first a response to the publication of Voltaire's correspondence with the Président de Brosses and the second a "mystification" written in the name of a descendant of the "maid of Orléans" against the author who had impugned her virtue, show poignantly how the husband once playfully invoked in *The Gabrieliad* was decidedly *not* sleeping peacefully. "Voltaire," for example, trains a harsh beam on the calculating, undignified, even potentially cowardly and *dishonorable* behavior that the famous writer displayed in his strained relations with his patron Frederick II of Prussia (here of course we feel Pushkin comparing his own experiences with Alexander and Nicholas): once he has managed to insult Frederick publicly in a literary duel, Voltaire weighs his options, beats a retreat, and drops a phrase in his correspondence back to Paris that was bound to rankle and disgust the 1836 Pushkin: "I fear being like those cuckolded husbands who strive to con-

---

met with the poet in late fall 1819 and foretold, in addition to several facts that later came true, a long life "if in his thirty-seventh year a misfortune did *not* happen to him either from a white horse, or from a white head, or from a white man [*weisser Ross, weisser Kopf, weisser Mensch*], all of which he should fear/avoid" (cited I. S. Chistova, "K stat'e S.A. Sobolevskogo 'Tainstvennye primety v zhizni Pushkina,'" in *Legendy i mify o Pushkine*, ed. M. N. Virolainen [St. Petersburg: Akademicheskii proekt, 1994], 251). D'Anthès was, of course, fair-haired.

145. "Voltaire" was published in volume III of *The Contemporary* (1836); "The Last Relative of Jeanne d'Arc" (Poslednii iz svoistvennikov Ioanny d'Ark) in volume V, posthumously (1837). For additional information about Pushkin's feelings regarding Voltaire in the last years of his life, including the personal scores he is attempting to settle in these articles, see N. O. Lerner, "Zamaskirovannyi Pushkin," *Rasskazy o Pushkine* (Leningrad: Priboi, 1929), 190–98; D. D. Blagoi, *Dusha v zavetnoi lire* (Moscow: Sovetskii pisatel', 1977), 430–50; V. A. Saitanov, "Proshchanie s tsarem," *Vremennik pushkinskoi kommissii* 20 (1982): 36–47; S. A. Fomichev, *Prazdnik zhizni: Etiudy o Pushkine* (St. Petersburg: Nauka, 1995), 209–36; and Stennik, *Pushkin i russkaia literatura XVIII veka*, 283–89. In effect, Lerner (I think basically correctly) reads the details of the "mystification" of "The Last Relative" allegorically into the strained situation in the poet's personal life in the last weeks leading up the the duel; Blagoi expands on Lerner, but then differs with him by claiming (I don't think very convincingly) that the "Voltaire" of "The Last Relative" is not the "real" French author but an amalgam of the two Heeckerens; and finally Fomichev suggests that Blagoi has overstated the case and that, despite the "personal element" (*lichnostnoe nachalo*) in this last work by Pushkin, it is first and foremost a deliberately ambiguous and multifaceted "work of art," none of whose points of view reflects totally that of the author. My position, as will be seen from the analysis to follow, also builds on Lerner but ends being somewhere between that of Blagoi and Fomichev.

vince themselves of the fidelity of their wives."[146] It is the cynicism coupled with the theme of the pathetic husband that the poet cannot countenance. Pushkin then goes on to say that the aging Voltaire was not a figure that commands our respect and that Frederick, despite his faults, was better than the writer because he knew his own worth and because, without such provocation on Voltaire's part to begin with, he would not have "insulted his old teacher" or dressed the "first among French poets" in a "fool's motley" (*shutovskoi kaftan*).[147] Here the subtext is that (1) no matter what, the aging Pushkin *will* comport himself with honor and dignity, and that (2) *his* monarch has suited him up in similar motley (the uniform of the *kameriunker*) without cause and in a needlessly insulting way.

"The Last Relative," though entirely a product of Pushkin's imagination and based on no real documents, is even more provocative and closer to the "hot" truth of the poet's last days than "Voltaire."[148] Now the author who in *La Pucelle* made bold to mock a symbol of national virtue, courage, and spiritual beauty is called out to a duel by a relative of the maiden, who wants satisfaction in the straightforward language of deeds. The relative, moreover, happens to reside *in England* (Pushkin's positive alterity). The imaginary Voltaire of course finds a refined (but still craven) way to deny authorship and refuse the duel. But this *gentilhomme de la chambre du roy* does accept responsibility for *Genriada* (*La Henriade*), which sounds very close to the Russian *Gavriiliada*, after which he is lambasted by the plain-speaking Englishman for his "satanic" skepticism:

> Modern history knows no subject more touching, more poetical, than the life and death of the heroine of Orléans, and now look to what use he [Voltaire] has put his inspiration! With his satanic breath he blows on the sparks smoldering in the ashes of the martyr's pyre, and, like some drunken barbarian, dances around his amusing fire. He is like the Roman executioner who adds defilement to the mortal torments of the maiden. The poem of the laureate [i.e., Southey's 1796 epic *Joan of Arc*] is of course not worth, in terms of sheer inventiveness [*sila vymysla*], Voltaire's poem,

146. *Pss,* VII:285.

147. *Pss,* VII:286.

148. Scholars now believe "The Last Relative" was probably written in the first days of January 1837, that is, approximately three weeks before the poet's fatal duel with d'Anthès. See *Pss,* VII:505.

but Southey's creation is the deed of an honorable man and the fruit of noble rapture.[149]

That Pushkin is donning the mask of a fabricated Englishman to get at the tangle of his own Voltairean/"French" roots should not detract in any way from the high seriousness and powerful self-reflexivity of this mystification. For this is about as close as a reader can ever come to seeing Pushkin talk face-to-face *about himself*: the "purple" in this passage is both ventriloquized (a bit *too* grandiloquent) and completely, painfully real. Pushkin is using the liberating otherness of the English (Southey) and the phrase "deed of an honorable man" (the highest praise he could give the revered Karamzin for writing what he, Pushkin, believed to be a both truthful and ennobling book about Russia's past) to strip aside the enslaving otherness of his own formation. This Voltaire is made into a "barbarian" of refinement just as the French (La Harpe, Voltaire, the Guizot who introduced Pushkin to the Bard in the amended Letourneur prose translations[150]) had made Shakespeare into a northern barbarian whose smashing of the classical unities the ordered Gallic mind could not quite comprehend or appreciate. Now Pushkin, too late of course to save himself, is declaring his independence, "swerving" in a way that is *more* Russian.[151] The

149. *Pss*, VII:351–52.

150. Pushkin was introduced to Shakespeare in the 1821 Paris edition (Chez Ladvocat) of the *Oeuvres Complètes de Shakspeare*. This edition came with a long (150 pp.) essay by François Guizot (the historian Pushkin would subsequently polemicize with in his reviews of Nikolai Polevoi's *History of the Russian People*) on Shakespeare's life and times ("Vie de Shakspeare"). And in this essay Guizot takes up, more subtly but nonetheless definitely, the cultural bias of La Harpe (who called Shakespeare *un auteur barbare*) and Voltaire. Shakespeare becomes what for the French is a contradiction in terms, *the writer formed from nature* (*le poète que forme la seule nature*), just as his country, which lacks *l'empreinte universelle et profonde de la civilisation romaine,* is a melting pot of nondistinguishable conqueror and conquered (Saxons, Danes, Normans, etc.) — all *egalement barbares.* One suspects that the always proud Pushkin, upon reading such lines and realizing that, to the French, he too will always be a "northern barbarian," saw a kind of Shakespearean challenge in them. (It also helped that Shakespeare precisely *did not* have a well-documented life.) Representing another *civilisation du Nord*, he would use "Our Father Shakespeare" (*Pss*, VII:51) himself to show not only how "unsimple" was his own genius, but also how it could borrow the forms of other European cultures, *beginning with the French*, in a way that was by no means "natural" or unconscious.

151. One of Pushkin's alter egos in these last years is the very "Russian," very down-to-earth Fonvizin, who visited the homeland of Voltaire in the eighteenth century and

notion of dancing around a scene of one's own idolatry, of making fun of that which others feel is sacred, of acting like the pagan Roman at the cross/pyre of the self-sacrificing martyr — all this was striking too close to home in Pushkin's case. As the poet was reported to have said to d'Archaic, d'Anthès's second, "You French, you are very polite. You all know Latin, but when you fire in a duel, you take your place at 30 paces. With us Russians it is different: the fewer the explanations, the more merciless the duel." [152] One wonders if Pushkin was thinking about "The Last Relative of Jeanne d'Arc," written just weeks earlier, as he uttered these words, in preparation for the duel his imaginary former *kumir* (idol) avoids.[153]

In the end, and this is what finally brings the Bloomian/Freudian model back to earth and turns it into something real, something embedded with its own futurity, Pushkin understood that all his marvelous words could signify, and with them he could take his proper place in the tradition, only if he could make them speak *in deed.* The conventional phrases spoken by the insouciant speaker of 1820 — "Battle is familiar to me — I love the sound of swords" [154] — had to have, for the Pushkin of the 1830s, something more behind them than convention: he had "to see death" before he could be "worthy of the kisses" of his pretty Madonna.

---

refused in his "Letters from France" to pay homage to Gallic idol worship and trendsetting in a manner already familiar to Pushkin through his uncle Vasily Lvovich. As Vatsuro and Gillelson have demonstrated in their analysis of Pushkin's marginal commentaries made in 1832 in a manuscript copy of his friend Vyazemsky's study of Fonvizin, Pushkin was clearly on the side of the unwilling-to-bow-and-scrape playwright, who saw through the "self-serving quality and obsequiousness of the [French] philosophers" (cited Stennik, *Pushkin i russkaia literatura XVIII veka,* 285). It is this same Fonvizin, as we shall see in our discussion of Derzhavin, who played an important "truth-telling" role in one of Pushkin's earliest and more "private" works, "Fonvizin's Shade" (Ten' Fon-vizina, 1815).

152. B. L. Modzalevskii, *Pushkin* (Leningrad: Priboi, 1929), 379.

153. Not only with Voltaire, but also with Derzhavin, his principal precursor in the Russian tradition, Pushkin would try to prove himself in his last years as a person who was not afraid to act *in deed.* The issue of Derzhavin's reputed cowardice under fire (the Pugachev uprising) would be an important subtext in several of Pushkin's most important works of the 1830s, including *The Captain's Daughter* and "I have erected for myself a monument" (the Horatian/Derzhavinian "Exegi monumentum"). See Part II of this study.

154. The poem was not published by Pushkin during his lifetime, but was read (probably in early April 1820) by him before the "Green Lamp" society and preserved among its papers. The reference to battle here is presumably to the announcement of a revolution in Spain. See *Pss,* I:461.

✑ Jakobson
Why the Statue Won't Come to Life, or Will It?

Schools in the "human sciences" are bound virtually by their own phylogenetic principles to undermine and supersede their predecessors rather than disinterestedly, patiently, build on them. A prior school has to be razed and then a new one erected on the same spot, with the "school board" quickly forgetting the attractions and the still usable space of the now nonexistent building. Students get bussed to the new school without any knowledge (unless some teachers tell them so) that they are walking the halls of a place that once looked much different. The prior school is precisely not "refurbished" or "updated," not given a new heating system or graced with a handsome new wing, but torn down and rebuilt in some entirely new way. This, I take it, is what Lydia Ginzburg had in mind when she wrote in her notebook in 1927 that "I find extremely unpleasant both in myself and in my comrades that satisfaction with one's own bold steps and that pathos of broad horizons. When entering any cultural activity (science, art, philosophy), one ought to remember: what is easy is bad (just as when entering a shop one remembers that what is cheap is bad). To acquire theoretically broad horizons and universal acceptance [*vsepriiatie*] is much easier than constructing and using a system of fruitful limitations [lit. 'conditions of one-sidedness,' *odnostoronnosti*]." [155] Where a *school of thought* is concerned, which depends greatly on the works *and personality* of its first thinker, it seems simpler to begin anew with the "theoretically broad horizons" than to use the already existing "system of fruitful limitations." Here Freud's notion of oedipal struggle—destroying and seemingly wiping away the existence of a controlling father—really does appear to be the operative principle.

I say all this by way of introducing the thought of Roman Jakobson, the great structural linguist, whose work only a generation ago was the cornerstone of every major Slavic program in the country (if not the world) and whose emphasis on the "Slavic word" (the interlocking systems of languages,

155. *Chelovek za pis'mennym stolom* (Leningrad: Sovetskii pisatel', 1989), 55.

89

cultures, folklores, verse forms, etc.) was the heart of "philology" as it was then practiced. How times have changed, how linguistics with its "system of fruitful limitations" has become a stepchild discipline, how the mention of "philology" makes the contemporary student's (and perhaps his faculty advisor's) eyes glaze over! Jakobson is a truly remarkable example of the sort of human science school razing I have just been describing. Just as Freud's psychoanalytic metaphors (primarily archaeological) have remained and even thrived while the scientific basis of his findings has been in constant dispute, Jakobson's strictly descriptive structuralist terminology has *not* been superseded in the realm of (linguistic) science even as his presence (if not his reputation per se) in current debates about the humanities and "whence literary studies?" has been reduced to what can only be called a spasmodic blip on our culture's radar screen. Moreover, essentially the same thing can be said about the relative reputations in the west of Bakhtin and Lotman (to be discussed in the final section of this first part): the former, primarily a philosopher, offers ways (and alluring vocabularies) for making literature not an object of study but a *place* where *subjects and subjectivities* interact; the latter, on the other hand, clearly Jakobson's equal in the field of semiotics and one of the most fertile minds of the second half of the century, hews to the descriptive, scientific/"enlightenment" episteme perfected by his illustrious predecessor, and *for that reason* continues to be less well known.

But why is this, why are we so much more apt to *listen to* Freud and Bakhtin, to try to glean the vectors behind their thought, and yet to *ignore* Jakobson and Lotman, to reduce them to the "mere" structuralist and semiotician? The cruder response is that Freud and Bakhtin allow us, relatively painlessly (unless we are sufficiently self-aware and scrupulous), to enter into dialogue with our texts and with their now silent authors. That is of course more intriguing, more inherently interesting. Jakobson and Lotman require us to *know* a great deal more before we speak and then to speak about what we do know in a way that is not itself a subjective, that is, metaphorical, embrace of its own subjectivity. Jakobson, for example, would not have used Mandelstam's flying machine metaphor in a manner that suggested that this kind of thinking was not something to be "studied" (analyzed) but something to be "lived" (experienced); rather, he would have described what Mandelstam was doing as an example of the (note the depersonalization) "poetic *function*": "The poetic function projects the principle of equivalence from the axis of selection into the axis of combination. Equivalence is promoted to the constitutive device of the sequence."[156] It makes no difference whether it is Jakobson's famous "I like Ike" example (internal rhyme) or the flying machine metaphor of Russia's greatest twentieth-century poet: both exhibit the same principle of language drawing attention to its own simultaneity (i.e., the coexistence of different "axes"), to its ability to say more than one thing at the same time. One doesn't need such slippery notions as "charisma" (the personality in and around the words) to talk about "poetry" in terms of the poetic function: one can merely say that "verse [as an orientation] actually exceeds the limits of poetry, but at the same time verse always implies the poetic function."[157] The poet can be "beside himself"[158] if he wants to, but language can't, and it is the latter (or so it seems!—see below) that is the only thing we can accurately describe and study. "Poetry" and "metalanguage" (the language that talks *about* poetic functions) are simply mirror inversions of one another, the former building on the principle of pure equation (simultaneity), the latter building on the principle of pure sequence (difference). Absolutely everything Jakobson says about texts (poetic and otherwise), messages, and the retrieval of information encoded therein—the speech event, the different functions of language (referential, expressive, conative, metalingual, etc.), study that is diachronic versus study that is synchronic, the dominant, verse organization, rhythm versus meter, sound symbolism, lexical versus grammatical tropes, etc.—is couched in a (meta)language that remains on this side of the scientific divide, that resolutely refuses to be "turned on," that describes the poetic function at work but will not itself be contaminated by the "poetic." The one glaring exception is an article that is itself framed by its own hortatory trope, the brilliant "On a Generation That Squandered Its Poets" (1931), which is Jakobson's homage to his own youth (the formalist-futurist symbiosis) and to the suicidal poet of the revolution (Mayakovsky) who more than any other symbolized the impossibility of embodying a revolutionary poetic over time. But this, one hastens to add, is only the exception that proves the rule.

There is an essential paradox in Jakobsonian thought, which I have likened in the title to this section to the statue that refuses to come to life. It is fascinating that this man, who was clearly a genius, returned in his last years to

156. "Linguistics and Poetics," *Language in Literature*, ed. Krystyna Pomorska and Stephen Rudy (Cambridge: Harvard University Press, 1987), 71.

157. Jakobson, "Linguistics and Poetics," 72.

158. Again, see Stewart, "Lyric Possession," 35 (see n. 66, above).

the "trans-sense" verse (*zaumnye stikhi*) of his youth not simply as object of study, but as something belonging to his own once-open past, as he filled the summer air of his Peacham, Vermont, dacha with the hilarious sounds of gods run wild (or was it beasts?).[159] This is not another banal tale of the *poète man- qué*—for how many poems, even some great ones, are worth the *quality* of Jakobson's mind in its verbal traces?—but a case of one legendary hero, say Achilles, trying at the end of his quest to have a go at being, if only in jest, a very different type of hero, say Odysseus. The one's (analytical) muscles, as awesome as they are, cannot in certain situations stand in for the other's (poetic) craftiness. And the result is burlesque, something recognizably both more and less than Khlebnikov. Jakobson is at his best, which is for this reader routinely astounding, when he is describing a general situation in language acquisition, or its opposite, language loss: aphasia, with its "similarity dis- order" (the loss of the metalinguistic function, the inability of the speaker to *select* the right word—"knife" becoming "fork"—for the right slot) versus its "contiguity disorder" (the loss of the surrounding grammatical framework of "relations"—conjunctions, prepositions, etc.—so that the speaker begins to forget inflections and to talk in a "telegraphic style").[160] Such articles really do have the aura of "science" about them. Likewise, Jakobson is compelling and very much still "usable" today when he enters on the terrain of "how relations in one area *interact* with relations in another": his move (with Tynianov) in 1928 away from the excesses of early Formalism toward the more historicized and dimensionalized concept of "system" ("The history of a system is in turn a system"[161]) of the Prague School, or his identification of the "dominant"

159. A stimulus to Jakobson's thoughts and reminiscences about his own "trans-sense" verse was an article he was writing during the 1979 summer season in Vermont: entitled "Zaumnyi Turgenev" (Supraconscious Turgenev), it retold and analyzed with consider- able panache an anecdote about how the great prose writer had resorted to screaming out a *zaumnyi* list of feminine Russian nouns ("Radish! Pumpkin! Mare! Turnip! Peasant Woman! Kasha! Kasha!") when confronted with a too orderly, ritualized, and masculin- ized setting at an exclusive London eating club (see Jakobson, *Language in Literature*, 262–66). The story of the early Jakobson as aspiring futurist poet is found in Bengt Jang- feldt, ed., *Jakobson-Budetlianin* (Stockholm: Almqvist & Wiksell, 1992; Acta Universitatis Stockholmiensis, Stockholm Studies in Russian Literature, 26). My thanks to Jakobson's biographer Stephen Rudy for this information.

160. "Two Aspects of Language and Two Types of Aphasic Disturbance" (1956, in col- laboration with Morris Halle), *Language in Literature*, 95–114.

161. "Problems in the Study of Language and Literature" (1928, with Yuri Tynianov), *Language in Literature*, 47–49; this quotation is taken from p. 48.

(*dominanta*) as a way of properly focusing attention in a historical context, of bringing together the diachronic and synchronic realms.[162]

Above all, however, this greatest of structural linguists is "on top of his game" when he analyzes a poem that itself draws meaning from *grammatical* (i.e., strictly relational) categories: the readings of Pushkin's two short pieces "I loved you" (Ia vas liubil, 1829) and "What is there in my name for you" (Chto v imeni tebe moem, 1830) in "Poetry of Grammar and Grammar of Poetry," for example.[163] These readings succeed so admirably, they seem to "deliver" a meaning that is completely adequate in this case to the exhaustiveness of the formal analysis, because they relate to a virtually "imageless poetry"[164] and because their compensatory play with pronouns (personal and interrogative) so totally overwhelms and in effect takes the place of the "axis of selection." There is a geometric elegance to these readings—the author even suggests that what geometry is for the visual arts grammar is for the verbal arts[165]—that foregrounds beautifully Jakobson's genius (but not necessarily Pushkin's). If one could put it this way, Roman Jakobson is the "Deep Blue" of poetic analysis: his way of looking at things as *relations* of abstract chess pieces on a chess board has no equal in its realm, where the category of "poetry" can be more or less subsumed into the category of "system" and "artificial intelligence." "Deep Blue" can defeat the world's greatest chess player, for it has no equal when it comes to abstract *relational* strategy, but it could never create something with the ontological status of a poem because it has no biography and no personality, only "on" and "off" switches. And even if it could simulate what a "good" poem would sound and look like, something essential (the relation of the "life" to the "art," which even "poets without biographies" possess as a consciously adopted absence) would be left out. Achilles cannot become Odysseus.

Jakobson's Achilles' heel makes itself felt most palpably in those exhaustive structural analyses of poems—Baudelaire's "Les Chats" and Shakespeare's sonnet 129 ("Th' expense of Spirit")[166]—where the strictly relational cate-

---

162. "The Dominant" (from unpublished Czech lectures on Formalism given in Brno in 1935), *Language in Literature*, 41–46.

163. "Poetry of Grammar and Grammar of Poetry" (1960), *Language in Literature*, 121–144.

164. "Poetry of Grammar and Grammar of Poetry," 129.

165. "Poetry of Grammar and Grammar of Poetry," 133.

166. "Baudelaire's 'Les Chats'" (1962, with Claude Lévi-Strauss) and "Shakespeare's

gories and the "geometric" qualities of form (say, symmetries of person, gender, nasal vowels, rhyme words, etc., in and among lines and stanzas) do not seem to bring the reader closer to a "feel" for the artistic structure and its ability to generate meaning. Whether lines 7 and 8 of "Les Chats," those referring to the cats' unwillingness to serve ("L'Érèbe les eût pris pour ses coursiers funèbres, / S'ils pouvaient au servage incliner leur fierté"), form a chiasmuslike pivot between two sestets and whether the configuration of the sonnet is ultimately tripartite or bipartite seem questions better suited to the reader-qua-chess-player type. Only on the very last page of the article, when Jakobson and Lévi-Strauss link up the cats, the Sphinx, the principle of the "feminine" in the context of the "supervirility" of the poem's grammatical gender, and the poet as the one who is capable of bringing these notions to life and endowing them with graceful movement, does the structure begin to be successfuly "semanticized." But it seems too little too late, something akin to trying to get from "here" to "there" by casting a rope across a chasm the width of the Grand Canyon. It is not this sexiest of poets who needs to be "delivered" from the piece's final words and purported feline message, "the scholar's austerity," [167] but the authors themselves. What Helen Vendler has written contra Jakobson's reading of Shakespeare's sonnet 129 could be applied with equal validity to the analysis of "Les Chats" and indeed to all Jakobsonian texts where the object of study is an *internal system of relations:*

> Jakobson had hoped, it is clear, to find a useful method that could be applied to all poems, or at least to very many poems. In this method, one compares all possible combinations of parts: odd strophes against even strophes, early strophes against late strophes, outside strophes (beginning and end) against inside strophes (middle), pre-center strophes against post-center strophes, quatrains against couplet, middle two lines against the lines preceding them and following them. This method, so extraordinarily bizarre when applied to a poem, does not I think yield useful interpretations, and the linguistic features remarked by Jakobson could be described independently of his binary method. The method militates against any notion of *the evolution of feeling* in the poem, any progressive expansion or contradiction of thought, and especially in this poem, *the indispensable sequence of emotional logic* which makes the poem a whole.

Verbal Art in 'Th' Expense of Spirit'" (1970, with L. G. Jones), *Language in Literature,* 180–197 and 198–215.

167. Jakobson, "Baudelaire's 'Les Chats,'" 197.

The linearity of the poem is wholly lost sight of, and the many small points of suspense and climax ignored.[168]

In other words, the statue remains itself, a frozen system of symmetries; it does not come alive.

In 1937, the centennial of Pushkin's death, Jakobson wrote perhaps his greatest work as literary scholar: originally published in Czech, "The Statue in Pushkin's Poetic Mythology" was translated into English, equipped with a host of photographs, and reissued in 1975 as *Puškin and His Sculptural Myth*.[169] The study is remarkable because it shows, in a very striking way, both the power and the limitations of the author's structural linguistic episteme. On the positive side, it demonstrated for the first time, on a sampling of a great many texts, that the theme of sculpture was absolutely crucial to the poet's personal mythology. More to the point, however, it isolated with considerable elegance and conceptual power such "magnetized" issues as: (1) when the theme (the "destructive statue") first began to become foregrounded as a subject in its own right (i.e., near the time of Pushkin's marriage); (2) how concerns arising in Pushkin's private life (i.e., his continual difficulties with money and his questionable reputation as freethinker and borderline radical) that stood athwart the path to his marriage could be seen to be reworked as plot "invariants" in three important works of the 1830s, *The Stone Guest* (Kamennyi gost', 1830), *The Bronze Horseman* (Mednyi vsadnik, 1833), and "The Fairy Tale of the Golden Cockerel" (Skazka o zolotom petushke, 1834), that also represented the poet's final efforts in these respective genres (drama, narrative poem, fairytale); (3) how this notion of graven image had a very real (not merely "metaphorical") biographical resonance for Pushkin that went back to his Lyceum days (e.g., the monuments in the parks at Tsarskoe Selo that celebrated some of the empire's victories during Catherine's "Golden Age" and that implicated the poet's own relatives) and that continued into his year of courtship (1830) (and beyond) with the repeated reference in his correspondence to the "bronze grandmother" (a bust of Catherine belonging to

168. "Jakobson, Richards, and Shakespeare's Sonnet CXXIX," in *I. A. Richards: Essays in His Honor* (New York: Oxford University Press, 1973), 179–98; this passage is from pp. 197–98 (my emphasis).

169. *Puškin and His Scuptural Myth*, ed. and trans. John Burbank (The Hague-Paris: Mouton, 1975). The version I am using here ("The Statue in Pushkin's Poetic Mythology") is based on the Burbank translation, slightly revised, and is found in Jakobson, *Language in Literature*, 318–67.

the Goncharov family) that he believed he would have to have melted down and sold in order to produce sufficient dowry funds in order to get married; (4) how the reversible idea of "the statue that comes to life" and "the human being that turns to stone" seems to have been one with which Pushkin became increasingly obsessed, especially with the onset of his married years; and (5) how the plot invariant in each case is what we might call today a "triangulated" (after Girard) relation involving a woman and competing lovers, one usually a husband (with his "rights") and the other a potential seducer or "kidnapper" of the woman who may be endowed with a different kind of power (i.e., political). It would seem that any reader of Jakobson's study must come to the conclusion that he has made some major, if not seminal, discoveries and that he has caused us to read "Pushkin" in a new and exciting way.

But has he? I would argue that this otherwise foundational work suffers, from my point of view fatally, from the same structuralist "bricolage," the same inability to glean in proper perspective *the evolution of feeling* and *the indispensable sequence of emotional logic,* that we noted above in Vendler's response to the Jakobsonian reading of Shakespeare's sonnet 129. Which is to say, Jakobson is brilliant at isolating "structure," but he seems next to helpless at showing the "dominant" as an organizing figure of emotion, as a way of understanding *how* structure interacts with feeling in order to tell its own story. Jakobson's calcified binaries can't tell the tale that arises out of their flesh-and-blood tensions. His way of presenting how Pushkin's biographical and aesthetic concerns interact is, despite the disclaimers,[170] extremely mechanical. All he can do is protect the new world of his structuralist discoveries by planting the flag of his own scientific "colonizing": he is against both "vulgar biographism" and "vulgar autobiographism,"[171] which seems to mean any of the "noise" he comes upon that cannot be pressed into the service of his binaries. It is not, I would argue, the "repeated correspondences between a

170. "The analysis of poetic language can profit greatly from the important information provided by contemporary linguistics about the multiform interpenetration of the word and the [biographical] situation, about their mutual tension and their mutual influence. We do not wish mechanically to derive a work from a situation, but at the same time, in analyzing a poetic work, we should not overlook significant repeated correspondences between a situation and the work, especially a regular connection between certain common characteristics of a poet's several works and a common place or common dates; nor should we overlook the biographical preconditions of their origin if they are the same" (Jakobson, "Statue in Puškin's Poetic Mythology," 320).

171. "Statue in Puškin's Poetic Mythology," 320.

[biographical] situation and the work," [172] i.e., the so-called invariants, that attract us to Pushkin and his "life of the poet," although to see that they are there is necessary to comprehend what is taking place, but rather the *difference* (the "story") those invariants generate when they are placed in contact with new, unpredictable information. It is this more telling (in various senses) story, this constant shuttling back and forth between what is fixed and what is free in life and art, *both of which always already implicate each other,* that Jakobson's model cannot replicate. To narrate this story successfully one cannot simply describe, one must evaluate, interpret in a such way that emotional coloring perforce enters the picture. For just as Chomsky's transformational grammar (another type of structuralism) works neatly for the simple declarative sentence, but quickly becomes unwieldy, a virtual skyscraper of embedded rules, when a complex and emotionally nuanced (i.e., potentially "poetic") utterance is diagrammed, so too are Jakobson's invariants both too much (they see structure where structure is not necessarily meaningful) and not enough (they don't convey the poet's awe and enchantment before the idea of *living form*). Moreover, Jakobson's own ideological vectors, which are not by the way a priori or "scientifically" arrived at, cause him, when they do surface to shape the material, to see Pushkin as more atheist/nonbelieving ("iconoclastic" in terms of the graven image myth) and more inherently radical (his complicated feelings toward Alexander and Nicholas) than he was in fact, especially later in life. This is a not insignificant distortion, about which I will be speaking more in a moment. Therefore, despite his remarkable findings, Jakobson is not I would say successful at *realizing* the sculptural metaphor in the larger context of the poet's personal mythology.

It will be the task of the remainder of this section to show how Jakobson's findings (together with some additional ones) might be used to bring Pushkin's statue back to life. Let us begin again by opening, in a manner that is precise and not arbitrary, the hermeneutic circle to Pushkin's own cultural context: to repeat, from his earliest days the poet was deeply superstitious, a tendency that seems to have played to his pagan, popular side and to his sense that there are signs in the world (and in his own biography) that he may interpret but over which *he has no control.*[173] Equally if not more important, after a

172. Jakobson, "Statue in Puškin's Poetic Mythology," 320.

173. I take, for example, Pushkin's statement in the voice of one of his favorite heroes (Petrusha Grinev) to be closely reflective of his own feelings: "I hope the reader will forgive me, for he probably knows from experience how easy it is for people to fall into superstition, however great their contempt for unfounded beliefs may be" (*Pss,* X:269;

certain point (1826 and "The Prophet"/"Prorok" can be cited as watersheds[174]) he *stops* treating Christian thematics in his work with Voltairean irreverence. Why this is so is a matter of some speculation, but his own humiliating exile in the south and then in Mikhailovskoe, the dismal failure of the Decembrist uprising and the sad fate of implicated friends and classmates, and his own maturation as thinker and writer must all have been factors. In other words, rather than the on/off switch of Jakobsonian binaries, what we have with the "sacred"/"demonic" space of superstition and religion is a rather large fuzzy band of pure feeling or awe governed by "forms" ("rites" in the case of religion) that are not susceptible of analysis or direct cognition. This, I submit, is where we must start in order to try to understand Pushkin's sculptural myth,

---

CPF, 276). Recent scholarship suggests that it was during the Mikhailovskoe exile (1824–26) that the actual theme of *sud'ba* (fate), as a concept suffused with superstitious dread and bearing a message of cosmic retribution for past sins, began actively to enter Pushkin's lyrics. A. F. Belousov was the first to explore the notion of a superstition-laden fate in Pushkin's post-1825 lyrics in his "Khudozhestvennyi smysl stikhotvoreniia A. S. Pushkina 'Zimnii vecher,' " *Prepodavanie literaturnogo chteniia v Estonskoi shkole* (Tallin: Tallinskii Pedagogicheskii Institut, 1981), 6–27. Belousov shows that a cluster of poems, "Zimnii vecher" (Winter Evening, 1825), "Niane" (To [My] Nanny, 1826), "Dar naprasnyi, dar sluchainyi" (Gift futile, gift accidental, 1828), "Predchuvstvie" (Foreboding, 1828), "Besy" (Devils, 1830), and "Stikhi, sochinennye noch'iu vo vremia bessonnitsy" (Verses composed at night during insomnia, 1830), are united into an informal cycle by several factors: (1) they are composed (with the sole exception of "To Nanny") in a trochaic meter that has "folk" connotations; (2) several feature the presence of an old woman spinning or knitting (cf. the Parcae); (3) they seem obsessed by the viciously circular movement of snow or leaves and, especially, by the recurrence of an uncertain but ominous noise that the lyrical speaker strains, but fails, to comprehend. It is through this notion of gathering dread, which appears to commence in Mikhailovskoe alongside the poet's newfound respect for sincere religious faith (see next note), that time and history shed their playful ("salon") guises and become "irreversible" in Pushkin.

174. Actually, the watershed years are 1824–26, i.e., those coterminous with Pushkin's northern exile in Mikhailovskoe. The thematic links between the ninth poem in the cycle "Imitations of the Koran" (Podrazhaniia Koranu), "And the weary wanderer grumbled at God" (I putnik ustalyi na boga roptal, wr. November 1824), and "The Prophet" (wr. September 1826) show how Pushkin's ideas regarding the high calling of the poet were evolving in these years of his greatest, most soul-searching isolation. Although humor, scabrousness, and an unwillingness to moralize directly will be features of Pushkin's work right into the 1830s, there is not a shred of the strictly "Voltairean" element, i.e., the "atheistic" mocking of religious sensibilities, after 1826. I take my trajectory for Pushkin's treatment of religious themes here from Sergei Davydov, "Puškin's Easter Triptych," in *Puškin Today,* ed. David M. Bethea (Bloomington: Indiana University Press, 1993), 44–45.

because it is this sacred space that he traduced in the Voltairean exuberance of his starting out. Hence, it is not the statue per se that we find in the early verse as an example of the demonic, but the "shade" or the "specter" (*ten'*), which only over time takes on three-dimenional form. In Pushkin's early poetry, say "Recollections at Tsarskoe Selo," monuments such as the Kagul obelisk and Chesma column function purely as links to the historic past (again, the heroic age of Catherine), to the poet's own family history (the Pushkins as warriors), and to the sacred site-in-the-making of his schooling and friendships (the Lyceum). Such graven images are perceived as exclusively, benignly *commemorative* — they are the tangible evidence of the "immortality" of brave and glorious deeds. The fact, for example, that Derzhavin, the Russian poet with greatest claim to a historic biography, and the one who wanted to see his own bust among those of Catherine's favorites at Tsarskoe Selo, is present at this soon to be mythopoeticized inauguration of Pushkin's career must be viewed as enormously significant, as we shall see in Part II of this study. But the statue itself does not become a serious fact of Pushkin's personal, and what is more important, erotic mythology until the prospect of his marriage to Natalia Goncharova. In this Jakobson is certainly right.

But what exactly does this mean in terms of the *indispensable sequence of emotional logic* surrounding the poet's "created life"? What was going on in and around his words and their experiential residue to precipitate this shift to the "embodied ghost," the destructive statue, or, to borrow Jakobson's terms taken from Russian ethnology, from *lekan* (statue as pure "external representation") to *ongon* (an "incarnation of some spirit or demon").[175] Here I think we might start with "To a Young Widow" (K molodoi vdove, 1817), a poem written during the Lyceum period:

> O priceless friend!
> Is it to be forever that you shed tears,
> forever that you summon
> from the grave your dead spouse?
> Believe me: from cold sleep
> the prisoners of the grave cannot be awakened.[176]

---

175. "Statue in Puškin's Poetic Mythology," 322.

176. *Pss*, I:214. The original reads: «О бесценная подруга! / Вечно ль слезы проливать, / Вечно ль мертвого супруга / Из могилы вызывать? / Верь мне: узников могилы / Беспробуден хладный сон.»

This little piece of silliness (only extracted here), which was not published in Pushkin's lifetime, was written fully thirteen years before *The Stone Guest,* yet it already displays certain structural attributes of the later drama, especially the notion that the speaker's challenge is to woo not just anyone, but precisely the young wife of a dead husband. In this case, the fetching widow was a certain Marie Smith, née Charon la Rose, who was visiting at the home of the Lyceum's director, E. A. Engelhardt. What is important to understand is that *already* the schoolboy Pushkin must maintain his independence against all forces, living and dead, and that in order for him to get to his happiness (a night with Marie Smith) he must *get by* a dead, hence potentially ghostly,[177] rival. But that rival has certain legitimate claims on the object of affection, claims which, when we come to issues of the "Muse" and the poetic tradition, will have to do with the other's (for our purposes, Derzhavin's) *earned* position as a genuinely historical figure. Thus, in order to establish his bona fides (and "be born," as it were) as artist and lover, the young Pushkin must willingly mock, and as it turns out in the most provocative sacrilegious terms (here hinted at with the imperative of the verb "to believe," *ver'*), those others already fixed in place — whether husbands, whose wives he eagerly pursues, or dead poets, whose muses he willingly woos away. And his challenges are particularly bold and fraught with risky (i.e., superstition-laden) consequences when they join jokes at the expense of the other world with the notion of "dead" + "husband/lover." The speaker who says at the end of "To a Young Widow" "No, a jealous one full of rage / Will not emerge from the eternal darkness"[178] is, as we might put it today, whistling in the dark.

The next stage in the psychic evolution of this ghost story occurs at the end of a poem that later in life Pushkin would, one assumes, have done anything to take back. But then to take it back would have meant that he wouldn't have been "Pushkin":

> But days fly by, and time, imperceptibly,
> flecks with gray my head,
> and serious marriage will unite me
> at the altar with an amiable wife.
> Wonderful comforter of Joseph!

177. At the end of the poem the speaker refers to the absent husband as a *zavistlivaia ten'* (envious shade) who (he hopes!) won't come back from the dead. *Pss,* I:215.

178. *Pss,* I:215. The original reads: «Нет, разгневанный ревнивец / Не придет из вечной тьмы.»

I beseech you, on bended knee,
O defender and protector of cuckolds,
I beseech — so bless me,
Grant me lack of care and humility,
Grant me patience again and again,
Tranquil sleep, and confidence in my spouse,
In my family peace and love for my neighbor.[179]

Written in 1821 in Kishinev at the height of Pushkin's Voltairean phase, *The Gabrieliad* is, despite its great charm, truly one of the most brazenly sacrilegious pieces ever penned, in Russia or elsewhere. It is also at its very center about infidelity: about as conscious of what she was doing as the apple eaten by her primordial mother, Mary was such a ripe and available piece of fruit ("Ah, how that Jewess was lovely!"[180]) that not to pluck her was itself a sin. And so each, first the serpent, then a weak-willed Gabriel, and finally the holy spirit (the dove) itself, has his/its way with her, but God, the ultimate patriarch and husband figure, all-knowing in other respects, is ironically kept in the dark about the escapades of the generous "virgin." It is this playfulness that Pushkin, through his speaker in "The Last Relative of Jeanne d'Arc," clubs in his old teacher and author of *La Pucelle* (just as Gabriel kicks Satan in the groin in *The Gabrieliad*), when he says three weeks before his fatal duel with d'Anthès that "Modern history knows no subject more touching, more poetical, than the life and death of the heroine of Orléans, and now look to what use he [Voltaire] has put his inspiration! With his satanic breath he blows on the sparks smoldering in the ashes of the martyr's pyre, and, like some drunken barbarian, dances around his amusing fire. He is like the Roman executioner who adds defilement to the mortal torments of the maiden." Pushkin could not help himself from authoring his sacrilegious joke at the time, but then after the fact, once he had set this "ontological rhyme" in motion in his life, he realized he had trod upon sacred territory, territory dear to many countrymen, who were

179. *Pss*, IV:119. The ending of "Gavriiliada" (1821) reads in the original: «Но дни бегут, и время сединою / Мою главу тишком посеребрит, / И важный брак с любезною женою / Пред алтарем меня соединит. / Иосифа прекрасный утешитель! / Молю тебя, колена преклоня, / О рогачей заступник и хранитель, / Молю — тогда благослови меня, / Даруй ты мне блаженное терпенье, / Молю тебя, пошли мне вновь и вновь / Спокойный сон, в супруге увереньс, / В семействе мир и к ближнему любовь.»

180. «Ах, как была еврейка хороша!» (*Pss*, IV:117).

after all Russians and not French, and territory that was the source of "poetry" of another sort. Yet I would even go so far as to say that the "after the fact" is a bit of an optical (or "scholarly") illusion, since there is the sense in almost everything Pushkin wrote that he *knew* what he was doing (not merely cognitively, and not merely emotionally, but precisely cognitively and emotionally at the same time, which has no other name than *poetic* knowledge). The passage above begins *as a prayer*—"Amen! Amen!"—that the speaker utters, challengingly, into the just concluded space of his elaborate off-color joke. He enjoys making fun of the ultimate cuckold if the prize, the apple waiting to be plucked, is worth it. But then, as always with Pushkin, he puts the shoe on the other foot. He, only twenty-one, projects forward to his own future days as husband and prays to the comforter and protector of cuckolds that he too, in the name of family peace and quiet, be kept in the dark about his wife's extracurricular activities. "Grant me lack of care and humility, / Grant me patience again and again, / Tranquil sleep, and confidence in my spouse, / In my family peace and love for my neighbor" is precisely *not* what will be given to the intensely jealous future husband of Natalia Nikolaevna, *and he knows it.*[181] Indeed, given the poet's self-mutilating call in the post-watershed "Prophet" to have a six-winged seraphim tear out "my sinful tongue, / both cunning [*lukavyi,* in popular tradition 'from the Evil One'] and full of idle speech,"[182] one can only imagine how Pushkin saw these lines coming back to haunt him.

Our third example brings us to the watershed years and to the premonition that the shade is about to be embodied as the retributive statue. In *Boris Godunov* (1825), we find a Pushkin who is well into "living down" the lessons of Byronic romanticism and is now interested more in *Russian* history,

---

181. For the record, Pushkin could be consumed by feelings of jealousy, especially when he sensed that the object of his desire was deliberately toying with his passionate need in the presence of a rival. See, in this respect, the consciousness of the speaker in the poem "Will you forgive me my jealous dreams" (Prostish' li mne revnivye mechty, 1823), in *Pss*, II:146, which was supposedly written under the influence of the poet's feelings for Amalia Riznich. On the other hand, Pushkin, like the Othello to whom he often implicitly compared himself, was trusting by nature. If during the last months of his life he came to experience overpowering jealousy toward his rival Georges d'Anthès, who continued to make public display of his feelings for Mme. Pushkina, he as far as we know never questioned the intentions, the implicit rectitude, of his "Madonna-like" wife. Thus, the jealousy that would come back to haunt the poet was directed at the end not toward the "spouse" in whom he lacked "confidence," but rather toward the "neighbor" who was threatening, in public, to shatter the "family peace."

182. *Pss*, II:304: «грешный мой язык, / И празднословный и лукавый.»

Karamzin, Shakespeare, and a notion of time that is maximally risk-laden and nonreversible. Here the primary shade or specter is the one haunting Tsar Boris and his claims to legitimacy. Yet even that shade, renegade priest Grigory Otrepev-cum-arisen Tsarevich, has its own shade to worry about. In the famous scene at the fountain, the Pretender, clearly the most "Pushkinian" character in the play and the one closest to the status of "poet in history," [183] declares in frustration to his exquisitely cool fiancée, Marina Mniszek,

> Don't torment me, charming Marina,
> Don't tell me that it is my [high] office, and not myself,
> that you have chosen . . .
>
> .   .   .   .
>
>   No! Enough!
> I have no wish to share with a corpse
> a lover belonging to him.[184]

Marina is a Polish (i.e., alluringly western) amalgam of Juliet on the balcony and Lady Macbeth uttering her dark visions of power into the ear of her spouse. She is also described externally, in the scene immediately preceding this one, as a "marble nymph: eyes, lips, without life, without a smile." [185] In other words, her beauty is potentially statuesque, and the one way the Pretender can bring that beauty to life as erotic feeling is through the assumed presence of a rival, that of the murdered Tsarevich, to whom she believes, or wants to believe, she is betrothed. It is only when the Pretender *becomes* the Tsarevich, when he enters sufficiently into his role as proud scion to make that role believable—a fact Pushkin underscores brilliantly by switching the stage direction from "Pretender" to "Dimitry (proudly)"—that the Polish ice goddess begins to melt. But then again, this is another sort of infidelity, since it is, in Pushkin's rendering, the Tsarevich (or his power) that Marina loves but it is the Pretender with whom she will eventually sleep.

The Boldino autumn of 1830, that tremendously fertile and anxiety-laden eve of the poet's marriage, provides the next series of examples. It is during this year, and especially during this autumn, of courtship that we for the first time

183. "I believe in the prophecies of poets" (*Ia veruiu v prorochestva piitov*), says the Pretender to a poet at one point (*Pss*, V:236).

184. *Pss*, V:242–43: «Не мучь меня, прелестная Марина, / Не говори, что сан, а не меня / Избрала ты . . . / Нет! Полно! / Я не хочу делиться с мертвецом / Любовницей ему принадлежащей.»

185. *Pss*, V:238: «Да, мраморная нимфа: / Глаза, уста, без жизни, без улыбки.»

come face to face with the full presence of the sculptural myth. Here it must be said that Jakobson and his descriptive method are both stunningly correct and immensely helpful — the very building blocks on which those coming after can erect their versions of a "truer" story. Even so, however, some significant adjustments are in order. First, there is the deadly erotic play in *The Stone Guest* with *statuia* (statue) and *stat'* (to stand erect): in scene iii, Don Guan mocks his rival's gender by calling the man embodied in the static form *ona* (*statuia* is feminine in Russian), and then he invites him to stand erect — the ultimate insult — at his wife's chamber door while he himself is taking his pleasure within.[186] What is distinctly Pushkinian about this encounter with the fixed other (i.e., "dead" + "husband" — > "statue"/embodied ghost) is that the plainly superstitious hero, as opposed to the more cowardly and down-to-earth Leporello, decides to carry out his fatal plan (the assignation) even *after* the *komandor*'s graven image has nodded to him. In other words, the utterer of the challenge knows at some level, just as he did in *The Gabrieliad,* its *cost.* Yet no matter what, this man with a reckless past, who, as Akhmatova pointed out, is a poet not only "in love" but in the more conventional sense,[187] will have his chance at rebirth[188] at the feet of his initially chaste but eventually desiring beauty.[189] As Donna Anna says, in lines that resonate unmistakably with Tatiana's famous rejection of Onegin, written contemporaneously:

> Diego [i.e., Don Guan in disguise], stop [your talk]: I sin
> listening to you — I am forbidden to love you,
> a widow must be faithful even to the grave. . . .[190]

And as Guan retorts,

---

186. To be sure, the unprefixed *stat'* is not the same verb in Russian for "to have an erection" (*vstat'*, *vstavat'*) or "to be erect" (*stoiat'*), but the root is identical and, given the context, it seems clear that Pushkin is playing off these meanings.

187. "Don Guan is a poet. His verses, transposed to music, are sung by Laura, and Guan himself calls himself an 'improvisatore of the love song' " (Anna Akhmatova, " 'Kamennyi gost' Pushkina," *Sochineniia* [Munich: Inter-language Literary Associates, 1968], II:260).

188. *Pss,* V:347: "It seems to me I have been reborn entirely" (*Mne kazhetsia, ia ves' pererodilsia*).

189. Cf. the psycho-erotic evolution of the already mentioned "No, I do not prize" (Net, ia ne dorozhu), in *Pss,* III:356.

190. *Pss,* V:343: «Диего, перестаньте: я грешу, / Вас слушая, — мне вас любить нельзя, / Вдова должна и гробу быть верна . . .»

Don't torment my heart,
Donna Anna, with eternal mention [lit. "remembrance," *pominan'e*]
of your husband. You have punished me enough,
even though it could be that I deserve execution.[191]

An important shift has taken place here along with the notion that the statue is retributive: not only is Guan in competition with the dead husband (actually, the husband that he killed), but the rights of that husband are legitimately *sacred* and not to be tampered with. That's where the embodiment comes from, since it is Pushkin's own body that is about to step into the role of the potentially ridiculous *komandor*. Hence it is the *husband*, and not the *father*, as in other versions of the Don Juan story, who comes to protect the honor of Donna Anna;[192] hence it is the striking *difference* between the massive physical monument, with its static grandeur, and the dead man's tiny, seemingly insectlike[193] stature in real life that draws the attention of the ironic, though still admiring ("He was proud and bold and possessed a stern spirit"[194]) Guan, hence it is that, for all the Spanish decor and the synecdochic mention of lemon and bay trees, a more accurate parallel for Laura and her guests would be, as Akhmatova also divined, some scene from Pushkin's days as a Petersburg "scapegrace," seated gaily among "members of the 'Green Lamp' society who are dining at the home of some celebrity of the time, such as [the actress Alexandra] Kolosova, and discussing art";[195] and hence it is that all the demonic/atheistic connotations in the drama are, strangely enough, associated not with the graven image of Orthodox loathing but with the "godless" man who is about to take what is not his in the name of love.[196] In this respect, I believe that Akhmatova's evaluation of the ultimate meaning of *The Stone Guest*,

191. *Pss*, V:343: «Не мучьте сердца / Мне, Дона Анна, вечным поминаньем / Супруга. Полно вам меня казнить, / Хоть казнь я заслужил быть можст.»

192. Mentioned in Akhmatova, " 'Kamennyi gost' " Pushkina," 262.

193. Don Alvar is described as a "dragonfly" (*strekoza*) impaled on Guan's sword (*Pss*, V:332); Pushkin was known among his Arzamas brethren as the "cricket" (*sverchok*).

194. *Pss*, V:332: «. . . а был / Он горд и смел — и дух имел суровый.»

195. " 'Kamennyi gost' " Pushkina," 265.

196. "The shameless, godless Don Guan" (monk), "Your Don Guan is an atheist [*bezbozhnik*] and a scoundrel" (Don Karlos), etc. Guan's reputation as an *Ateista fulminado* is mentioned at least four times in the play: see discussion in Akhmatova, " 'Kamennyi gost' " Pushkina," 264.

coming as it does through a poet's sensibility, possesses a kind of spiritual acuity that cannot be even hinted at in the midst of all Jakobson's findings:

> And so, in the tragedy *The Stone Guest* Pushkin is punishing himself — his young, carefree, sinful self, and the theme of jealousy from beyond the grave (i.e., the fear of it) sounds as loudly here as the theme of retribution.
>
> Therefore, a careful analysis of *The Stone Guest* brings us to the firm conviction that behind [these] externally borrowed names and situations we have, in essence, not merely a new reworking of the universal legend of Don Juan, but a profoundly personal, original work by Pushkin, the basic character of which is determined not by the *sujet* of the legend, but by the personal lyrical feelings, inextricably bound to real-life experience, of Pushkin himself.
>
> Before us is the dramatic embodiment of the inner personality of Pushkin, the artistic exposing-to-view [*obnaruzhenie*] of that which tormented and captivated the poet.[197]

This explains, and beautifully, Pushkin's feelings toward his own version of Guan, but even that is not enough to account for the massive "simultaneity" of this situation. For the poet is both Guan and the jealous husband-cum-statue. That is the point. There is a reason he is willing, even now, to hurl challenges at his own image of future pain and humiliation. It has to do with the actual beauty, Natalia Goncharova, at whose altar he is willing to sacrifice everything. For the image of stone (marble) also is associated *with her,* or at least with her image in the tragedy, almost as much as with the jealous statue guarding her virtue. Recall, for example, what the seductive (or is it genuinely worshipful?) Guan says to her at the pedestal of her husband's monument:

> It is only from afar that I with reverence
> look on you when, bending down quietly,
> you strew your black locks onto the pale marble —
> and it seems to me then that secretly
> an angel has paid a visit to this tomb,
> [and] in my troubled heart I can then no longer
> find prayers [i.e., Guan is playing the role of monk]. I marvel wordlessly
> and think: happy is he whose cold marble

---

197. "'Kamennyi gost'' Pushkina," 273.

is warmed by her heavenly breath
and watered by the tears of her love. . . .[198]

This, I would say, is the missing second element in Pushkin's intricately realized sculptural metaphor, what we have been referring to elsewhere as his
"Pygmalion myth": it is both what the stone will do to him (it will come for
him as his death) and what it will do *for* him (it will bring him back to life even
as he seems to be the one doing the touching and the creating). Pygmalion was,
in Ovid's poetic rendering, the legendary king of Cyprus who, disappointed
in love ("Pygmalion loathed the vices given by nature / To women's hearts"),
created a statue of such beauty ("Meanwhile he carved the snow-white ivory /
With happy skill; he gave it a beauty greater / Than any woman's") that he
became enamored of it ("The sculptor / Marvelled, and loved his beautiful
pretense") and prayed to Aphrodite to give him a wife resembling his creation.[199] But poets shouldn't ask to have their prayers answered: Aphrodite not
only heeded the supplicant, but gave Pygmalion precisely *his own statue* come
to life:

> When he returned [from the festival of Aphrodite],
>   he went to his ivory image,
> Lay on its couch and kissed it. It grew warm.
> He kissed again and touched the ivory breast.
> The ivory softened, and its carven firmness
> Sank where he pressed it, yielded like the wax
> Which in the sunlight takes a thousand shapes
> From moulding fingers, while use makes it useful.

198. *Pss*, V:333: «Я только издали с благоговеньем / Смотрю на вас, когда,
склонившись тихо, / Вы черные власы на мрамор бледный / Рассыплете — И мнится
мне, что тайно / Гробницу эту ангел посетил, / В смущенном сердце я не обретаю /
Тогда молений. Я дивлюсь безмолвно / И думаю — счастлив, чей хладный мрамор /
Согрет ее дыханием небесным / И окроплен любви ее слезами.»

199. The translation is Gilbert Highet's, as found in *Latin Poetry in Verse Translation*,
ed. L. R. Lind (Boston: Houghton Mifflin, 1957), 164–65. The Latin originals for these
quotes read: "Quas quia Pygmalion aevum per crimen agentis / viderat, offensus vitiis,
quae plurima menti / femineae natura dedit, sine coniuge caelebs / vivebat thalamique diu
consorte carebat"; "interea niveum mira feliciter arte / sculpsit ebur formamque dedit,
qua femina nasci / nulla potest, operisque sui concepit amorem" (Ovid, *Metamorphoses*,
2 vols., with an English translation by Frank Justus Miller [Cambridge: Harvard University Press, 1951], II:80–82).

Pygmalion was aghast and feared his joy,
But like a lover touched his love again.
It was a body, beating pulse and heart.
Now he believed and in an ardent prayer
Gave thanks to Venus: pressed his mouth at last
To a living mouth. The maiden felt his kiss —
She blushed and trembled: when she raised her eyes
She saw her lover and heaven's light together.[200]

This metamorphosis feels eerily like the speaker's reaction to the gift of eros
in the very private "No, I do not prize." But isn't our detective work here simply
another case of figurative language run wild, for what could it mean, *really,* to
claim that Pushkin-Pygmalion had, in his disenchantment over his amorous
past, fallen in love with his own creation and had prayed for a wife resembling
what he had made? I think not. During this very same Boldino autumn Pushkin wrote, as it turns out mainly for himself, a series of responses to his critics
("Refutation of Criticisms"/Oproverzhenie na kritiki). In this quite personal
essay format, while defending himself against various ad hominem attacks
in the periodic press referring to his physical appearance, his genealogy, and
what some with unseemly glee saw to be the waning of his talent, he decided to
"explain himself," with tetchy sarcasm and a sturdy sense of amour propre. He
told his imaginary reader that, contrary to the simpleminded opinion of his
critics, it was logical and psychologically convincing to have Maria, his lovely
young heroine in *Poltava* (1828), fall in love with the gloomy and aging hetman
Mazepa. Why? Because "love is the most capricious of passions," because there
happen to be myths about such miraculous reversals, *including Ovid's story of
Pygmalion,* that inspire us with their own special poetry, and because, to cite
another example that for Pushkin was close to home, "Othello, the old moor,
captivated Desdemona with stories about his wanderings and battles." [201] Here

200. *Latin Poetry in Verse Translation,* 165. The original reads: "ut rediit, simulacra suae
petit ille puellae / incumbensque toro dedit oscula: visa tepere est; / admovet os iterum,
manibus quoque pectora temptat: / temptatum mollescit ebur positoque rigore / subsidit
digitis ceditque, ut Hymettia sole / cera remollescit tractataque pollice multas / flectitur in
facies ipsoque fit utilis usu. / dum stupet et dubie gaudet fallique veretur, / rursus amans
rursusque manu sua vota retractat. / corpus erat! saliunt temptatae pollice venae. / tum
vero Paphius plenissima concipit heros / verba, quibus Veneri grates agat, oraque tandem / ore suo non falsa premit, dataque oscula virgo / sensit et erubuit timidumque ad
lumina lumen / attolens pariter cum caelo vidit amantem" (Ovid, *Metamorphoses,* II:82).

201. *Pss,* VII:132. The other Ovidian transformations/matings that Pushkin mentions

too Pushkin was talking, obliquely but nonetheless unmistakably, about himself and his own situation as potential Pygmalion and potential Othello. If the statue might be coming for him as repayment for past sins (his Guan incarnation), then in return for this fatal barter he could enjoy ("Pygmalion was aghast and feared his joy"[202]) the sensation of the black tresses on his stone flesh (his statue incarnation, or the end of his protean movement) and the equally, if not more, arousing sensation of the cool marble coming to life (as Ovid's ivory had melted into warm, pliable wax) at the sculptor's touch.

Even so, even granting that the poet might have been thinking of one of Ovid's metamorphoses as he was writing furiously during that Boldino autumn, is there a concrete sense in which some*thing* created can, because it is adored so much and because it so seems to have a life of its own, become some*one*? Not Natalie by herself, but the statue that predated her and into which she seemed to have entered? Yes. There are, it turns out, two other contemporaneous texts that show how powerfully and seemingly alchemically Pushkin was *realizing* this double-sided sculptural metaphor in the year of his courtship. The first involves his letter to Natalie's mother (N. I. Goncharova), dated 5 April 1830, on the occasion of their betrothal; the second the final, eighth (originally the ninth) chapter of *Eugene Onegin*, which he was also finishing that fall. The letter, which I quote virtually in full, reads:

> When I saw her for the first time, her beauty was just beginning to be noticed in society. I fell in love with her; my head began to whirl; I asked for her hand. Your answer, all vague as it was, gave me a moment of delirium. I

on this page all involve *women* — Leda, Philyra, Pasiphaë, and Myrrha — a fact that would make the example of Pygmalion even more significant. Ovid of course had been an important early interlocutor (the "poet as exile") in Pushkin's work: see, e.g., "To Ovid" (K Ovidiiu, 1821), *Pss*, II:62–64. Pushkin had at least three different editions of Ovid, two French and one Latin, in his library as catalogued by Modzalevsky: (1) *Amours mythologiques, traduits des Métamorphoses d'Ovide par De Pongerville*, 2d ed. (Paris, 1827) (no. 1231 in catalogue); *Oeuvres complètes d'Ovide*, ed. "imprimée sous les yeux et par les soins de J. Ch. Poncelin" (Paris, 1799) (no. 1232 in catalogue); and *Publii Ovidii Nasonis opera*, ed. "recognovit, et argumentis distinxit J. A. Amar" (Paris, 1822) (no. 1233 in catalogue). See B. L. Modzalevskii, "Biblioteka A. S. Pushkina," *Pushkin i ego sovremenniki. Materialy i issledovaniia* 9–10 (1910): 304.

202. Akhmatova correctly surmises that what Pushkin fears is not death but the *loss of happiness*, which he knows his too tormented heart cannot withstand. He repeatedly describes his wish for marriage and family life as his try *for happiness*. Akhmatova, " 'Kamennyi gost' ' Pushkina," 267 (see n. 187, above).

departed the same night for the army. You ask me what I was doing there? I swear to you that I do not know at all, but an involuntary anguish was driving me from Moscow. There I would not have been able to bear either your presence or hers. I wrote you. I hoped, I waited for an answer—it did not come. The errors of my first youth presented themselves to my imagination. They were only too violent, and calumny had added to them further; talk about them has become, unfortunately, widespread. You might have believed it; I dared not complain, but I was in despair.

What torments awaited me on my return! Your silence, your cold air, Mlle. Natalie's reception of me, so nonchalant, so inattentive. . . . I did not have the courage to explain myself, I went to Petersburg with death in my soul. I felt I had played a rather ridiculous role; I had been timid for the first time in my life, and timidity in a man of my age could hardly please a young person of your daughter's age [Natalie was eighteen at the time of the Pushkins' marriage in February 1831]. One of my friends [i.e., Vyazemsky] went to Moscow and brought me back a kind word which restored me to life, and now when those gracious words which you have been so kind to address to me should have overwhelmed me with joy [i.e., news that the proposal was being looked on favorably]—I am more unhappy than ever. I shall try to explain.

Only [force of] habit and a long [period of] intimacy could win for me your daughter's affection. I hope in time I can awaken in her feelings of attachment toward me, but I have nothing with which to please her [in the sense of "giving pleasure," "je n'ai rien pour lui plaire"].If she consents to give me her hand, I shall see only the proof of the calm indifference [la tranquille indifférence] of her heart. But surrounded as she will be [in society] with admiration, with homage, with enticements, will this calmness last? She will be told that only unfortunate fate has prevented her from forming other ties, more fitting, more brilliant, more worthy of her—perhaps such remarks may be sincere, but she will assuredly believe them to be so. Will she not have regrets? Will she not regard me as an obstacle, as a fraudulent ravisher [un ravisseur frauduleux]? Will she not take an aversion to me? God is my witness that I am ready to die for her, but that I should die to leave a dazzling widow, free to choose a new husband tomorrow—this idea is hell.

Let us speak of finances; I set little store on that. Mine have sufficed me up to the present. Will they suffice me, married? Not for anything in the world would I bear that my wife should come to know privations, that she should not go where she is invited to shine, to amuse herself. She has the right to insist upon it. In order to satisfy her, I am ready to sacrifice to her all my tastes, all the passions of my life, a mode of life quite free and quite reckless. Still, will she not murmur if her position in society is not as brilliant as that which she deserves and which I would wish for her?[203]

I find this document to be one of the most remarkable, and poignant, examples in all world literature of a great and proud artist exposing his own vulnerabilities and displaying his readiness to shed all the outward trappings of a previous identity in order to have a "try at happiness" — love, family, domestic life — which, we recall, he *already suspected to be doomed*. Pushkin, to repeat, was someone who was fastidiously guarded about his feelings. Only his desperate situation (he had in recent years already been rejected several times by other young ladies, including a first time by Natalie and her mother[204]), together with the relative freedom of a "noneroticizable" female correspondent and the glorious limitation of his idiomatic French, could have made him so fully place his cards on the table. This is not Don Guan, the man who claimed that his wife was his "113th love," but the man who correctly suspects that one day in the not so distant future he will be nothing more than a dragonfly caught on the rapier of a younger, more desirable opponent. With all his verbal gifts, with all his protean genius he is willing to sacrifice in her name, he has nothing *of value* to offer to the other side. What he has earned in the eyes of society, which is what concerns the mother, is a bad name. He sees this and he knows it. He can worship at the altar of this beauty, he can hope that one day it will be well disposed toward him, but he knows in his heart that this maiden's *tranquille indifférence* (the attitude of a statue) will not be (for her) the same as pleasure, desire, love: "I have nothing with which to please her." And he doesn't (and as far as we know he never will) *resent this in her*: it is not her fault. If anything, it is his. The extent to which Pushkin sees everything and even now, at the moment in his life when he is most exposed and most needful, resolutely refuses to write himself into the role of the victim simply takes the reader's breath away. If the source of inspiration can exist in a document that is not, strictly speaking, aesthetically shaped, then this is it.

203. Pushkin, *Letters*, 405–6; *Pss*, X:217–18.

204. Technically speaking, Natalie's mother did not reject Pushkin during his initial suit for her daughter's hand; what she did was *not accept* that suit, which is to say, she did not completely "shut the door," but at the same time she continued to look about for a more attractive prospect.

The final chapter of *Eugene Onegin* provides us the example we need of the female statue come to life — what in Pushkin's erotic mythology might be called not the destructive, but the grace-bearing, *ongon*. It is important to keep in mind here the details of Ovid's plot: Pymalion creates a statue of such charm that he falls in love with it, but it is only through prayer (to Aphrodite in Ovid, to God in Pushkin's Madonna poem) followed by the intercession of the other that the statue comes to life. At the beginning of chapter 8, the speaker lists all the incarnations of the Muse in his works up to that point, and then, as he brings Onegin together with Tatiana for the story of their second round of meetings and *his* obsessive infatuation, we are introduced to his (the speaker's) current, and what will turn out to be ultimate, version of the Muse — the village miss (*uezdnaia baryshnia*) become the comme il faut society princess.[205] The metamorphosis of Tatiana is so shockingly total and unaccountable that many have faulted the author for failing to realize the *novelistic* expectations of this finale. But then Pushkin was writing a novel *in verse,* which is a "devil of a difference," as he said. I would like to suggest, therefore, that the psycho-erotic structure of this last chapter replicates certain crucial aspects of the Pygmalion myth as they apply to Pushkin's situation: (1) the change in Tatiana as she navigates the treacherous waters of high society makes her beauty now superior to, because alive and somehow coming from within, that of marble ("She sat at a table / with the brilliant Nina Voronskaya, / that Cleopatra of the Neva; / and in truth you would have to agree, / that Nina, *with her marble beauty* / could not outshine her neighbor, / although she was dazzling"[206]); (2) Onegin, the narrator's Byronic alter ego and rival for the affections of Tatiana, is struck dumb, paralyzed, virtually turned to stone himself by this change he cannot explain ("But Onegin could find / no traces of the former Tatiana. / He wanted to start up a conversation with her / and — and he couldn't. She asked / whether he had been here for a long time, whence he was coming / and whether it might be from their parts? / Then she turned to her husband / a weary glance, and glided away . . . / And he [Onegin] remained there motionless"[207]); and (3) the gen-

---

205. A recent reading of Tatiana that mounts a spirited and well-reasoned challenge to her status as Muse is Caryl Emerson, "Tatiana," in *A Plot of Her Own: The Female Protagonist in Russian Literature,* ed. Sona Stephan-Hoisington (Evanston: Northwestern University Press, 1995), 6–20.

206. *Pss,* V:148: «Она сидела у стола / С блестящей Ниной Воронскою, / Сей Клеопатрою Невы; / И верно б согласились вы, / Что Нина мраморной красою / Затмнить соседку не могла, / Хоть ослепительна была.»

207. *Pss,* V:149: «Но и следов Татьяны прежней / Не мог Онегин обрести. / С ней

eral who is Tatiana's husband and Onegin's relative is there in the background as the necessary third party—not a shade, not an avenging statue himself, but simply a decent man who has *earned*, through his deeds as a warrior, a place of honor in society and to whom the statue-come-to-life is faithful even if she does not love him. In this reversal of the *Stone Guest* plot (this Donna Anna does not yield to the lover's words), Pushkin places the husband in the virtuous and now departing wife's boudoir at the climactic moment when the failed hero freezes on the spot: "She left. There stands Evgeny / as though thunderstruck."[208] The only hint of the husband's vulnerability—not developed in the plot—are the war wounds fixed on by the Freudians. But the general need not be a Russian Jake Barnes. Rather he is, in the psychological space of the poem, together with the thoughts of the narrator who is clearly "on his side," that everyday other into whose hands is committed the living statue. In other words, the general (who is bound by the storyline) + the narrator (who possesses the mythopoetic sensibility "behind the scenes") = Pushkin-Pygmalion *after the fact* of Aphrodite's gift. In terms of the poet's *erotic* mythology, there is no more story to tell—it passes beyond the veil, and almost (but not entirely) from view, into the privacy of the Pushkins' domestic life.[209]

In conclusion, in my reworking of Jakobson's findings I have been stressing how all the different aspects and details—some random, others "bioaesthetically" shaped—of Pushkin's sculptural mythology came together on the eve of his marriage to produce poems, dramas, prose writings, doodlings, and other verbal artifacts seemingly "alive" with their own haunting prescience. And, to be sure, the myth of the graven image come to life did not disappear from the poet's work after the Pushkins' wedding. It did, however,

речь хотел он завести / И—и не мог. Она спросила, / Давно ль он здесь, откуда он / И не из их ли уж сторон? / Потом к супругу обратила / Усталый взгляд; скользнула вон . . . / И недвижим остался он.»

208. *Pss*, V:162: «Она ушла. Стоит Евгений / Как будто громом поражён.»

209. I say "not entirely" because out of political considerations (i.e., tsarist censorship), Pushkin was not allowed to become a completely *private* citizen. As he writes to his wife in a letter of 18 May 1834 after he has become angered by the intrusion of the postal censors into his domestic sphere: "Look, little wife [*zhenka*]. I hope that you won't give my letters to anybody to make copies of. If the post has unsealed a husband's letters to his wife, then that's its affair. But there is one unpleasant thing in that: the privacy of family relationships, intruded upon in a foul and dishonorable manner. But if you are to blame, then that would be painful for me. Nobody must know what may take place between us; nobody must be received into our bedroom. Without privacy there is no family life" (*Pss*, X:377; *Letters*, 652).

fuel itself on a different sort of economy: now Pushkin was concerned not so much with winning a Madonna (that prayer had been granted), but with protecting the modest domesticity that he did possess and with returning to the values and figures of the eighteenth century with a view to how he might be measured against them when his time, sooner or later, came. To put it rather crudely, Pushkin wanted to demonstrate again and again, over a broad swath of genres, how the power of the poet and the power of the tsar were and were not commensurate, and how Russia needed them both to move forward out of her troubles. As the poet wrote to his wife several months after completing *The Bronze Horseman* and while gathering material for his history of Peter: "And suddenly I shall cast a bronze monument that can't be dragged from one end of the city to the other, from square to square, from alley to alley." [210] In other words, the "material" quality of his legacy was always on his mind during these years. On the other hand, he continued to be superstitious about any graven image *in his own likeness* (as opposed to his wife's): "Here [in Moscow] they want a bust of me to be sculpted," he complains in another letter of the mid-1830s to Natalia Nikolaevna, "but I don't want it. Then my Negro ugliness would be committed to immortality in all its dead immobility." [211] Any attempt to translate the poet's monument into something fixed and three-dimensional is understood instinctively to belong to the semantic field of the "demonic," a concept we will be visiting in greater depth in our discussion of Derzhavin and Pushkin.

In this respect, *The Bronze Horseman* and "The Fairy Tale of the Golden Cockerel" are indeed, as Jakobson copiously argued, deep-structural siblings to *The Stone Guest,* although he didn't push the parallelism (the *difference* in sameness) quite far enough. In the more realistically motivated narrative poem, where the poet's contest with his greatest rival (Peter as both creative and destructive historical force) must be given a more or less "verisimilar" outcome, the now *déclassé* hero and little man is destroyed along with his sweetheart and dreams of domesticity. The statue come to life is that of the titanic tsar trying to protect *his* legacy—the city, the empire—the cost of which is the "happiness" of the unprepossessing subject. In the peculiarly

210. Pushkin, *Letters,* 654; *Pss,* X:379. The letter was written no later than 29 May 1834, that is, very close to Pushkin's birthday (26 May).

211. Pushkin, *Letters,* 767; *Pss,* X:452. The letter was written between 14 and 16 May 1836. For a revealing early self-portrait that touches, even in 1814, on some of the same themes (e.g., *Vrai singe par sa mine*), see "Mon Portrait," in *Pss,* I:80–81.

Pushkinian fairy tale, on the other hand, where the power and legacy of the adviser to Tsar Dadon are presented with a kind of "dream" logic, the astrologer-castrate (*zvezdochet-skopets*) is betrayed by the tsar, but it is *his* statuette-cockerel, as small as Peter's monument is large, that whirls into motion and gets, so to speak, the last word. The adviser and his magic helper are heeded only so long as they serve Tsar Dadon, which by 1834, as Akhmatova was the first to demonstrate in another article,[212] likely alludes to Pushkin's role as post-Karamzinian "court historian" and to his ambiguous feelings toward Alexander and Nicholas. At the same time, the astrologer is *castrated,* which is Pushkin's *addition* to Irving's "The Legend of the Arabian Astrologist," [213]

212. Anna Akhmatova, "Posledniaia skazka Pushkina," *Sochineniia,* ed. G. P. Struve and B. A. Filippov (Munich: Inter-language Literary Associates, 1968), II:197–222. The reading of "The Fairy Tale of the Golden Cockerel" as political satire, initiated by Akhmatova in the early 1930s, has become in recent years the work's dominant mode of interpretation, although very rarely (if ever) can it be said (and one has to assume that Akhmatova herself would not have said it) that Pushkin's artistic design is politically or ideologically motivated *tout court.* Perhaps the most extreme example of this tendency (fairy tale = political cryptotext) is found in Andrej Kodjak, "Skazka Pushkina 'Zolotoi Petushok,' " in *American Contributions to the VIII International Congress of Slavists* (Columbus: Slavica, 1978), II:332–74. For an outstanding recent study of "The Golden Cockerel," with thorough exposition of the scholarly debate and of the tensions between folkloric and nonfolkloric (i.e., literary, biographical, etc.) sources, see V. E. Vatsuro, " 'Skazka o zolotom petushke': Opyt analiza siuzhetnoi semantiki," *Pushkin: Issledovaniia i materialy* 15 (1995): 122–33.

213. First noted in Jakobson, "Statue in Puškin's Poetic Mythology," 328 (see n. 169, above). The theme of the "compensatory" interrelations between worldly power (wealth, status) and artistic power (inspiration), with the striking variable of castration (the absence of sexual potency) added in, seems to have been on the poet's mind, for obvious reasons, in his last years. See, for example, his 1835 off-color poetic joke (not intended for publication) "Once a violinist came to a castrato" (K kastratu raz prishel skrypach), in *Pss,* III.322. Another possible subtext here was Pavel Katenin's poem "An Old True Story" (Staraia byl'), which, in a gesture of prickly "friendship," the bilious archaist dedicated to Pushkin and sent to him in 1828. In that work Katenin presents a competition between a "Greek castrate" (*ellin-skopets*) and an old "Russian warrior" (*russkii voin*) over who can best create a song to honor Prince Vladimir. Although the competition is won without a fight by the Greek, Katenin's ironic point is that the post-December 1825 Pushkin (i.e., the castrated Greek) is too willing to sing the praises of autocracy (here the allusion is to Pushkin's advice, perceived by some as too close to flattery, that Nicholas follow the generous impulses of his great forebear Peter, as presented in "Stanzas" [Stansy, 1826]), while the still "disgraced" Katenin (i.e., the old Russian warrior in exile on his estate) is content to remain silent. By the mid-1830s Pushkin may have agreed with Katenin's "castrate"

and thus symbolically denied direct access to power (but not to desire). In other words, read back into Pushkin's biography, the imposed position of aging *kameriunker* made him more of a *jester* (he constantly refers in private to his uniform as his "fool's motley") than a distinguished confidant. All the fairy-tale character wants in return for his kingdom-saving counsel is the one request he has coming to him, the "maiden, the Tsarina of Shemakha" (*devitsa, Shamakhanskaia tsaritsa*), but it is this request that Dadon, himself now struck by the maiden's beauty, denies. For a poet as sensitive to logosemantic play as this one is, is it any wonder that "*petushok*" (cockerel) can be anagrammatically decoded as *Pushk*in? Yes, the wonder-working *zvezdochet* is struck down by the tsar's phallic staff (*zhezl*), but then the *petushok*, which could only be the poetic/historical "truth" that exists independent of its author, comes to life and avenges, *after the fact,* the injustice. If Nicholas will ignore the implicit message of *The History of Pugachev,* then he will do so at his own risk. Thus, just as in his own doodles of himself Pushkin caricatures or even *disfigures* his laurel-enshrouded human likeness, so too does he *refigure* himself as a fantastic bird elsewhere: the sketch, for example, of what may well be this very same cockerel that was bizarrely inserted into the manuscript of *The History of the Village Goriukhino.*[214] (See illustrations 5 and 6.) Vadim Vatsuro's astute conclusion about the "Golden Cockerel" — "Pushkin makes the 'magical helper' an autonomous figure and very nearly the genuine hero of

---

label with regard to his historical person (hence the wry reinvocation of the insult), but not with regard to the power of his word (the *petushok*). See the illuminating discussion of the Katenin-Pushkin competition in Iu. Tynianov, *Arkhaisty i novatory* (Leningrad: Priboi, 1929), 160–77.

214. See *Pss,* VI:119. There is considerable debate about when precisely Pushkin wrote *The History of the Village Goriukhino* (Istoriia sela Goriukhina), although most scholars now agree it was probably during the first Boldino autumn (1830). It is also hard (if not impossible) to determine when Pushkin made his sketch of the fantastic bird and inserted it into the manuscript of his mock history. One thing is certain, however: as M. P. Alekseev first established, Irving's *A History of New York* was one of Pushkin's sources for *The History of the Village Goriukhino;* and likewise, after Akhmatova's discovery it has become impossible not to take into account "The Legend of the Arabian Astrologist" as Pushkin's primary textual point of departure in "The Fairy Tale of the Golden Cockerel." Thus, even if Pushkin didn't know Irving's legend in 1830, when we think he was working on *The History of the Village Goriukhino,* he still could have done the sketch a few years later (based on Akhmatova's chronology) and then interleaved it after the fact, as a kind of mnemonic trace of the cockerel's "power" and message, in his own (in various senses, i.e., Boldino = Goriukhino) history.

his fairytale narration" — is, in this reader's opinion, wrong in one crucial respect. No, the impression that "evil is punished, but good does not triumph" is a false one, since it is not the life of the astrologer (or the tsar) that the logic (the embedded desire) of the tale would or should preserve, but the message — the (poetic) truth will out — of the statuette.[215] Likewise, to anticipate our own story for a moment, the poet will make every effort, throughout his ultimate self-sculpting in "Exegi monumentum," to undo both the tsar's (the "other" Alexander's) and the poet's (Derzhavin's) literalism and boastfully three-dimensional immortality. To repeat, Pushkin's immortality, if he has any choice in the matter, will be of the *nerukotvornyi* (not made by hand) variety. And the maiden, the occasion for the conflict? Well, she simply disappears.

215. Vatsuro, "Skazka o zolotom petushke," 133.

∞ Lotman
The Code and Its Relation to Literary Biography

Perhaps no two thinkers in the latter decades of the twentieth century have changed more our ability to conceptualize Russian literature, the Russian literary context, and ultimately verbal reality regardless of national origins, than Mikhail Bakhtin (1895–1975) and Yuri Lotman (1922–93). Yet, once outside the orbit of Russian literature specialists (*russisty*), Bakhtin is by far the better known and more celebrated—an interesting phenomenon of cultural reception in its own right. (Curiously, Bakhtin has appeared almost singlehandedly to make up for much of the traditional "time lag" in Russian culture by being "ahead of his time," a Western postmodernist—whether he would have agreed with this designation or not—*avant la lettre.*) And as strange as it may sound to the noninitiate, Bakhtin and Lotman are, by some "Hamburg account" measuring the ability of the human mind to mimic the speed of light, comparable to no one of their time and place except each other, a fact they apparently were coming to realize in the early 1970s. Not by chance was Lotman often compared, both in how he looked and how he thought, to Albert Einstein.

The purpose of the present section is to show how Lotman the Push-kinist learned from Bakhtin, adapting the latter's "dialogism" (in its various incarnations) to open up the more mechanical structural-semiotic "modeling systems" made famous in the works of the Moscow-Tartu School of the 1960s and 1970s. This shift in Lotman has been duly noted by several commentators. What has not been noted, however, is the potentially positive or "energy-releasing" aspects of the one concept Bakhtin found most "closed" and "deadening" about structural analysis—the so-called *code*,[216] which stood

216. "In the course of his research Lotman realized that a code identified in a culture is much more complex than that which can be identified in a language and his analyses became increasingly subtle and took on a rich, complex historical awareness" (Umberto Eco, Introduction, in Yuri M. Lotman, *Universe of the Mind: A Semiotic Theory of Culture*, trans. Ann Shukman [Bloomington: Indiana University Press, 1990], xii). For a succinct description of Lotman's own understanding of how "code" functions in Saussurean versus Jakobsonian linguistics, see his "Three Functions of the Text," in *Universe of the Mind*, 11–

to a given text or cultural moment as the Saussurean *langue* stood to the *parole* of individual utterance. My main interest here is simply to demonstrate that, while Lotman learned from Bakhtin and thus under the power of the latter's arguments was able to, as it were, organicize and "soften up" the harder edges of the structuralist-semiotic worldview,[217] he still remained very much his own thinker, and he did so precisely in this area of the *creative potential* in what might be termed "code wrestling." In this, as I will suggest, Lotman remained true to the genres and the literary period he began with and was our greatest pioneer in (re)discovering — Russian *poetry* and *poetic consciousness* of the Karamzin-Pushkin era. Lotman emerges then as the antipode to Bakhtin, our greatest theorist of the novel and of the novelistic consciousness associated with Dostoevsky and (by Bakhtin's distinguished students) Tolstoi. And the divide, crudely put, between these two thinkers rises up over their orientations, positive and negative respectively, toward the categories of "code," "model," "structure."

Thereafter, in the final pages of this section, I will turn to the major works of Lotman's last decade — his biography of Pushkin in particular. Among other things, these later works apply, in nonspecialist language, the lessons of "code wrestling" to concrete examples of what might be called "poetic thinking." It is my hypothesis that Lotman, who has learned from Bakhtin but has also learned where he departs from his antipode, is trying to use his method to get as close as possible to the headwaters of poetic creativity itself — how poets use the material of life, beginning with its implicit codes, not only to write but to *live* creatively. The connection between life and art, text and code, can

---

19. It is here, inter alia, that Lotman, expanding on Jakobson's "poetic function," speaks about a semiotic code as potentially including "not only a certain binary set of rules for encoding and decoding a message, but also a multi-dimensional hierarchy," which can have a "creative function" — that is, it can do more than transmit ready-made messages, it can "serve as a generator of new ones" (13). Lotman then shows in "Autocommunication: 'I' and 'Other' as Addressees" how the Jakobsonian communication model can be modified, precisely at the level of code, in certain "I-I" situations involving complex or "secondary-modeling" speech (the poetic speaker delivering a "message" to himself): "the 'I-I' system qualitatively transforms the information, and this leads to a restructuring of the actual 'I' itself" (*Universe of the Mind*, 22). It is the element of human *choice* and *self-creation* in this "recoding" that we will be examining in the pages below.

217. For more on the later Lotman's turn toward "organicist" models under the influence of Vernadsky ("biosphere") and Bakhtin ("logosphere"), see Amy Mandelker, "Semiotizing the Sphere: Organicist Theory in Lotman, Bakhtin, and Vernadsky," *PMLA* 109 (1994): 385–96.

be, Lotman comes more and more to see, *generative of meaning*—the ultimate semiotic gesture. In this context, Pushkin and Karamzin were Lotman's greatest exemplars, models, and, not by chance, *personal* sources of inspiration. In other words, Lotman kept growing as a thinker at a truly astonishing rate: at the end he was returning to the concrete lives and texts studied by the literary historian and critic not so much as an expression of the entropy of his conceptualizing ardor (quite the opposite in fact, to judge by his adventuresome 1980s pieces on the semiosphere and its relation to intracranial function), but as an expression of his most real, most living, and, one might foretell, most durable idea—poets need the biologically, existentially, and aesthetically *encoded* constraints of a single life lived in time in order to create something whose exemplary ("modeling") power appears *greater than* the constraints giving rise to it.

How, on one level, does the straitjacket of the rhyme scheme, say the Onegin stanza, *enable* the verbal movement standing in for the physical grace of Istomina dancing on stage? How, on another, do the dueling or gambling or nobleman's honor codes of Pushkin's milieu shape but also challenge, *bring out not automatically but through struggle,* the behavior we have come to associate with the quintessential poet's life? In short, what *choice* is there in a life that takes codes seriously? By discussing these matters in a language that itself was simpler, more direct, and at the same time more metaphorical, expressive, and *multiply coded* than the metalanguage of the semiotician, Lotman was taking a risk, but one he could not apparently in good conscience avoid. He was, courageously, testing the limits of his own codes and sense of generic propriety (the scholar/scientist who has the right only to reconstruct faithfully, but not to invent). He was bending the sharp edges of his structural-semiotic model as far as they could legitimately go in the direction of "life." He was trying to touch the hot core of "creativity" across the threshold of a cognitive lucidity perhaps unmatched in the history of Russian culture. And so the actual lives of Pushkin and Karamzin became the necessary ballast, the compelling exempla, making the "castles in the air" of scientific/semiotic theory real, alive, *nonrepeating,* and therefore inspiring. Very few Russian thinkers, or any thinkers for that matter, have dug as deeply and broadly in the past for Mandelstamian horseshoes—that is, the chance discovery that casts a poetically lived life in a new, meaningful light. If the rather technical discussions about culture as semiosphere, functionally asymmetrical hemispheres of the brain, neurolinguistics, and so on, were the dialectic scaffolding, the "rhyme scheme" that allowed mature Lotmanian thought to soar across interdisciplinary boundaries into the outer reaches of scientific speculation, then here was Istomina's dance—the beauty of an individual life that does not merely replicate a model/code but itself *generates meaning* against those codes.

One of the core components of Bakhtinian thought is its relentless emphasis on the dialogic, uniquely specific, and unreplicable nature of an utterance (*vyskazyvanie*), broadly defined.[218] It is the very *ongoing, in-process, interpersonal* (*mezhlichnostnyi*) aspect of dialogue that makes it, in Bakhtin's language, forever unfinalizable, open. Thus, if the process of semiosis requires signs to generate thought and meaning in the first place, then the originary pivot of the Bakhtinian position is away from Saussurean *langue* and toward a somewhat eccentric version of *parole*, or *vyskazyvanie*. As has been pointed out by Ponzio and Grzybek, in this orientation Bakhtin is virtually of one mind with the American pragmatist and pioneering semiologist Charles Sanders Peirce: "for Bakhtin (as well as for Peirce) these signs [creating meaning/semiosis] 'belong not to the closed and defined system, the code (*langue*), but rather engage each other in the process of interpretation.'"[219] It is completely logical, therefore, that Bakhtin would be critical of the mechanical, "artificially intelligent" (linguistic competence *predicted* by codes) trajectory of structuralism, from Saussure's positings of a codifying *langue* to Chomsky's transformational unpackings of "deep structure": "My attitude toward structuralism: I am against enclosure in a text";[220] and "a code is a delib-

---

218. See, e.g.: "Every utterance is only a moment of continuous discursive interaction" (V. N. Voloshinov, *Marksizm i filosofiia iazyka: Osnovnye problemy sotsiologicheskogo metoda v nauke o iazyke*, 2d ed. [Leningrad: Priboi, 1930], 97); or "There is no such thing as an isolated utterance" (M. M. Bakhtin, "Iz zapisei 1970–1971," *Estetika slovesnogo tvorchestva* [Moscow: Iskusstvo, 1979], 340); or "Every word (every sign) of a text leads beyond its boundaries. Any understanding is the correlation of a given text to other texts . . . and their reinterpretation [*pereosmyslenie*] in a new context (mine, the present's, the future's). . . . We emphasize that this contact is the dialogic contact between texts (utterances)" (M. M. Bakhtin, "K metodologii gumanitarnykh nauk," *Estetika slovesnogo tvorchestva*, 364). One of the first to note Bakhtin's different emphases in his use of the terms "utterance" and "language" (as opposed to the "message" and "code" typical of Jakobsonian usage) was Tzvetan Todorov in *Mikhail Bakhtin and the Dialogic Principle*, trans. Wlad Godzich (Minneapolis: University of Minnesota Press, 1984), 54–56.

219. A. Ponzio, "Semiotics between Peirce and Bakhtin," *Recherches Semiotiques-Semiotic Inquiry* 4 (1984): 274; cited P. Grzybek, "Bakhtinskaia semiotika i moskovsko-semioticheskaia shkola," in *Lotmanovskii sbornik I*, ed. E. V. Permiakov [Moscow: Its-Garant, 1995], 252)

220. "K metodologii," 372.

erately established, killed [*umershchvlennyi*] creative context."[221] Not unlike some phenomenologists, Bakhtin was interested in what could be generated *that was genuinely new* out of a given dialogic encounter, and so, in his thinking, because a "context is potentially incomplete [*nezavershim*]," while "a code should be complete/finished off [*zavershim*]," "the code . . . does not have cognitive, creative significance."[222]

There is a potentially subtle paradox here in Bakhtin's thought, not so much in its logic (which is unerring) but in its at times eccentric application. Crudely speaking, one might phrase the contradiction thus: Bakhtin's exclusive emphasis on — indeed, his obsession with — openness meant that his ideas, however rich and provocative, could never be "tightened up," made more "scientific," even the slightest bit "closed." They attach to real texts and contexts (that is, to Bakhtin's rather specialized use of literary and cultural history) only in the most general way. Why? Because their chief goal was to trace the human being's cognitive drive toward greater communicative openness — of verbal forms (dialogism), of novelistic structure (polyphony), of space-time relations (chronotope), of language that breaks down stylistic boundaries and argues with itself (heteroglossia), of the "authorizing" process (*chuzhaia rech'*, another's speech), of bodies that celebrate their multiple orifices (carnival). Bakhtin assumed that little could be learned by studying how the human personality interacted with the "closed" or coded aspects of certain verbal forms. Poetry became in his thinking, which in the end could not do without its own binary oppositions, the necessary monologic antipode to the genre chosen by history for its dialogic adaptability and closeness to "life" — the novel. However, as one of Bakhtin's most perceptive students has recently suggested, his

---

221. "Iz zapisei 1970–1971," 352. Bakhtin mentions Lotman at least twice in these late writings, both times somewhat critically. See, e.g., the following from "Iz zapisei 1970–1971," 339: "The understanding of multiplicity of styles [*mnogostil'nost'*] in *Evgenii Onegin* (see Lotman) as a *recoding* [*perekodirovanie*] (of romanticism to realism, etc.) leads to the falling away of the most important *dialogic* moment and to the transforming of a dialogue of styles into the simple existence of different versions of the same thing. . . . The code assumes some sort of ready state of content and the realization of a choice among *given* codes." Elsewhere Bakhtin complains that, while Lotman sees the "logical" categories of "opposition" and "shift in codes," he "hears voices" ("K metodologii," 372). For a useful discussion of Bakhtin's comments about Lotman, see Allan Reid, "Who Is Lotman and Why Is Bakhtin Saying Those Nasty Things about Him?" *DISCOURS SOCIAL/Social Discourse* 3 (Spring–Summer 1990): 311–24.

222. "Iz zapisei 1970–1971," 352.

spirited defense of the living context is itself strangely decontextualized, bereft of *real biography:* "Bakhtin embraces struggle, but at the level of words, not personal fates. For him, the novel is above all the home of many wonderful, unwinnable, unloseable *wars with words.*"²²³ In this sense, Bakhtin had something to learn from Lotman.

Lotman's orientation to the code/text/context force field of course differed fundamentally from Bakhtin's. To the end of his life he did not reject the principal scientific assumptions of Saussurean linguistics, beginning with the notion that there was a dialectical tension between *langue* and *parole,* code and text, in every formal discursive encounter.²²⁴ It took someone of Lotman's immense curiosity, flexibility, common sense, tact, and unparalleled concrete knowledge about both the history of literary forms and the history of social behavior to see this complex tension in a way that was more than Saussure-Jakobson and less than Bakhtin-Peirce. Here one might argue that, precisely because Lotman was less of a speculative phenomenologist with one powerful idea (history's drive toward novelization) and more of a pragmatic "enlightener" and scientific thinker, he could in a way utterly alien to Bakhtin and indeed rare for any tradition conjoin the roles of code taxonomer, text reader, and context reconstructor. My point here is simply that, to use the same metaphor, Lotman could "loosen up," "organicize" his original Saussurean stance, which he did in the late 1970s and especially in the 1980s, whereas Bakhtin, who saw semiotics as interested *only* in the "transmission of a *ready-made* message with the help of a *ready-made* code,"²²⁵ could not see a reason for

223. Caryl Emerson, "Russian Theories of the Novel," in *Cambridge Companion to the Russian Novel,* ed. Malcolm V. Jones and Robin Feuer Miller (Cambridge: Cambridge University Press, forthcoming).

224. See, for example, his Preface to *Universe of the Mind* (1990), which he concluded with a section entitled "After Saussure." In these pages, Lotman cites all the advances in "scientific thought" about language made by those such as Bakhtin, Propp, Jakobson, and Peirce, but he reserves a special place for Saussure, "whose works . . . remain in force as the foundation stones of semiotics" (5). Thus, even at this late date Lotman is absolutely comfortable speaking about semiotics as both a "scientific discipline" and a "method of the humanities" (4). By the same token, two of Saussure's ideas remain valid to Lotman, undergirding his work as theorist (i.e., explorer of semiotic *langue*) and literary scholar/historian/critic (i.e., explorer of semiotic *parole*), right to the end: "the opposition language [*langue*] and speech [*parole*] (or code and text)," and "the opposition: synchrony and diachrony" (Preface, 5).

225. Bakhtin, "Iz zapisei 1970–1971," 352; my emphasis.

"tightening up" his. Bakhtin could not move—paradoxically, the "maximal-ism" of his dialogism would not permit it—from the position that "In living speech the message, strictly speaking, is created *in the process* of communica-tion, and so, in essence, *there is no code.*"[226] But Lotman could move, and the reason why is a tantalizing imponderable.[227] It is to this move that we now turn in the second part of the essay.

Lotman authored and/or edited four works on Pushkin and Karamzin in the 1980s: *A. S. Pushkin's Novel "Eugene Onegin": Commentary* (Roman A. S. Pushkina "Evgenii Onegin": Kommentarii, 1980); *Alexander Sergeevich Push-kin: A Biography of the Writer* (Aleksandr Sergeevich Pushkin: Biografiia pisa-telia, 1981); the "Literary Monuments" (Literaturnye pamiatniki) edition of Karamzin's *Letters of a Russian Traveler* (Pis'ma russkogo puteshestvennika, 1984); and *The Creation of Karamzin* (Sotvorenie Karamzina, 1987). These works are among Lotman's most significant, and it is clear from his corre-spondence of the time that they were also dear to their author/editor and, the biographies of Pushkin and Karamzin especially, summational or "stocktak-ing" with regard to his career.[228] It was here that Lotman, now often reminded of his own deteriorating health, set out to demonstrate the full human poten-tial of his semiotic science.[229] What is striking from our point of view is that these works provide their own *textual* evidence of Lotman's turn, begun in

226. "Iz zapisei 1970–1971," 352; my emphasis.

227. Perhaps because he never doubted the fundamental ("scientific") truth of the Saussurean oppositions? Perhaps because these first truths belonged to Saussure and to science "in general," and so their refinement over time was natural and expected (Lotman was apparently not threatened with the loss of intellectual "copyrights," whereas Bakhtin, who was not possessive with regard to his own "authorship," could not imagine his own thought developing outside its original dialogic framework)? In fairness to Bakhtin, how-ever, it needs to be stressed that his critical comments about semiotics and Lotman come in random *notes* he wrote near the end of his life and may never have intended to publish.

228. As Lotman confides to his friend B. F. Egorov in a letter of 18 February 1986, "In general I researched and wrote the book [*Sotvorenie Karamzina*] for income ('such am I in the nakedness of my cynicism,' as Pushkin said), but it turned out as something not devoid of meaning, a kind of summing-up of my works [*itog rabot*] over a number of years" ("Pis'ma o Karamzine," in *Lotmanovskii sbornik I,* ed. E.V. Permiakov, notes and commentary B. F. Egorov [Moscow: Its-Garant, 1995], 77).

229. See Lotman's comments in the same letter cited above: "For some reason I've gone downhill seriously [*ia kak-to sil'no sdal fizicheski*] over the last months. I look calmly at the approaching far shore of the crossing" ("Pis'ma o Karamzine," 78).

the late 1970s and fully realized in the 1980s,[230] toward a modified Bakhtinian position with regard to code: in other words, these works are textually oriented both in terms of their subjects (the concrete "texts" of Karamzin's and Pushkin's lives and works) and in terms of the more "natural" (thus multiply coded, potentially *personal*)[231] language of Lotman's own writing. One document is particularly useful to us as we examine Lotman's mature application of code: the until recently unpublished preface to the Polish edition of the Pushkin biography.[232]

Lotman begins the preface in his characteristically tactful fashion by appealing to his Polish readership: his work was not written with the present audience in mind, so he begs the Poles' indulgence for his own potential cultural bias and points them to an excellent biography in Polish (by W. Woroszylski) for additional "context." Then he proceeds—in a way that is never

230. "In the second half of the 1970s the concept of the text was reconsidered by the Moscow-Tartu School, especially in a series of articles by Lotman [for example, 'Kul'tura kak kollektivnyi intellekt' (1977), 'Mozg-tekst-kul'tura-iskusstvennyi intellekt' (1981), 'Semiotika kul'tury i poniatie teksta' (1981), 'Kul'tura i tekst kak generatory smysla' (1983), 'K sovremennomu poniatiiu teksta' (1986)]. It is noteworthy that in these articles the original [that is, the one given by the Moscow-Tartu School] definition of the text is subjected to some adjustments in the spirit of Bakhtinian semiotics" (Grzybek, "Bakhtinskaia semiotika," 247 [see n. 219, above]). It is not fortuitous, in my opinion, that the later and more explicit of these theoretical articles were written contemporaneously with the text-oriented biographies of Pushkin and Karamzin.

231. Lotman places "natural language" (*estestvennyi iazyk*), as in normal, everyday speech, in a position of "inside-between" (*vnutri-mezhdu*), which is to say, it can be located somewhere between artificial/metalanguages, on the one hand, and artistic or complex semiotic ("secondary modeling") languages, on the other. In this sense, "natural language" by nature is heterogenous and thus more "dialogic" (the connection here with Bakhtin's notion of heteroglossia should be obvious) than the metalanguage of the semiotician. (See Iu. M. Lotman, "Kul'tura i tekst kak generatory smysla," *Kiberneticheskaia lingvistika* [Moscow: n.p., 1983], 26; "K sovremennomu poniatiiu teksta," *Uchenye zapiski Tartuskogo gosudarstvennogo universiteta* 736 [1986]: 104; "Three Functions," 14 [see n. 216, above]; and Grzybek, "Bakhtinskaia semiotika," 248–49.) By writing the Pushkin and Karamzin biographies in a version of "natural language," Lotman was aesthetically complicating (not simplifying) his texts in order to bring them (and himself) closer to the threshold of personal "meaning *generation*," which in the language of the poets is called inspiration. Not by chance, the "explosion" of inspiration will be one of the central topics of Lotman's last book, *Kul'tura i vzryv* (Culture and Explosion, 1992).

232. Iu. M. Lotman, "Aleksandr Sergeevich Pushkin: Biografiia pisatelia" (Predislovie k pol'skomu izdaniiu), in *Lotmanovskii sbornik I*, 85–88.

made so explicit in the Russian edition—to explain the challenge he set himself in writing such a biography: he was trying to show the human, personal (as in *lichnoe, lichnost'*) element in the science of semiotics.

> I have come to hear more than once that semiotic research, by occupying itself with the analysis of texts, loses sight of the complexity of the living human personality [*zhivaia chelovecheskaia lichnost'*]. History, say the opponents of semiotics, is the history of people, and not of texts and codes. And it is precisely this—the human—aspect of history that remains, in their opinion, outside the possibilities of semiotic research.[233]

This is the bias that Lotman is trying to overturn by telling Pushkin's story: "social man" or the "man mixing with others" (*obshchaiushchiisia chelovek*) is also, whether we like the scientific pretensions of the language or not, "semiotic man" (*semioticheskii chelovek*). But the humanizing element in this scientific approach comes through the presence of dialogue, and here Lotman must have known for certain that his words had a definite Bakhtinian ring to them: "The life of man is a continuous dialogue with those around him and with himself, and it can be examined according to the laws of the dialogic text."[234]

Thus, technically speaking, Lotman has set himself the task of examining the writer's "biography as the object of semiotic culturology."[235] But the fact of the matter is that Lotman does not, in this most important of cultural cases (Pushkin's biography!), want to speak technically. Indeed, he imposes a genre on himself—a "textbook for pupils" (*posobie dlia uchashchikhsia*) at the publishing house "Enlightenment" (Prosveshchenie)—that is maximally "simple," straightforward, nontechnical:

> Assuming that any scientific truth, once it has attained a certain level of maturity, can be expressed in a generally accessible language, and [assuming as well] that a complex system of specialized metalanguage can be likened to scaffolding around a building—it is necessary while the building is being constructed, but can be removed when the latter is ready—I wanted to attempt to write a book in such a way that to read it one would not need any specialized training in semiotics, and that to the reader a

233. "Aleksandr Sergeevich Pushkin," 85.
234. "Aleksandr Sergeevich Pushkin," 86.
235. "Aleksandr Sergeevich Pushkin," 86.

semiotic view toward life would seem not only natural but for this very same reader long since familiar [lit. "characteristic"].[236]

Lotman was hoping, at least explicitly, that by writing such a biography he would be demonstrating that semiotic science had come of age. This was the actual test case to prove all the semiotic calculations and "formulas." However, in taking on this genre, much the same way that Pushkin would take on a genre as a test of his own ingenuity, Lotman was simultaneously moving in the opposite direction. toward the personal, as opposed to the abstract and purely descriptive; toward the unique, as opposed to the predictable and replicable; and finally toward the creative (the linguistically heterogenous and potentially *unpredictable*), as opposed to the monologic and "closed" (his semiotic metalanguage). In other words, the "protean" nature of Lotman's experiments with "scholarly" genres in the 1980s had a familiar ring to it.

But Lotman had yet another challenge in mind when he undertook to write the Pushkin biography, and it is at this point that we come face to face with his simultaneous convergence on and divergence from the Bakhtinian animus toward codes. First, the distinction:

> The study of cultural semiotics introduces us to two possible situations:
>
> 1) General codes for the given collective determine the nature of texts generated by the personality. [Such] texts do not have an individual character and present themselves merely as the automatic realization of the laws of sociocultural grammars.
>
> 2) Texts are generated by the personality according to the laws of a grammar arising ad hoc. With respect to already existent sociosemiotic norms, [these] texts present themselves as a shift, a violation, a "scandal."[237]

It was of course the first category of *texts determined by codes* that Bakhtin had taken issue with in his "Iz zapisei 1970–1971" and that Lotman had come to realize was not sufficently flexible to cover all situations in cultural semiotics. Bakhtin saw, a priori, the dialogic situation as happening between the two (or more) concrete, actual consciousnesses involved. A person, say a Decembrist like Lunin or Pestel, could model his behavior on that of the Greeks or Romans, but the "dialogue" that ensued from this modeling process

236. "Aleksandr Sergeevich Pushkin," 86.
237. "Aleksandr Sergeevich Pushkin," 86.

would necessarily be different, if in nothing other than its "context" (Russian, nineteenth-century, post-Napoleonic, and so on), from that in the original source (for example, Hector's leaving for battle, Caesar's death, Cato's glorious deed).[238]

But what Lotman had pointed out, and correctly, in his pathbreaking work on the Decembrists is that much of these young nobles' behavior *did* have a monologic/monolithic cast to it: because the situation demanded resolve, they were consciously inserting their own lives into ancient *plots* that obliged them to act in certain honorable, brave, chivalrous ways—ways neither playful nor "double-voiced." Hence they were creating texts, to use Lotman's formulation, not of "individual character" (except that each would, as a member of the collective, enter History in this significant way) but ones that "automatically realized the laws of sociocultural grammars." To be sure, there were numerous plots, whose variations meant that this behavior was never absolutely predictable or marionettelike, but all the same the use of a "modeling" approach to the "texts" of these lives appeared entirely appropriate. The pathos of the Decembrists' situation was that they *willingly* emplotted their lives after such ancient types of heroic civic duty.[239] This was their romanticism, their "poetic" as opposed to "novelistic" behavior: their lives, even their everyday lives, had to signify in precisely this *emplotted* manner. All else was insignificant and thus not worthy of comment/inclusion, which is to say, for these individuals the "prosaic" could not yet "mean."[240] In this case, the unfinalizable speech

238. Iu. M. Lotman, "The Decembrist in Daily Life (Everyday Behavior as a Historico-Psychological Category)," in *The Semiotics of Russian Cultural History,* ed. Alexander D. Nakhimovsky and Alice Stone Nakhimovsky (Ithaca: Cornell University Press, 1985), 110; *Izbrannye stat'i,* 3 vols. (Tallinn: Aleksandra, 1992–93), I:307.

239. "The difference [between 'routine behavior' and 'signifying activity'] is essential: individuals do not select routine behavior but rather acquire it from their society, from the historical period in which they live or from their psychological or physiological makeup; there is no alternative to it. Signifying behavior, on the contrary, is always the result of choice. It always involves individuals' free activity, their choice of the language they will use in their relations with society" (Lotman, "Decembrist," 129; *Izbrannye stat'i,* I:321).

240. Lotman gives the illustrative example of Ryleev's semiotically marked *Russian* lunches (for example, in the "Spartan," pre-14 December climate it was considered "effete" to stress "Gallic" values): one of the participants in these lunches, Mikhail Bestuzhev, remarks how he would see his colleagues pacing around the room with *cigars* and appetizers of *cabbage* while criticizing Zhukovsky's "obscure romanticism." The non-Russian cigars were semiotically "invisible," which is to say there was no bad faith in smoking them, because they were *just there,* as part of the nonsignifying background. The Russian

act did not encompass the urge for an integral, finalizable biography, but the other way around.

That Lotman could study this type of behavior in context and not see it as something inevitably to be overcome on the path to "novelization" is one of his distinctive accomplishments. However, it is his second formulation that for us deserves special attention because in it he broaches more explicitly than heretofore a biographically generative definition of code. In this instance, the texts (of art, of a life) are not determined beforehand by a plot or code, but *created individually, on an ad hoc basis, according to an emerging grammar.* This shift sounds almost Bakhtinian, but is it really? As Lotman continues in the following paragraph:

> It is precisely this second instance that can be characterized as the activity of semiotic creation [*semioticheskoe tvorchestvo*]. As applied to the "text of life" these instances can be characterized as alternatives: either circum-stances impose norms of behavior and a type of action on the individual [i.e., the Decembrist model], or the individual transforms [lit. "transfig-ures," *preobrazuet*] circumstances according to the laws of his own inter-nal norm. In the first instance, the person's life acquires the character of a "model biography" [*tipovaia biografiia*], while in the second, even when what finally awaits him is defeat or destruction, the person becomes a cre-ative participant in his own life.[241]

Lotman is suggesting that the second type of personality (here Pushkin) has a special orientation toward the text of his life. He finds a way *to use* the codes and behavioral norms for its own benefit, as an artist works with his medium:

> One can liken him [the creative personality] to a sculptor and the circum-stances of life to the stone with which he enters into struggle, opposing the stubbornness of his design to the stubbornness of the material. A sculptor cannot complain of the fact that the granite presented to him is too hard, because the resistance of the material enters into the energy-supplying [*energeticheskii*] moment of creation.[242]

---

cabbage, on the other hand, had a semiotically loaded, ideological import. See Lotman, "Decembrist," 137; *Izbrannye stat'i,* I:327.

241. "Aleksandr Sergeevich Pushkin," 86.

242. "Aleksandr Sergeevich Pushkin," 86. Lotman uses this same metaphor of the sculptor working with stone—he even uses the concrete image of Michelangelo—in an October 1986 letter (unpublished) to Boris Egorov explaining the central idea behind the

This is, I would submit, one of Lotman's most profound insights. For the genuinely creative personality the "code" exists only as precondition, firm footing from which to push off, but after that it exists *to be overcome*. Whether meter or rhyme scheme or strophic design in a poem or rules for dueling or gambling in life, the code is not a ready-made plot (as in the case of the Decembrists' modeling from Roman sources). It is not a totalizing model to follow. Rather it is a formal occasion that guarantees *in advance* that the emerging plot (that is, the finished poem, the completed duel or card game) will produce a change, *but one that is itself not necessarily predictable.* Signifying turning points in a biography, which to a literary sensibility always evoke the specter of preexisting codes, are perceived by the later Lotman as belonging more to the authoring personality than to the modeling codes. Pushkin and Karamzin were creative precisely because the literary roles/masks they routinely donned at various stages of their careers (for example, that of Byronic apprentice in Pushkin's case, that of student and naive, sentimental traveler in Karamzin's) allowed them freedom in the privacy of their own thoughts to develop personalities that had little to do with those masks and indeed could be seen in retrospect actually to oppose them. Also fascinating in this connection is the fact that the only way the lucid and always reasonable Lotman can himself tap the "energy-supplying moment of creation" is by bending his own language toward the slightly "murky" pole of poetic expressiveness — the metaphor of the sculptor and his stone.

Pushkin biography: everything the poet touched in life he, like King Midas, turned with fabulous alchemical efficiency to the gold of art. But King Midas's story ends sadly, as did Pushkin's, because he turned his food to gold as well, and by so doing starved. Lotman is in this letter quite passionate and even moving in defense of his idea: the fact that Pushkin worked with, struggled with, codes did not seem to him a matter of facile or cold-blooded "manipulation." Nor did it make Pushkin's biography less "tragic," quite the opposite in fact, so that Pushkin's story emerged as a "tragedy of strength" rather than a "tragedy of weakness." Lotman was responding to his friend Egorov, who himself had argued that Lotman's Pushkin came across as too conscious, too predetermined: once again, the notion of codes as "fixed, mechanical." I might add that this, significantly, is not the only time Lotman resorts to the King Midas metaphor for creative behavior: in his preface to *Universe of the Mind,* he writes that the semiotic researcher (including of course himself!) "has the habit of transforming the world around him/her so as to show up the semiotic structures. Everything that Kind Midas touched with his golden hand turned to gold. In the same way, everything which the semiotic researcher turns his/her attention to becomes semioticized in his hands" (5). My thanks to Mikhail Lotman and Boris Egorov for providing me a copy of the October 1986 letter.

While certain of Bakhtin's students could successfully apply the philosopher's ideas to aspects of Pushkin's work (for example, Sergei Bocharov on "prosaic" versus "poetic" voice zones in *Eugene Onegin*), Bakhtin appeared less original, less "himself," when the topic was Pushkin. The reason is that Bakhtinian thought, with its concealed teleology, its drive toward ever-emerging novelization, cannot account for the poetic *use* of codes—the idea that a personality can fully acknowledge the arbitrariness of a fixed form and yet willingly adopt that form to generate energy and construct a life that is, yes, open. Pushkinian thought, in Bakhtinian terms, is balanced *between* the epic and the novel, understanding both yet giving itself fully to neither: as opposed to the Decembrists, it already sees the potential for "prosaic" signification, but as opposed to the great realists of the next generation, it is not yet ready to "monologize" fully the "poetic"—that is, to expose artistic convention as not only arbitrary but *false* and *wrong* because it is so. The visual *ostranenie* (making-strange) of Natasha Rostova's visit to the opera or the verbal/psychological "double-voicedness" of Ippolit Terentev's confession, where one can plead in public for one's own dignity, is unthinkable to Pushkin.

The mark of the mature Pushkinian hero is an awareness of the necessity of codes together with the inability of any one "plot" to encompass "life." This is what Lotman grasps. To repeat, a set of rules for behaving in a conventional situation (such as a duel) is not the same as a literary plot or the ancient recording of a heroic life. The one is merely a point d'appui, the other an actual "situational" template.[243] One reason Pushkin as authoring consciousness cannot allow his character Germann in "The Queen of Spades" to win is that the latter wants to cheat the code: to gamble is just that, to follow the code in the *chance* that one's fortunes might improve. A change will take place that one is not allowed to know in advance. Likewise with Masha Mironova and Petr Grinev in *The Captain's Daughter:* here the code, the starting point, is a nobleman's honor and his oath to his sovereign, while the "game," a brutal peasant rebellion, is much more complex and much less formalized. As long as the code is followed in good faith, however, the plot will take care of itself. In Pushkin's "purer" fiction, say *Tales of Belkin,* where the historical theme is less pronounced and characters are allowed to engage in metaliterary games,

---

243. Lotman was apparently approaching this idea when he applied A. Zorin's distinction between "role" and "situational" behavior, between a mask affixed to a persona as opposed to a mask attached to a *bytovaia situatsiia* (everyday situation), in the closing pages of *Sotvorenie Karamzina* ([Moscow: Kniga, 1987], 318–19).

we find examples such as Aleksei and Liza in "Mistress into Maid" (Baryshnia-krestianka), who know all along they are *acting out* aspects of other writers' *siuzhety* (plots), but use those various emplotments to get at their genuine, exuberant natures. They end up being *greater than* the ability of any one plot to contain them. "Life" emerges triumphant, but it is a life uniquely aware of literary role-playing and conventions.

This logic, which Lotman more than any other recent commentator was aware of, was applied by him with inspiring elegance to Pushkin's own biography. Together with Stella Abramovich, whose outstanding work on the last year of Pushkin's life confirmed his own hypotheses,[244] Lotman came to the view that the Pushkin who dueled with d'Anthès was neither "seeking death" (the romantic fallacy) nor at the moment of his fatal encounter any longer "at the mercy" of the court society that had been threatening his reputation over the final months (the sociological fallacy).[245] In other words, Pushkin forced the use of the dueling code on the other side, knowing that *some change* (for example, exile to the country with his wife and family or death on his terms) would take place. And far from causing anxiety, this turning of his fate over to an artificial code gave him, for the first time in months, peace of mind and, possibly (had he lived), renewed *creative energy*. What Pushkin was willing to do was *gamble,* in the true spirit of gambling; what he was not willing to do was be the pitiful figure, the cuckolded husband, in someone else's lowbrow comedy of manners. This, for example, is how Lotman describes Pushkin at the time of the final duel:

> Having taken the decisive step [i.e., having written Baron Heeckeren such an insulting letter that the latter's adoptive son d'Anthès would have no choice but to answer the challenge], Pushkin immediately, according to the accounts of contemporaries, calmed down and became "especially jovial." He was planning on living, full of literary projects; setting off for the duel, he wrote the children's writer A. O. Ishimova a business letter

---

244. See Lotman's afterword ("O dueli Pushkina bez 'tain' i zagadok"), in Stella Abramovich, *Predystoriia poslednei dueli Pushkina. Ianvar' 1836-ianvar' 1837* (St. Petersburg: Petropolis, 1994), 326–38. This piece, first published as a review of Abramovich's 1984 edition of the same book, is important not only as a statement of Lotman's ideas vis-à-vis the "plot" of Pushkin's death but also as perhaps his most eloquent defense of the proper "rules" for undertaking biographical research.

245. See Iu. M. Lotman, *Aleksandr Sergeevich Pushkin: Biografiia pisatelia* (Leningrad: Prosveshchenie, 1981), 245–46.

asking for translations for *Sovremennik* [The Contemporary]. The letter, written just hours before the fatal duel, ended with the words, "Today I accidentally opened your *History in Stories* [Istoriia v rasskazakh], and, not intending to, fell to reading it. That's how one should write!" These were the last lines written by Pushkin's hand.[246]

Pushkin, then, was using the code, not the finished plot, in order to be the author of his life *up to the end.* As terrifying as it sounds, it really did not matter what happened: in any case, it would be on Pushkin's terms. There were things that mattered to Pushkin more than merely staying alive (his honor, his family's privacy, his reputation in the eyes of History). But the code, itself a closed set of rules, guaranteed a "poetic" merging of text and context because Pushkin had both the cognitive awareness and the daring to gamble on a new meaning. Lotman's language toward the end of the biography, his use of elevated diction when describing the hero ("Pushkin died not defeated [*pobezhdennym*], but victorious [*pobeditelem*]"[247]) and of emotionally tinged, even sarcastic terms when describing the court and the Heeckeren faction ("light vaudeville" [*legkii vodevil'*], "young good-for-nothings" [*molodye shalopai*], "their pygmylike nonentity" [*ikh nichtozhestvo pigmeev*][248]), shows to what extent he himself has been drawn into this drama, how much he personally is *inspired* by it. Thus, the code, rather than being synonymous, in Bakhtin's phrasing, with "an intentionally fixed, killed context," is that formal unit which, while not determining the outcome, enables poetic behavior in life. It gives an element of choice, not the free choice of result but the opportunity to provoke change, back to the authoring *lichnost'*.[249]

246. *Biografiia pisatelia*, 244.
247. *Biografiia pisatelia*, 245.
248. *Biografiia pisatelia*, 245.
249. As the reader can guess, *lichnost'* (personality, personhood) is a kind of god-term for the Lotman of the last years: the site of the "miracle" of poetic speech and, by analogy, "poetic behavior"; the place where the predictable "explodes" into the unpredictable and becomes, simultaneously, aware of it. By invoking this vaguely—for the Russian context—Christian concept and by thus making permeable the hermetic language of the semiotician, Lotman is coming close to but never actually reaching, the superstitious-cum-religious sensibility of his subject.

PART II

Pushkin, Derzhavin, and
the Life of the Poet

non omnis moriar . . .
— Horace

So! All of me won't die . . .
— Derzhavin

No, all of me won't die . . .
— Pushkin

The name of the
great Derzhavin is
always pronounced
with a feeling of bias,
even superstition.
— Pushkin

✑ Why Derzhavin?

Perhaps the greatest mystery of Pushkin's life was, as I argued in the preceding section, his death, or at least the manner in which he set the terms of his potential demise. In a matter of months after penning the Stone Island cycle, a series of lyrics that in their internal progression put the poet's life and legacy in perspective with great valedictory power and restrained elegance, the man Pushkin was setting out for his fatal duel with d'Anthès-Heeckeren. It was, according to the historical clock, 4 P.M. on 27 January 1837 when he met Danzas, his second, at the sweetshop on the corner of Nevsky Prospect and the Moika, and the two proceeded together to the place of the duel. But earlier in the day, as Lotman reminded us, Pushkin had written the children's author A. O. Ishimova a letter soliciting translations for his journal *The Contemporary* and taking the occasion to praise her stories which he that very morning, "not intending to, fell to reading" (*ponevole zachitalsia*).[1] How are we to make sense of a personality that, on the one hand, appears to map its creative path onto the Orthodox Easter Week calendar in the magnificent cycle,[2] and, on the other, writes a business letter in the shadow of death and, serenely undistracted,[3] takes active pleasure in another's artistic accomplishments ("That's how one should write!" [*Vot kak nadobno pisat'!*])? The cardinal principle of Pushkin's personality would seem to be then *its resistance to definition from the*

---

1. *Pss*, X:486.

2. See V. P. Stark, "Stikhotvorenie 'Ottsy pustynniki' i zheny neporochny . . .' i tsikl Pushkina 1836 g.," *Pushkin: Issledovaniia i materialy* 10 (1982): 193–202, and Sergei Davydov, "Pushkin's Eastern Triptych," in *Puškin Today*, ed. David M. Bethea (Bloomington: Indiana University Press, 1993), 38–58, for fine recent treatments of the internal structure of the Stone Island cycle and for arguments about a possible "paschal" sequencing of the lyrics.

3. There are, for example, no traces of sprayed ink around the words formed by Pushkin in his letter to Ishimova, which is a sign of his calmness during composition. In other letters, where the occasion of writing made him angry or distraught, this ink spray often appeared as a telltale sign of the inner state. My thanks to Tatiana Krasnoborodko of the Manuscript Section of Pushkinskii Dom (St. Petersburg) for this information.

outside: ready for death, it is not necessarily "courting" it (the "suicidal" argument); putting its artistic house in order, it *chooses,* without being sure of the outcome, its moving day from history to History. Thinking about Pushkin, we as readers can never come to rest, a fact both exhausting and intoxicating. As soon as we fix the man going to the duel as someone calm and making future plans, we remember earlier lines of verse such as "And so it seems, my turn has come, / My dear Delvig is calling me" or "No, all of me won't die."[4] Yet as soon as we give a "fatalistic" shape to those lines, which in human terms could only mean that the man provoked his own death, we must remember his last written words to Ishimova.

In the first part of this study I tried to situate Pushkin in contemporary critical discourse by suggesting that it was the elusively oscillating "stand-in-relation-to" that often gets left out of scholarly/"scientific" approaches to his life and work, whether they be psychoanalytic (psychology as biology), structural-linguistic, or semiotic. By the same token, a more aggressively rhetorical (or "postmodern") approach, such as that of Harold Bloom, that foregrounds verbal confrontations with poetic authority figures at the near total expense of existential ones also does not adequately seem to account for the sensation of *risk,* of psychic *cost,* everywhere present in Pushkin's life and writing. Only by focusing on the powerful co*incidence*/*coincidence* of *freedom within limitation,* both in the poet's life and in his art *and* in their interaction, can we begin to pin down, if only momentarily, this Russian Proteus. The essential Pushkin, in this reading, is never pure structure and never pure feeling, but always their fruitful and larger-than-life embrace. Also, while mention was made in the first part of those male authority figures, beginning with Voltaire, with whom the poet did battle in order to make a place for himself within the tradition, our concern was primarily with the erotic component of Pushkin's sculptural myth — that female embodiment of pure form (the Muse) which had to be brought to life and then protected from rival interest if the poet was to have any chance at "happiness."

Pushkin lived in a time, and was himself very much a product of that time, in which the erotic and the intellectual/cognitive were tightly compartmen-

4. *Pss,* III:215: "I mnitsia, ochered' za mnoi, / Zovet menia moi Del'vig milyi"; *Pss,* III:340: "Net, ves' ia ne umru." The "No, all of me won't die" line, crucial in the 1836 "Exegi monumentum" ("I have erected for myself a monument not made by hand" [Ia pamniatnik sebe vozdvig nerukotvornyi]), actually goes back to Derzhavin's poem of the same name (given to it, as in Pushkin's case, not by the author but by literary history), and ultimately to Horace. The significance of these sources will be addressed later in this part.

talized and "gendered." He could share ideas with smart women (say, Vera Vyazemskaya), just as he could recognize that literary intelligence (say, that of a Mme de Staël) need not come in "male" form, but it is highly unlikely that he was *erotically aroused* by such intelligence. As he wrote, provocatively, in "Excerpts from Letters, Thoughts, and Remarks" (1827):

> People complain about the indifference of Russian women toward our poetry, positing as a cause their ignorance of the Russian language. But what woman will not understand the verse of Zhukovsky, Vyazemsky or Baratynsky? The fact of the matter is that women everywhere are the same. Nature, having endowed them with subtle mind and with the most touchy/irritable sensitivity [*chuvstvitel'nost' samaia razdrazhitel'naia*], has denied them almost totally a sense of the graceful. Poetry slips by their ear/hearing without reaching their soul; they do not feel its harmony. Note how they sing stylish romances, how they distort even the most natural verses, upset the meter, destroy the rhyme. Listen in to their literary judgments and you will be amazed at the incorrectness (lit. "crookedness," *krivizna*] and even the crudity of their understanding . . . Exceptions are rare.[5]

I cite these ungenerous (was Pushkin smarting from some recent wound?) dicta not to debate their dubious truth value for our more civilized space-time but rather to set the stage for the second half of the poet's story. A sense of the "graceful," a feeling of "harmony," required in his mind that such formal matters as meter and rhyme *be felt* as a natural and necessary aspect of a poem—its skeleton or backbone, so to speak. Play with that backbone too capriciously, bend it in the wrong places, and it is no longer a backbone, but something else, something not very "poetic." But where exactly did that skeleton, in Russian terms, come from? Here we must turn not to eros and its embodiment (the Pygmalion myth) but to the male pursuit of "glory" and its embodiment in a monument worthy to be immortalized even in an iron age.

One of the most fascinating and heretofore not systematically studied aspects of Pushkin's creative biography is his relations with contemporaneous Russian writers of his own "aristocratic/noblemen's" (*dvorianstvo*) party whom he knew personally at some point in his life.[6] This is not to say that

---

5. "Otryvki iz pisem, mysli i zamechaniia," in *Pss*, VII:38. The piece was published in Delvig's almanac *Northern Flowers* (Severnye tsvety) for 1828 (but appeared in December 1827).

6. The words "aristocrat" (*aristokrat*) and "nobleman" (*dvorianin*) were not synonymous in Pushkin's time, with differences in meaning that went back to Peter's project

some impressive work has not been done in this area, especially by Vadim Vatsuro,[7] but rather to say that the precise psychological mechanisms of Pushkin's responses to such figures as Karamzin, Dmitriev, Batyushkov, Zhukovsky, Katenin, Griboedov, Delvig, Küchelbecker, Baratynsky, Vyazemsky, Gnedich, and Chaadaev have not been analyzed in the aggregate. We know, for example, that Pushkin was much more willing to "take off the gloves" in print against someone not of his party—say, Kachenovsky or Bulgarin or Polevoi—than against one of his own. And what was at work here was not only the expected solidarity of literary parti pris, but something else—the "noblesse oblige" of social class/background that stated that one should not promote one's personal interests at the expense of another worthy individual (*honnête homme/chestnyi chelovek*).[8] Over and over again Pushkin had to be very careful not to appear, in a self-serving way, to be attaching clay feet to the gods of Russian literature's heroic age. All of his behind-the-scenes skirmishes over politics, literary and otherwise—his epigram(s) on Karamzin as paraphrastic apologist for tsarist despotism, his response to Dmitriev's criticisms of *Ruslan and Lyudmila,* his polemic with Küchelbecker over elegiac "croaking" versus odic civic-mindedness, his portrait of Salieri that touched the linguistically "archaic" Katenin to the quick—had to follow this same formula of "noblesse oblige" whenever his words on a related topic reached the public, were *published.* The same holds true of those reverse instances—say, Pushkin's praise, posthumously, for the Karamzin who authored the history and the Gnedich

---

of forming a "meritorious" or service nobility to replace the "hereditary" one (*stolbovoe dvorianstvo*), whose independence of spirit had historically caused the tsar trouble. Pushkin's six-hundred-year-old family belonged of course to the old and now increasingly impoverished nobility, a fact that would cause him consternation as his social status (as "aristocratic") became mocked by the rising "democratic" journalists (Bulgarin, Polevoi, etc.) in the 1830s. It was also true that the "tiers état" of the writing community in Russia was made up, in the first three decades of the nineteenth century, primarily by persons of noble birth who were trying to support themselves in a system rapidly moving away from the eighteenth-century model of patronage (e.g., Derzhavin). For our purposes here, however, I will be using the terms "aristocrat" and "nobleman" more or less interchangeably.

7. See V. E. Vatsuro, "Podvig chestnogo cheloveka," in Vatsuro and M. I. Gillel'son, *Skvoz' umstvennye plotiny* (Moscow: Kniga, 1972), 32–113.

8. For a critically astute introduction to the interaction between Pushkin-era social and literary codes, see the first two chapters ("A Russian Ideology" and "Institutions of Literature") in William Mills Todd III, *Fiction and Society in the Age of Pushkin* (Cambridge: Harvard University Press, 1986), 10–105.

who translated Homer—where something positive was said in print about a fellow aristocrat. Here too one had to take every precaution not to seem to be raising oneself or one's work on the wings of a departed angel. To be able to constitute accurately, within this relatively narrow semantic space, the force field of Pushkin's loyalties and rivalries will be extremely useful to us as we proceed to investigate the male side of his creative life.

It is against such a background that I pose the initiating question of this second part—why precisely Gavrila Romanovich Derzhavin (1743–1816)? Why this aging warhorse who, by the time of his one and only brief encounter with our poet, was ready, or so it seemed to the younger generation, for the cultural glue factory? Because, first of all, Pushkin's "relationship" with Derzhavin was one that was, potentially, marked with the greatest residue of superstitious awe—that combination of dread and attraction that signals the presence of mythological space. The fact that Pushkin began and ended his career by addressing Derzhavin, a parallel that could not have been lost on someone as sensitive to formal shaping and "composition" as he was, only confirms this presence. Because, second, Derzhavin was universally acknowledged to be the greatest Russian poet before Pushkin, the one whom Pushkin's friend Vyazemsky called at the time of his death "a living *monument*"[9] of the Age of Catherine and Suvorov and the same one whom Pushkin's literary opponent Nikolai Polevoi was still calling sixteen years later a "moral giant" (*nravstvennyi ispolin*) and the only cultural phenomenon on Russian soil comparable to Pushkin himself.[10] But not only that. Equally if not more important, it would

9. "Over the course of three tsardoms rang out the sounds of Derzhavin's songs. But it was the brilliant age of Catherine, this poetic age of the glory of Russia (of which it seemed as if Derzhavin was the living and eloquent monument among us), that was the greatest epoch of his fame as well. This age found him in the full flower of his manliness and strength. The present days, rich in the threatening tempests and grandiose deeds of the people's courage [i.e., Russia's lead role in the defeat of Napoleon], witnessed the setting of his genius, dispirited by the years. But the deeds of Suvorov's sons often awakened his [the general's] Singer and drew from the latter's now cool lyre sounds worthy of former days. Two or three of these poems, written by Derzhavin over the past three years, could be called the parting song of the dying swan" (P. A. Viazemskii, "O Derzhavine," *Syn Otechestva* 37 [1816]: 169; the entire necrologue is found on pp. 163–75). The reference to the swan is to Derzhavin's poem on his immortality that will be played upon by Delvig as he passes the torch from Derzhavin to Pushkin in his "Who like the swan of flowering Ausonia" (Kto, kak lebed' tsvetushchei Avzonii, 1815). See below.

10. Polevoi's expansive review of Derzhavin's new collected works (4 vols., by the publishing house of A. Smirdin) appeared in *Moskovskii telegraf* 15 (1832): 362–98; the

Figure 7. Gavrila Romanovich Derzhavin (1743–1816), generally recognized as Russia's greatest poet up to the time of his death. In *Eugene Onegin* (VIII.ii.1–4) Pushkin writes, "Old Derzhavin recognized / And blessed us, descending to his grave." From an original oil painting by V. Borovikovsky, 1811.

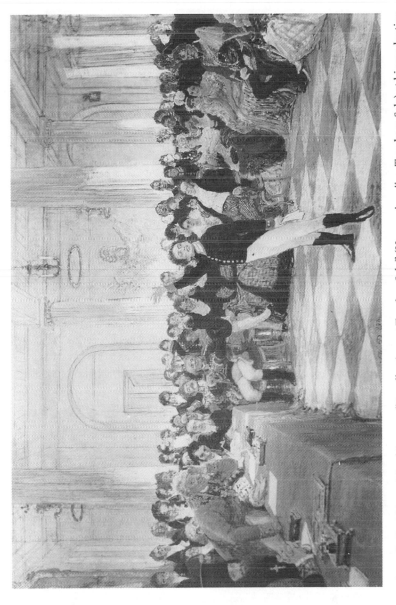

Figure 8. Pushkin reciting his poem "Recollections at Tsarskoe Selo" (Vospominaniia v Tsarskom Sele) at his graduation exercises at the Lyceum on 8 January 1815, while Derzhavin (leaning over the table to the left) looks on with delight. A painting by Ilya Efimovich Repin, 1911.

Figure 10. Pavel Voinovich Nashchokin (1801–54), another close friend of Pushkin. Pencil drawing by K. Mazer, 1839.

Figure 9. Baron Anton Antonovich Delvig (1798–1831), poet, editor of *Northern Flowers* (Severnye Tsvety) and *Literary Gazette* (Literaturnaia gazeta). Probably Pushkin's closest and most beloved friend; after his death Pushkin said of him, "No one on earth was nearer to me." Watercolor by P. L. Yakovlev, 1818.

Figure 11. A view of the Lyceum and Sadovaya Street. Lithograph by K. Shultz from an original by I. Meyer, 1850s.

Figure 12. The Chesma column. Lithograph by V. P. Langer, 1820.

Figure 13: The Cameron Gallery at Tsarskoe Selo. An engraving by Galaktionov from an original by Svinin, 1817.

be the *life* of Derzhavin and the options he offered as *historical man* that would be definitive, as already exhausted plot, for Pushkin. No other literary figure of the eighteenth century offered this potent combination, *poet + life in history,* to the same degree as did the "singer of Felitsa." This is what Pushkin himself meant, for instance, when he placed Derzhavin at the ultimate position of a list of great eighteenth-century personages (Catherine, Suvorov, Bibikov, Voltaire, etc.) *for whose sake* he set out to preserve the past in his *History of Pugachev,* as he tells us in the preface.[11] And because, third, the childless Derzhavin did a great service for the schoolboy Pushkin and then promptly (but apparently not promptly enough) died and entered the category of "shade" *before* his appointed successor could repay the debt in the proper coin. With other substantially older and respected literary figures ("fathers" and "uncles," so to speak) whom Pushkin knew, such as Karamzin, Dmitriev, and Zhukovsky, or with those who were just a few years older (senior "siblings"), such as Vyazemsky, Chaadaev, and Katenin, there was the sense that the poet could encounter them in an open present, on terms that were not necessarily a priori magnetized with the comings and goings of a revenant. Not so Derzhavin, who departed the scene before Pushkin became "Pushkin." These various considerations will constitute the leitmotifs in the story to follow.

Yet there is still another important issue in our preliminaries about "why Derzhavin?"—the ontological status of the older poet's language vis-à-vis that of the heir apparent waiting in the wings. Pushkin, as I have tried to make clear earlier in this study, does not appear to have what Bloomians and Lacanians might call *linguistic* anxiety toward his predecessors. To all appearances, he thought his language adequate to the task of its telling within the rules de-

---

quote about "moral giant" appears on p. 362. The review then continued over two other issues: 16 (1832): 523–55 and 18 (1832): 213–44, 293–95. In his essay Polevoi continuously made the point that Derzhavin's civic-mindedness and willingness to "take up the deed" (*priniat'sia za dela*) *at the expense of his own poetry* still spoke to the Russia of 1832. See *Moskovskii telegraf* 15 (1832): 381, 386, 390. At the same time, while finding essential to Derzhavin's temperament the blend of "grandee and man, functionary and poet," Polevoi asserted boldly that "with the exception of Pushkin, we have not had such an *exclusively poetic* character, from the time of the formation of Russia, as Derzhavin" (*Moskovskii telegraf* 16 [1832]: 523). On the last page of the article Polevoi spoke about the monument to Derzhavin that was being erected at the time near the poet's estate in the Novgorod province. By the 1830s Pushkin would have been very sensitive to this use of the Derzhavin icon. See below.

11. *Pss,* VIII:109.

fined by "genre consciousness." However, this very adequacy also comes at a
cost, even if that cost is not purely linguistic. Derzhavin brought to an apo-
theosis the quality of vivid, spontaneous, originary "Russianness"[12] that Pushkin, with his Karamzinian/"Gallic" linguistic bias and his early Arzamasian
playfulness, could not but see as his total opposite and even negation.[13] He
often boldly intermingled the "high" and the "low," the Church Slavonicisms
whose presence Lomonosov had associated with proper odic diction and the
Russianisms whose presence Lomonosov had associated with less prestigious
genres, in a manner suggesting that, stylistically, he knew no fear. In other
words, it was his ability to be *uniquely excessive* that was characteristic. At the
same time, the way the insouciantly "archaic" Derzhavin could see things and
give them their names really did give his work the impression of something
being gloated over by a Russian God on the seventh day of Creation: his water-
falls are upside-down mountains that burst into the lapidary hues of millions
of sparkling diamonds and pearls, his dinner tables groan with all manner of
peacock-colored staple and delicacy (e.g., one four-line stanza yields *crimson*
ham, *green* cabbage soup, *rosy-yellow* pie, *white* cheese, *red* crawfish, *jet-black*
and *amber* caviar, the *light-blue* fin of a pike) done in their *echt*-native preparation, etc. If Pushkin is subtle and elegant, Derzhavin is flamboyant and
expressive. And if Pushkin begins with a verbal base of "salon speech" and
only subsequently, under the influence of Pavel Katenin and others, backs
away somewhat from the original Karamzinian admonishments to write as

12. "This *Russianness*, this national quality [*national'nost'*] of Derzhavin has been
overlooked [by us] up to the present. Speaking about Derzhavin's lyric verse, everyone
has forgotten the *Russian* singer in him. . . . If Derzhavin had been more familiar with
Russian antiquity, if he had not gotten carried away with a false idea of it, according to
which Karamzin thought it necessary to *deck out* [*skrashivat'*] that which is native to us,
even in History itself, perhaps it would have fallen to his lot to begin the period of our
truly national *Poetry*" (Polevoi, "Sochineniia Derzhavina," *Moskovskii telegraf* 18 [1832]:
224–25; emphasis in original).

13. Boris Eikhenbaum, for example, puts his finger on this Derzhavinian quiddity
when he writes "to poets of a nonsymbolist school Derzhavin can still to this day give
much. He who wants to speak about the world *through things* [my emphasis], he who feels
the genuine fullness of the living word, that one will find for himself much of value in his
poetry." Likewise, when Eikhenbaum says that "Derzhavin speaks *about his own inspiration* [my emphasis] too powerfully and with too much conviction not to believe him,"
he is citing an aspect of the great precursor's linguistic temperament with which Pushkin
himself would have to struggle. See below. B. M. Eikhenbaum, *Skvoz' literaturu: Sbornik
statei* (rpt. The Hague: Mouton, 1962), 16.

one speaks, to show good taste, and to embrace French calques at the expense of the clumsily homegrown, Derzhavin is aggressively, confidently *pre-Karamzinian*. He seems to write his own rules in a language that is more prone, syntactically and lexically (i.e., his roughened, inversion-saturated syntax and striking compound epithets), to be magnificently "unspeakable."

Hence all the "Gallo-Russian" locutions that entered the vocabularies and thought patterns of educated Russians, and Pushkin in the first instance, as a result of Karamzin's reforms — e.g., words and phrases such as *Bozhe moi!* (*mon Dieu!*), *chort voz'mi* (*diable m'emporte*), *interesnyi* (*interéssant*), *ser'eznyi* (*sérieux*), *moi angel* (*mon ange*), *ocharovatel'nyi* (*charmant*), *v svoei tarelke* (*dans son assiette*), *Sdelaite chest'* (*faire honneur*), etc.[14] — did so too late to have any significant impact on the philosophically "German" but linguistically ebulliently "Russian" Derzhavin. In this respect, what Boris Uspensky has formulated about Pushkinian language in the post-Karamzinian world applies to Derzhavin as to a photographic negative:

> If [Church] Slavonicisms are viewed by Pushkin [over time] as something stylistically possible, as a conscious poetic device, then Gallicisms can be perceived as neutral elements of speech. In this way the linguistic distinctiveness of the mature Pushkin can be expressed, with a certain amount of crudity, in the following formula: Gallo-Russian substratum + Slavono-Russian superstratum. This formula, it seems, defines in general the subsequent development of the Russian literary language.[15]

The "substratum" of Derzhavin's language and thought patterns, to reverse Uspensky's formula here, is clearly "Slavono-Russian."[16] Mérimée, who once

14. See discussion in B. A. Uspenskii (with Iu. Lotman), "Spory o iazyke v nachale XIX v. kak fakt russkoi kul'tury," *Izbrannye trudy. Tom 2. Iazyk i kul'tura* (Moscow: Gnozis, 1994), 398–99.

15. "Spory o iazyke," 402.

16. As Uspensky writes in another recent article, "De cette façon la perspective de Derjavine est radicalement différente de celle de Pouchkine: c'est celle d'une langue poétique slavonisée qui sert de fond pour une mise en jeu de la langue familière. Pour utiliser une image, on peut dire que le rapport entre Pouchkine et Derjavine en ce qui concerne leur approche des slavonismes et des russismes est le même que celui qui existe entre un positif et un négatif.

"On peut dire que les éléments relevant de la langue familière sont marqués chez Derjavine exactement de la même façon que le sont les slavonismes chez Pouchkine; en ce sens il sont comparables dans leur fonction. Dans les deux cas un effet de distanciation est obtenu, mais si chez Pouchkine ce sont les slavonismes qui sont mis à distance dans la per-

wrote to Sobolevsky that Pushkin's intonation, even in a mature work such as "The Queen of Spades," sounded "completely French,"[17] could never have said the same thing about the "other" great poet in the Russian tradition. It is this fact, that of Derzhavin's radical linguistic alterity, that Pushkin will wrestle with as he returns in his maturity to the themes of the eighteenth century and to the "primary naming" (and "odic" praising/condemning) associated with his illustrious precursor.

In addition, however, and perhaps more to the point, this question of which stratum came first in the language, the "Russian" or the "French"/"European," had a direct impact on the one concept — that of inspiration — central to both Derzhavin's and Pushkin's views of themselves as poets in language and "in history." It will be another of my theses that the distinction in etymology and meaning between *vostorg* and *vdokhnovenie,* words that run like a red thread through much of Pushkin's creative life, encompassing important friendships and rivalries, and that appear in certain significant polemical contexts, is not fortuitous, but always goes back to the poet's urge to define himself as someone linguistically and temperamentally different from his predecessor. I will have further comments about the specific meanings of these words in context in due course, but for now suffice it to say that *vostorg* is defined by Dal as something very close to the Russian sublime: its etymology involves a violent "wrenching" or "expelling" quality (*vostorgat', istorgat'*), a "ripping out" (*vyryvat'*) and a "lifting up" (*podnimat' vverkh*) that suggest that one is completely under the sway of an all-powerful force. To experience *vostorg* is to be jettisoned out of oneself. Through it one comes to know "benign frenzy, rapture, the forgetting of oneself, the temporary release of the spirit from the world and its vanities, the soaring of the spirit, and [that feeling's] temporary domination to the point where it sometimes sees visions."[18] Virtually everyone in Pushkin's circle, and especially such friends as Delvig and Küchelbecker, who grew up under the sway of Derzhavin's rough-hewn genius, knew that the older poet possessed his generation's "copyrights" to *vostorg*—

---

spective de la langue parlée, chez Derjavine ce sont les éléments appartenant à la langue parlée qui sont distanciés par rapport à la langue livresque. Aussi bien les slavonismes chez Pouchkine que la langue parlée chez Derjavine ont la fonction de *procédés littéraires*" (B. Uspensky, "La langue de Derjavine," in *Derjavine: un poète russe dans l'Europe des Lumières,* ed. Anita Davidenkoff [Paris: Institut d'études slaves, 1994], 114).

17. Cited Uspenskii, "Spory o iazyke," 401.

18. V. I. Dal', *Tolkovyi slovar' zhivogo velikorusskogo iazyka,* 4 vols. (St. Petersburg-Moscow: izd. t-va M.O. Vol'f, 1912), I:614.

it was *his* word, it defined *his* poetry, most of all his odes.[19] Pushkin, on the other hand, as we recall from our opening discussion, used the French calque "inspiration"/*vdokhnovenie* to describe a state not of losing oneself in the sublime, but of finding oneself at the precise moment where impressions (sense) and understanding (cognition) come together: "*Inspiration?* It is the disposition/orientation of the soul to the most vivid reception of impressions, and consequently, to the rapid grasp of ideas, which aids in the explanation of the former."[20] Hence it is also not by chance that Pushkin uses a "Gallo-Russian" expression to show his awareness of an otherness capable of seeing and *grasping from the outside* a Derzhavinian *vostorg* no longer adequate, either linguistically or experientially, historically, to *his* generation's Russianness.

Finally, as mentioned above, this part of our study will attempt to elaborate and deepen the heuristic guidelines of the first part: how creative anxiety is a positive, "forward-moving" concept; where Freudian and Bloomian models do and do not apply; what aspects of poetic structure have emotional as well as cognitive functions, etc. With this in mind, Part II will isolate three psycho-

---

19. This is not to say that Derzhavin did not use the term *vdokhnovenie*—he did. But my point is that when he did speak of "inspiration" he had in mind "ecstasy," "the sublime," in its post-Lomonosovian incarnation, and it is this connection with which Pushkin will polemicize.

Yuri Lotman's student Elena Pogosyan has written a study of the development of the concept of odic *vostorg* in the three decades of the eighteenth century (1730s–1760s) during which the panegyrical tradition was meticulously working out the "rules of address" when praising the Russian monarch: who does the "we" or "I" represent, is the work recited or written down and submitted, what constitutes "sincerity" (*iskrennost'*) and what does not, etc.: Elena Pogosian, *Vostorg russkoi ody i reshenie temy poeta v russkom panegirike 1730–1762 gg.* (Tartu: Tartu Ülikooli Kirjastuse, 1997). The fact, as Pogosyan points out in her conclusion, that the later Lomonosov could address the empress as "You, Catherine" (*Vy, Ekaterina*), a phrasing that went back to the heartfelt language of Trediakovsky's love lyrics, meant that *private* emotions were at last admissible when speaking of this august personage; moreover, as the scholar continues, "the culmination of this evolution [in the panegyric] was the adoption [of a type] of contact with the monarch that was printed, which is to say public, yet not [necessarily] direct, which [in turn] meant that the author was no longer presented with the inevitability of deciding the question of the sincerity of his emotion and the genuineness of his performance" (128). Derzhavin's odic production and his own notion of *vostorg* belong to this post-Lomonosovian era, when, despite the fact of the great number of odes being written to honor the empress, "the development of the literature was oriented not toward the struggle to belong to official culture, but toward [the effort to] break with it" (128).

20. *Pss*, VII:29.

logical "vectors" of Pushkin's personality—his independence and *stremlenie pervenstvovat'* (urge to be first), his superstition and sense of play/risk with cosmic forces, and his passion for formal symmetry and composition[21]— in hopes of arriving at a more complex and dimensionalized understanding of his relationship with Derzhavin. I consider these tendencies—which work in concert, as simultaneous extensions of one another, and often in hidden, paradoxical ways—to be determinative in the poet's psychological makeup. For instance, what is superstition but an "ontological rhyme" (cf. coincidence/coincidence) given to one by an outside force? And what is a strong poetic personality but one that has a particularly developed sense of how ontological rhymes become verbal ones and vice versa? Our main interest, then, will be in how Pushkin makes use, at different turning points in his life and in situations both strictly artistic and nonartistic, of his famous first meeting with Derzhavin—the reading of "Recollections at Tsarskoe Selo" (Vospominaniia v Tsarskom Sele) during the 8 January 1815 public examination at the Lyceum. (See illustrations 8 and 11.) Pushkin's relations with his two closest friends, Delvig and Nashchokin, to whom he made his strongest and most psychologically ambiguous statements about Derzhavin, will also be examined for their potential, in this context, for crossover from nonliterary to literary biography.

21. Though not published in his lifetime, Pushkin's oft-cited statement about "symmetry" could be applied to much of his work and to the "shape" he gave his own life as poet: "Proportionality, correspondence (symmetry) are characteristic of the human mind; herein lies the secret . . . of harmony in verse" (*Sorazmernost', sootvetstvennost' [simetria (sic)] svoistvenna umu chelovecheskomu—v etom zakliuchaetsia i taina . . . garmonii stikhov*) ("large 'Academy,' " XI:303). For an ingenious analysis of the various possible compositional symmetries in several of Pushkin's well-known poems, see E. Etkind, *Simmetricheskie kompozitsii u Pushkina* (Paris: Institut d'études slaves, 1988).

❧ 1814–1815

Given the temporal limitations of any biography, there are just three stances or orienting attitudes that a poet can have toward a predecessor.[22] If a poet is beginning a career, he can experience the model as a point from which to commence his "creative path" (*tvorcheskii put'*); here the future is maximally open, to the extent that the younger poet himself has no biography of literary significance (in Tomashevsky's terms, no usable "biographical legend") *and* can imagine himself distinctly emerging from the shadow of the precursor. Young meets old or, as it often happens, dead, and it is natural that the young, if sufficiently confident, would experience itself as a vast field of creative possibility, while the other, having exhausted its potential for biography and entered the realm of myth, is viewed as fixed. The second stance occurs at any point in the poet's career when he has "defined himself" but is not yet seriously involved in composing his epitaph: when he now turns to the older model, he can start over but he can never begin for the first time. He knows he has some of his creative life behind him and he believes he has some of his creative life before him. From this vantage, the precursor, though dead, is bound to appear more complicated, more human, less mythical, as the younger man's understanding of "life" fills in and roughens the contours of the original meeting. The psychological operations of this second stance are such that, for the strong personality at least, irony shadows each confrontation with an earlier model ("I am and am not he"). The third stance is when the poet, now substantially older or old, turns to the original model to write his epitaph. Now the turning is final and recapitulative; the distinction(s) between the two poets involves not an irony of multiple potentials but a last sweeping gaze and affirmation that "this, and not that, is mine." Here the poet is maximally attuned

22. Two important and by now "classic" studies of how poets engage and reshape the traditions given them by precursors are the already discussed Bloom (see Part I of this study) and Lawrence Lipking, *The Life of the Poet: Beginning and Ending Poetic Careers* (Chicago: University of Chicago Press, 1981). Lipking's triad of initiation, harmonium, and tombeau has been particularly useful in the argument that follows.

to the understanding that his potential for creative biography is limited, perhaps even exhausted, and that he is close to entering mythical space. This general scheme will serve us as we examine four "turning points" in Pushkin's creative life, referred to for simplicity's sake by their temporal coordinates: 1814–15 (beginning), 1825–26 (first ironic midpoint), 1830–31 (second ironic midpoint), and 1836 (ending).

The ways in which the psychological dominanta of Pushkin's personality engage and challenge the myth of Derzhavin are fascinating, fraught as they are with the younger poet's special brand of serious play.[23] As I suggested in

23. Important modern treatments of Pushkin's engagement of Derzhavin include: M. P. Alekseev, "Stikhotvorenie Pushkina 'Ia pamiatnik sebe vozdvig . . . ,'" *Pushkin i mirovaia literatura* (Leningrad: Nauka, 1987), 200–210; Dmitrii Blagoi, *Literatura i deistvitel'nost'* (Moscow: Khudozhestvennaia literatura, 1959), 212–31; Sergei Davydov, "Pushkin's Merry Undertaking and 'The Coffinmaker,'" *Slavic Review* 44.1 (1985): 41–48; B. P. Gorodetskii, *Lirika Pushkina* (Moscow-Leningrad: Izd. Akademii Nauk SSSR, 1962), 45–53; G. P. Makogonenko, "Pushkin i Derzhavin," in *Derzhavin i Karamzin v literaturnom dvizhenii XVIII–nachala XIX veka* (Leningrad: Nauka, 1969), 113–26; G. S. Tatishcheva, "Pushkin i Derzhavin," *Vestnik Leningradskogo Universiteta* 14.3 (1965): 106–16; and A. Zapadov, *Masterstvo Derzhavina* (Moscow: Sovetskii pisatel', 1958), 237–58. But see also S. Bondi, *O Pushkine. Stat'i i materialy*, 2d ed. (Moscow: Khudozhestvennaia literatura, 1983), 446–67; G. A. Gukovskii, *Pushkin i problemy realisticheskogo stilia* (Moscow: Khudozhestvennaia literatura, 1957), 112–13; B. Meilakh, *Khudozhestvennoe myshlenie Pushkina kak tvorcheskii protsess* (Moscow-Leningrad: Izd. Akademii Nauk SSSR, 1962), 165–67; and Walter Vickery, "'Vospominaniia v Tsarskom Sele' (1814) i 'Pamiatnik': K voprosu o strofike," in *Slavic Poetics: Essays in Honor of Kiril Taranovski* (The Hague: Mouton, 1973), 485–97. Tatishcheva identifies two primary schools of understanding the Pushkin-Derzhavin connection in Soviet scholarship: the Blagoi-Zapadov approach, which sees Pushkin as gradually turning away from what Derzhavin stood for as a *proidennyi etap* (concluded stage), versus the Gukovsky-Makogonenko approach, which stresses Pushkin's turn toward the later "Anacreontic" and "protorealist" Derzhavin of "Life at Zvanka" (Zhizn' zvanskaia) ("Pushkin i Derzhavin," 106–7). The problem with this logic is that these two views are not in fact mutually exclusive: Pushkin could be seen to reject the more famous "public" and "odic" Derzhavin as he matured while he could also be seen to be attracted to the more private, "prosaic," and "Anacreontic" Derzhavin of the early 1800s. The most informed of all these scholars is Alekseev, whose analysis of Derhavin in the context of Pushkin's late poem "I have erected for myself a monument not made by hand" ("Exegi monumentum") is as brilliant as it is exhaustive. Still, as will become evident below, I disagree fundamentally with Alekseev's almost exclusively "positive" assessment of Pushkin's engagement with the older poet; it is, from my point of view, not dark or "anxious" enough: see, e.g., "It is well known that Pushkin liked his early 'Derzhavinian' verse, holding it dear in the same way as his memories of school-

the preceding section, if Pushkin "took on" a fellow writer later in his career, whether it was Byron or Walter Scott, Küchelbecker or Katenin, he did so as a poet who had defined himself sufficiently to be confident of escape from the other's shadow ("what is left after our confrontation will be more *mine* than yours"). Not so, however, with Derzhavin. This is because, first of all, Pushkin encountered Derzhavin before he had defined himself, that is, before he could realize the complex possibilities (or "fatedness") of his own historical moment and his poetic role in it; and because, second, the very notion of romantic (auto)biography was, at the time of the encounter, not yet thinkable. The notion, according to Lotman, that "the life of the poet, his personality, and his fate merge with his art, constituting for the public a unified whole . . . belongs to the epoch of Romanticism." But for previous generations, including that of the youthful Pushkin, "artistic works lived lives for their readers separate from their authors. . . . The biography of the author was perceived as something external to the creative work [*nechto postoronee po otnosheniiu k tvorchestvu*]." And so it was only in the wake of Napoleon and Byron—i.e., right about the time of Derzhavin's death—that "a poet's work began to be viewed as one huge autobiographical novel, in which lyric and narrative poems formed chapters, while the biography served as *siuzhet* [plot]."[24] Pushkin's original meeting with Derzhavin has to be understood in all of its *preromantic* potential. In short, there could be no sense of dual composition, where the status of the speaker in the text and the status of the writer outside the text were intentionally blurred and drawn to comment on each other. However, this does not mean that the self-references in "Recollections" are uttered into a void.

---

boy years" ("Stikhotvorenie Pushkina," 200). Also very useful and influential on my own thinking is Davydov's treatment of Pushkin's "return" to the early "Arzamasian" thematics of the Lyceum period in "The Coffinmaker" (Grobovshchik, 1830); where I differ with Davydov, however, is in the latter's stress on the bright side of parody ("Recollections" in this reading is straightforwardly acknowledged as a "brilliant imitation" ["Pushkin's Merry Undertaking," 45]) and on the essentially playful reinvocation of Derzhavin. Even though my argument will be that Pushkin is being at least partially playful and irreverent in his returns to Derzhavin, this strategy covers over an "anxious" and serious side of the relationship that is at least as important. Where these earlier studies of the Derzhavin-Pushkin relationship bear on my own analysis will be indicated periodically in the text below. A recent work that provides a wealth of useful information on Pushkin's relations with Russian writers and thinkers of the eighteenth century is Iu. V. Stennik, *Pushkin i russkaia literatura XVIII veka* (St. Petersburg: Nauka, 1995).

24. Iu. Lotman, *Aleksandr Sergeevich Pushkin: Biografiia pisatelia* (Leningrad: Prosveshchenie, 1981), 54.

Lotman, who has virtual perfect pitch in matters of Pushkin's psychology and development, warns the reader not to overdramatize the first encounter with Derzhavin: "The meeting of Pushkin and Derzhavin did not have in reality that conventionally symbolic (and, what's more, certainly not that theatrical) character that we involuntarily ascribe to it, looking back and knowing that on that day in the hall of the Lyceum the greatest Russian poet of the eighteenth century, who had but a year and a half to live, and the greatest of all Russian poets encountered each other." [25] But at the same time, while warning us not to mythologize, Lotman also claims, apparently not able at this point to expel entirely a poetic register from his own language, that Derzhavin "ordained" (*rukopolozhil*) Pushkin into the ranks of poets and that "for Pushkin himself this was one of the most important events of his life. He felt like a page who had been knighted" (*On chuvstvoval sebia kak pazh, poluchivshii posviashchenie v rytsarskii san*).[26] The image of knighting or ordination is well chosen: it stresses the one-time, unrepeatable nature of the ritual as well as the unquestioned, originary authority of the king. One cannot choose one's king, just as one cannot choose one's parents. In Pushkin's crossing from page to knight of poetic calling, he was not, despite the open fields of battle up ahead, wholly free to create himself. For one as insistent on keeping the terms of self-definition to himself, this would have to be an extremely potent realization.

Let us now look for a moment at the immediate psychological environment surrounding the poem and then at the work itself. Pushkin's teachers (Koshansky, Chirikov, Kunitsyn, Piletsky-Urbanovich, Kartsov, etc.), the Lyceum administration (Malinovsky), and memoirist-friends (Pushchin) are the primary sources we have for insights into his personality as a schoolboy. It is to them we must turn to reconstitute, however imperfectly, the youth who then stepped into the role of poetic speaker. The benefit of the teachers' evaluations is that they are not "touched up" by memory and are more unbiased (indeed, some of the *nastavniki*, already sensing Pushkin's almost congenital resistance to authority, are mildly oppositional) and objective; the benefit of the memoiristic treatments, especially Pushchin's, is that we are apt to get a closer approximation of Pushkin's point of view. In any event, the salient character traits and values that emerge from these accounts are: youthful patriotism and naive desire, in the context of 1812 and the Napoleonic campaigns, to be an active participant in History; the cultivation of a circle (*krug*) of friends whose

25. *Biografiia pisatelia*, 29.
26. *Biografiia pisatelia*, 25, 29–30.

nurturing framework would replace the notion of "family" (cf. Pushkin's cool relations with his parents) and the traditional starting point of "childhood"; a preference for vigorous physical activity that does not accord with Pushkin's studied pose, probably more appropriate to his friend Delvig, of languor and "laziness" (*len'*); an unwillingness to display his knowledge to superiors, possibly motivated by an urge not to appear to be currying favor (Pushchin); light-mindedness or flippancy (*legkomyslie*) and wittiness (*ostroumie*) (Kartsov, Piletsky-Urbanovich, Malinovsky); a powerful sense of competition (*chuvstvo sorevnovaniia*) (Koshansky), particularly with regard to literary contests;[27] touchiness (Pushkin was *razdrazhitel'nee mnogikh*), which in relations with others expressed itself as a combination of "boldness and shyness" (*smelost' i zastenchivost'*) (Pushchin); temperamental instability, which oscillated between generosity of spirit and the hot need to assert primacy (Chirikov called Pushkin *vetren, dobrodushen, vspyl'chiv*); "self-esteem together with ambition" (*samoliubie vmeste s chestoliubiem*) (Piletsky-Urbanovich); a love of friendly games and mystifications involving verbal dexterity and improvisational skill. All of these qualities are important to keep in mind as we move from the realm of the nonliterary to the literary, but those that are most formative, for our purposes, are Pushkin's sense of competition and his need to implicate—still in a preromantic context—his life in History.

"Recollections at Tsarskoe Selo" is, significantly, the first poem Pushkin published under his own name. "To a Versifier Friend" (K drugu stikhotvortsu) had been published in *The Messenger of Europe* in 1814, but through a ruse: Delvig, it seems, had sent it under the name "Aleksandr N. k.sh.p.," hiding the author by reversing the consonants in his surname. "Recollections" is, therefore, the poet's first *official* appearance in print. But it is also closely associated with his friendship with Delvig, who more than any other fellow student was responsible for *discovering* Pushkin (seeing his potential as far above that of other competitors such as Illichevsky)[28] and who himself, much

27. "An unloved child in his own family, developing early and extravagantly, Pushkin as a youth was, it appears, deeply unsure of himself. This in turn elicited his bravado, his fighting spirit [*molodechestvo*], his striving to be first. At home he was considered a layabout [*uvalen'*], and so he began to place highest value on physical adroitness, strength, ability to stand up for himself" (Lotman, *Biografiia pisatelia*, 23).

28. See. e.g., Delvig's lines from his poem "To Pushkin" (Pushkinu, 1815?) and his sonnet "To N. M. Iazykov" (N. M. Iazykovu, 1821): "Pushkin! He won't even be able to hide himself in the forests; / His lyre will give him away with its loud singing, / And from the mortals the immortal one will be carried off / By a triumphant Apollo to Olym-

more than his friend, had his own cult of Derzhavin.[29] (See illustration 9.) It would be no exaggeration to say that Delvig's warmth, generosity, loyalty, and what Anna Kern called his "childlike lucidity" (*detskaia iasnost'*),[30] his lively yet essentially *disinterested* imagination,[31] his sense of *serving* a muse without publicly straining after recognition or *slava* (glory)[32] were as close as Pushkin ever came in his own experience to the ideals of friendship and spiritual beauty in male form (Nashchokin is a somewhat different model, to be discussed below). That Delvig's inner beauty, which despite his contemplative nature was not shy but had a mischievous, scabrous streak,[33] was clothed in a

---

pus" (Пушкин! Он и в лесах не укроется; / Лира выдаст его громким пением, / И от смертных восхитит бессмертного / Аполлон на Олимп торжествующий); and "I took a shine to the infant Pushkin, / Sharing with him both sadness and delight, / And it was I who first heard his singing" (Я Пушкина младенцем полюбил, / С ним разделя и грусть и наслажденье, / И первый я его услышал пенье) (A. A. Del'vig, *Polnoe sobranie stikhotvorenii*, ed. B. Tomashevskii [Leningrad: Izd. Pisatelei v Leningrade, 1934], 191, 157). The "To Pushkin" poem is discussed at the conclusion of this study.

29. See, e.g., M. P. Alekseev, *Pushkin i sravnitel'no-istoricheskie issledovaniia* (Leningrad: Nauka, 1972), 16–17. In his unpublished obituary of Delvig, Pushkin states that his friend "never parted from Derzhavin [i.e., he always had a volume of his poetry with him]" (S Derzhavinym on ne rasstavalsia [*Pss*, VII:216]). The tradition, repeated by numerous memoirists (S. T. Aksakov, Glinka, Markevich), that Derzhavin used the occasion of Pushkin's reading of "Recollections" at the public examination to "appoint" his successor, gained special force in Delvig's 1816 poem, addressed to his friend, "On the Death of Derzhavin" (Na smert' Derzhavina). See Vatsuro's commentary in *Sll*, 549.

30. *Druz'ia*, I:211.

31. "The only thing noteworthy about him [as a student] was the liveliness of his imagination [*zhivost' voobrazheniia*]" (Pushkin, in his unfinished necrology, not later than 1834 [*Druz'ia*, I:207; *Pss*, VII:216]).

32. See, e.g., Pushkin's well-known lines in "19 October 1825" (19 October being the anniversary of the opening of the Lyceum and a date the poet was drawn to continually to commemorate his original circle of friends and their current fates, including his own): "From childhood two muses would pay us visits, / And our lot was made sweet by their caress: / But I already loved the sound of clapping hands, / [While] you, proud, sang for the muses and for your soul; / My gift like my life I wasted without thought, / [While] you cultivated your genius in quietude" (С младенчества две музы к нам летали, / И сладок был их лаской наш удел: / Но я любил уже рукоплесканья, / Ты, гордый, пел для муз и для души; / Свой дар как жизнь я тратил без вниманья, / Ты гений свой воспитывал в тиши); and "Service to the muses does not tolerate vanity; / The beautiful must be majestic" (Служенье муз не терпит суеты; / Прекрасное должно быть величаво) (*Pss*, II:246).

33. Pushkin notes, for example, in an unfinished article on his now deceased friend

"sluggish" exterior (Delvig apparently had a bad heart), and that he had little of the stronger friend's physical energy and resilience, elicited Pushkin's playfulness and humor in their private language, but his fierce loyalty and protectiveness in any exchange involving outsiders or public space. True, the Delvig who amused his classmates by falling to dreaming in a manner more literal than poetic could not be taken always very seriously, but for Pushkin this unprepossessing exterior concealed something he needed badly: *faith* in him and his poetic calling. For example, when Delvig describes in his 1822 sonnet "Inspiration" (Vdokhnovenie), a poem Pushkin admired, how it is the role of the "*ecstatic* poet" (*vostorzhennyi* piit) to place honor (*chest'*) above all other qualities and to fight betrayal and slander in this world with belief in a nobler form of immortality, he is speaking the language of the Lyceum years—language, as we shall see, that had a definite Derzhavinian cast to it. Similarly, the hymn Delvig wrote for the Lyceum's first graduating class, and the fact that it was Delvig and *not* Pushkin who wrote it, would become a sacred text for Pushkin, one steeped in a mythological time of separation and return, the cycle of life, tragedy (Decembrist classmates), death (Delvig's own), and ultimately transcendence (the "proud endurance," *gordoe terpen'e,* that triumphs over "misfortune," *neschast'e*).[34] Delvig, first in the 1810s and then in the 1820s, like Nashchokin in the 1830s, gave Pushkin, who from early on was skeptical of the blandishments of *slava* and of his need to pursue them, an example of a close friend who was, in this one important sense, *better, more generous* than he was, precisely because this friend did not appear to link his acts of kindness or solicitude with concrete rewards in this world. Delvig was the psychological glue holding Pushkin's sacred trivium (friendship, Lyceum, poetry) together.[35] His was a gift for living that Pushkin, so gifted in his way but also so competitive and ambitious, could admire and actually look up to. This presumably is what Pushkin meant, for example, when he wrote Khitrovo after Delvig's death that "C'était le meilleur d'entre nous,"[36] and he sadly admitted to Pletnev that "no one on earth was nearer to me than Delvig."[37]

that one of Delvig's defining traits was his "playfulness/liveliness of mind" (*igrivost' uma*) (*Druz'ia,* I:206).

34. See discussion in Lotman, *Biografiia pisatelia,* 20–21.

35. "It's sad, agonizing. This is the first death I have ever wept over. . . . Of all the ties of childhood he alone remained in view—our poor little band was collected around him. Without him we are as though orphaned" (*Pss,* X:261; *Letters,* 455).

36. *Pss,* X:262.

37. *Pss,* X:261.

Thus, along with Derzhavin the younger Delvig was, one assumes, a privileged addressee in the initial audience of "Recollections." In Pushkin's mind his official beginning would always be linked with Derzhavin *and* Delvig, with literary ambition (the look ahead) and with literary comradeship, fraternal love, and nostalgia (the look back). We should not lose sight of the fact, however, that when Pushkin returned subsequently to the topic of his beginning, he did so as a poet *with a biography* and, after a certain point (1825 turns out to be an important year in this regard), a sophisticated (including self-critical) understanding of romantic self-fashioning. The poet who could write, in 1830, when speaking of himself and Delvig, that "our beginning spoiled us" and that "We both appeared early / At the hippodrome, and not the market, / In the vicinity of Derzhavin's coffin, / And a noisy rapture it was that greeted us," [38] is presumably one who is well into the process of editing the myth of his own origins.[39] The same could be said for Pushkin's famous prose note describing from his vantage the one and only meeting with Derzhavin. Dating to 1835 but probably preserved from earlier autobiographical notes destroyed in the wake of the Decembrist uprising, this brief memoir is highly charged with the electric currents of its own mythmaking.[40] Here it is Delvig who, the first to make fun of himself, is scandalized that the Poet asks, on entering the Lyceum, "Where, brother, is the john?"[41] And it is the young Pushkin, who having read his poem two paces from Derzhavin and having heard his voice ring out at the mention in his own words of the precursor's name, *disappears* and cannot be found for a grandfatherly embrace. In other words, Delvig's good nature, idealism, and orientation toward the other are stressed, while Pushkin, aware at this point of the potential of dual (inside/outside) composition, moves in to take control of the terms of his "knighting" (*My* genius cannot be captured

---

38. *Pss*, III:185: «избаловало нас начало» and "Явилися мы рано оба / На ипподром, а не на торг / Вблизи державинского гроба, / И шумный встретил нас восторг."

39. Cf. the famous lines at the beginning of the eighth chapter of *Eugene Onegin:* "Old Derzhavin recognized / And blessed us, descending to his grave" (*Starik Derzhavin nas zametil / I, v grob skhodia, blagoslovil*) (V:142). See as well Pushkin's 31 January 1831 letter to Pletnev (the *second* following Delvig's death), where he speaks about reading Derzhavin and Zhukovsky together with the deceased in the context of *pervaia molodost'* (first youth) (*Pss*, X:262).

40. See discussion in Stephanie Sandler, *Distant Pleasures: Alexander Pushkin and the Writing of Exile* (Stanford: Stanford University Press, 1989), 210–11.

41. *Pss*, VIII:48: «где, братец, здесь нужник?»

by the old man's).[42] What is particularly marked from our perspective is that, despite the crowd at the public examination, the memoir includes just three people—Derzhavin, Delvig, and Pushkin himself.

Seen within its own immediate context, in the absence of foreshadowing, "Recollections" can still tell us a good deal about Pushkin's options as a beginner. The scholarly record shows both the brilliance and the obstructed vision of the Soviet textological approach, which while unsurpassed in identifying sources, is less subtle in dealing with the psychological dynamics of confrontation. Tomashevsky, in his effort to qualify the issue of Derzhavinian "odic" influence, a tradition that goes back to Shevyrev's statements in 1841, has demonstrated that Pushkin's language in the poem—his rhymes, his short-form adjectives, his phrasal locutions, even his strophic design—is mediated by other poets closer in age and temperament, especially by Batyushkov in his "historical elegy" entitled "On the Ruins of a Castle in Sweden" (Na razvalinakh zamka v Shvetsii, 1814).[43] Tomashevsky's point is well taken, and his findings, scrupulously arrived at, are in their way useful: the picture of this original meeting is significantly enriched when we realize that Pushkin was adjusting aspects of the older poet's manner to the linguistic practice of respected *current* models. Perhaps Vinogradov presents the "philological" perspective here in its most balanced and persuasive form: "To avoid Derzhavin's influence, whether in the Anacreontic or in the high odic genre, was difficult. However, even here Pushkin filters Derzhavin through the styles of Batyushkov, Zhukovsky, and Vyazemsky. 'Recollections at Tsarskoe Selo' [1814] is filled with reminiscences [*reministsentsii,* in the sense of textual echoes] from Derzhavin's style, but within the limits of norms derived from the styles of Batyushkov and Zhukovsky."[44]

42. One need not dispute the fact of Pushkin's disappearance following the reading, which other memoirists such as Pushchin have confirmed (I. I. Pushchin, *Zapiski o Pushkine,* ed. S. Ia. Shtraikh [Moscow: Goslitizdat, 1956], 60), but simply draw the reader's attention to the mature Pushkin's conscious framing of it.

43. B. Tomashevskii, *Pushkin, kniga pervaia (1813–1824)* (Moscow-Leningrad: Izd. Akademii Nauk SSSR, 1956), 56–63. It has also been argued by Vatsuro that the title of Pushkin's poem derives from earlier poetic "recollections" by Batyushkov. For more on the links between Batyushkov and the Pushkin of "Recollections," see B. Tomashevskii, "Strofika Pushkina," *Pushkin: Issledovaniia i materialy* 2 (1958): 91–93; V. V. Vinogradov, *Stil' Pushkina* (Moscow: Gos. izd. khudozhestvennoi literatury, 1941), 123–24; Dmitrii Blagoi, *Tvorcheskii put' Pushkina (1813–1826)* (Moscow-Leningrad: Izd. AN SSSR, 1950), 104–6; Vickery, " 'Vospominaniia,' " 485–97; and Vatsuro, in *Sll,* 550.

44. Vinogradov, *Stil' Pushkina,* 123–24.

But the encounter between Derzhavin and Pushkin was not only over language in the narrow sense, a kind of Shishkovite-Arzamasian shadowboxing here *avant la lettre*.[45] It was also over the role of the Poet in History, as these terms were understood in 1815. First, who *was* the mythical Derzhavin that sat in attendance at the public examination? To reiterate, at the time of "Recollections," Derzhavin was primarily the aging poet-warrior and poet-statesman; he was not, as was the Zhukovsky alluded to in the poem's final stanza, a "bard in the camp of Russian warriors." This latter distinction suggests a splitting of roles, a patriotic division of labor, that was, for Derzhavin, unthinkable. Derzhavin rose from obscurity to fight Pugachev, advise Catherine, serve in the highest state posts (governor, state secretary to Her Highness, senator, minister of justice), pass laws, see his fortunes climb and fall at the hands of powerful grandees and favorites; and in addition to all this, *as an avocation*, he wrote verse. As Derzhavin tells his patron Catherine in "Felitsa" (1782), the poem that finally brought him recognition and wealth in the form of a snuffbox filled with *chervontsy* (gold coins), "You do not number that man among prophets / Who can only string together rhymes."[46] And as he advises the out-of-favor hero-warrior, in a tone that by the late 1790s was clearly self-reflexive, in "On the Return of Count Zubov from Persia" (Na vozvrashchenie grafa Zubova iz Persii, 1797), one of Pushkin's favorite Derzhavin poems,

He who at the end of his joustings/battles
can in the distance behind him espy
a pathway of marvelous deeds,
having given an accounting to his conscience
in moments both bright and gloomy,
reads these hours with a smile,
of how he took pleasure in good things,
of how he saved others from misfortune, from need,
of how he hastened to be kind to all,
and was free of sighs and [feelings of] repentance. [Emphasis mine.][47]

45. "Cricket" (sverchok)—as Pushkin was nicknamed among the Arzamasians—would be formally accepted into the society only in autumn 1817.

46. G. R. Derzhavin, *Stikhotvoreniia*, ed. D. D. Blagoi (Leningrad: Sovetskii pisatel', 1957), 101: «Пророком ты того не числишь, / Кто только рифмы может плесть.»

47. Derzhavin, *Stikhotvoreniia*, 256: «Кто при конце своих ристаний / Вдали зреть может за собой / Аллею подвигов прекрасных / Дав совести своей отчет / В минутах светлых и ненастных, / С улыбкою часы те чтет, / Как сам благами насладился, /

It is this Derzhavin, the one whose name was always mentioned together with Suvorov (they both, by the way, wrote poetry, some to each other), the one who could claim, without exaggerating, that the monarch was his muse[48] (to the postromantic age, an amazing psychological maneuver!), the one who had to be thought of first as a Man of History *before* he could be understood as the greatest poet of the previous century, that Pushkin addresses in "Recollections." It is also this Derzhavin who in such poems as "An Outing at Tsarskoe Selo" and especially "Ruins" made a concerted effort to link his name and biography with the sacred space (Tsarskoe Selo) of Catherine's monument-decorated glory (and, as it providentially turned out, Pushkin's schooling).[49] Add to this the fact that Pushkin was uttering his lines in the wake of the fall and self-inflicted burning of Moscow (not simply a dramatic ploy in the poem, since the Lyceum itself had felt the threat of the growing conflagration and had been close to evacuation) and then the longed-for victory over Napoleon, and we begin to see the civic pathos animating the poem. When the schoolboy poet exclaims, "And I did not lay down my life avenging you [Moscow]; / In vain was my spirit aflame with anger,"[50] he is expressing the sentiments of all his comrades who followed their older brothers' regiments out of town and were desperate for news from the front. The power of Derzhavin's position, the almost hypnotic force it must have had over Pushkin's official debut, was that the hypostases of soldier, statesman, and poet were linked, *unreflexively* and *preromantically,* with the "Golden Age" (*vremena zlatye*) of Russian history. It was a position that was never to be duplicated, however much the schoolboy gestured after a return in his lines.

The combination of what, in terms of his own gift, the schoolboy Pushkin brought to this poem and what the very *public* nature of the reading brought to Pushkin lies at the heart of the confrontation. Already in "Recollections" we see that exquisite sense of composition that would be the poet's hallmark in all his work. Here the categories of balance and symmetry exist

---

Как спас других от бед, от нужд, / Как быть всем добрым торопился, / Раскаянья и вздохов чужд.»

48. See, e.g., the ending to "The Vision of the Murza" (Videnie murzy, 1783–84?): "I will be immortal through you" (*Toboi bessmerten budu sam*) (Derzhavin, *Stikhotvoreniia*, 113).

49. See "Progulka v Sarskom sele" (1791) and "Razvaliny" (1797) in Derzhavin, *Stikhotvoreniia*, 172–74 and 261–64.

50. *Pss*, I:73: «И в жертву не принес я мщенья вам и жизни; / Вотще лишь гневом дух пылал.»

within the poem, but even in the Lyceum period, in the Bakunina cycle for example (1816–17), Pushkin understood how to play with and transpose actual chronology (when a given work was written) in order to create a *cyclical* progression and the impression of psychological development as extension and return (the classical epistrophe) *among* poems — the first requirement for what later would become Pushkin's version of romantic (auto)biography.[51] The epistrophic structure of "Recollections" is clear enough: the poem begins in the liminal space of nocturnal memories, which the speaker, imagining himself as the stylized *ross* (Russian),[52] enters to breathe life into (and to be inspired by) the eighteenth-century setting of the parks at Tsarskoe Selo. The speaker then recollects a history for this place and for Russia that begins with the Golden Age of Catherine, proceeds through the "new age" (*novyi vek*) of war, *ekpyrosis* or apocalyptic destruction (the burning of Moscow), and the diabolical hubris of Napoleon (the *vselennoi bich*), and concludes with yet another age, the present, this one symbolized by Alexander's triumphant entry into Paris and the proffering of the olive branch in return for the tyrant's misdeeds. The notion of poeticized historiography as extension and return is embedded in the poem in several ways: (1) Alexander's gesture of peace and his rising above the fray initiate, proleptically, a second Golden Age (the *s olivoiu zlatoi* vs. the *vremena zlatye*); (2) the peace-bearing Russian in Paris (*V Parizhe ross!*) at the end of the poem is in mirror opposition to the destructive Gaul seen earlier on the Kremlin towers in Moscow (*Uvy! na bashniakh gall kremlia!*); (3) the singer of Catherine and of her heroes' martial exploits in the earlier age (Petrov, Derzhavin) is now answered by Russia's "scald" (Zhukovsky), who celebrates Alexander and the glory of the present. Perhaps most intriguing for our purposes is Pushkin's use of motifs — the age of Catherine, Derzhavin as interlocutor, the quest for *slava*, the erection of a monument (*pamiatnik*), Tsarskoe Selo as point of origin, the circle of comrades (*krug tovarishchei*), etc. — that will be raised to the status of "mythologemes" at the

---

51. See, e.g., Tomashevskii, *Kniga pervaia,* 119: "The elegist became the hero of his elegies, which [in turn] developed the history of his feelings. For that reason there could be observed an almost obligatory cyclicization of the elegies." See also S. A. Fomichev, "Liricheskie tsikly v tvorcheskoi evoliutsii Pushkina," in *Boldinskie chteniia* (Gorky [Gor'kii]: Volgo-Viatskoe knizh. izd., 1986), 94–104.

52. Vatsuro links the image of the contemplative *ross* with the figure of the *sedoi muzh* (gray-haired man) (Rumiantsev) in Derzhavin's "The Waterfall" (*Vodopad*, 1791 [*Sll,* 551]). In actuality, however, *ross* is a more recent form than *russkii* (Vasmer, for example, gives the first usage of *Rosiia* as 1517).

end of his career. Now these motifs, presumably because Pushkin himself has virtually no personal biography to recollect, are realistically motivated, that is, the monuments cited refer to an actual column and obelisk (commemorating real victories)[53] on the park grounds; later, however, in the "epistrophe" joining Pushkin's life inside and outside his texts at the end of his career, these motifs will be increasingly colored by personal myth. (See illustration 12.)

Thus, the young Pushkin has, on the one hand, positioned himself through the inner compositional logic of the poem as heir apparent to the Petrov-Derzhavin-Zhukovsky tradition of patriotic singing and imperial celebration. Yet the decidedly public nature of this debut conceals, on the other hand, its own risks, especially for an individual, like Pushkin, whose pattern almost invariably will be not to follow but to sidestep, to swerve creatively, from a regnant tradition. As Lydia Ginzburg has formulated this swerve, "[Push-kin] likes to test himself in a skirmish with limitations. A confining tradition is for him something like marble or granite, which he must, while creating, overcome."[54] Consider, for example, the ways in which the "rules" of this beginning were actually not under Pushkin's control: (1) the very genre of the poem (a blend of the "lyric" and the "odic"[55]) did not leave the poet any room for irony, just as its subject, a moment of national pride tinged with sadness (Moscow) and celebration (Paris), possessed a pathos the young poet and patriot was not inclined to complicate or undermine; (2) the motivation for writing the poem was not Pushkin's to begin with, but came at the instigation of his teacher A. I. Galich, who assigned the poem as an exercise for students passing from the "junior" (the initial three years) to the "senior" (the final three years) course of study;[56] (3) the Lyceum administration served as a

53. The monuments referred to in stanzas 5 and 6 (later edition) are: the column (*stolp, kolonna*) erected in the center of the large pond within the park to celebrate the famous naval victory over the Turkish fleet in the Chesma harbor (25–26 June 1770), and the Kagula obelisk, in Pushkin's time placed in the center of a pine-bordered lawn, honoring the victory over the Turkish army at the Kagula River (21 July 1770).

54. *O lirike*, 2d ed. (Leningrad: Sovetskii pisatel', 1974), 28.

55. In the plan conceived when he was still at the Lyceum for publishing a selection of his works, Pushkin placed this particular poem under the rubric of "lyrical" (*liricheskii*), which in that context — i.e., the presence of "public pathos" — was virtually interchangeable with "odic." See Tomashevskii, *Kniga pervaia*, 61 (see n. 43, above).

56. Pushkin's account in his much later diary entry (17 March 1834) that the "kind" (*dobryi*) Galich "forced" (*zastavil*) him to write the poem is ambiguous: "Here [at a gathering of literary men at Grech's] I came upon the kind Galich and was very happy to see him. At one time he had been my professor and had encouraged me in my chosen

kind of proto-censorship, screening out anything that might have threatened the atmosphere of public bonding; and (4) the reading of the poem aloud to a distinguished older audience made the occasion, again, much more "public" than any exchange of other Lyceum-period works steeped in a more private semantics (i.e., those written to an immediate circle of friends). The changes made by Pushkin before and after his public reading indicate to what extent ideological considerations and feelings of personal ambition entered into the dynamics of confrontation. Tomashevsky has argued in his textual commentaries, for example, that Pushkin added the last two stanzas, those relating to Alexander and Zhukovsky, when he learned, in December 1814, that Derzhavin would be in attendance; that he subsequently removed one stanza devoted to Alexander (the original penultimate) and toned down his other references to the tsar, presumably in response to the fact that the promise of a new era had not been lived up to; and that, when Derzhavin himself asked for a copy of the poem, Pushkin rewrote, in the original Lyceum version, a verse alluding to Zhukovsky so that it would reflect instead Derzhavin.[57] One wonders whether it was these maneuverings Pushkin had in mind when, after considerable vacillation, he decided not to include "Recollections" in his *Verse* (Stikhotvoreniia) of 1826 and when, in comparing his muse with Delvig's, he said, "Service to the muse does not tolerate vanity." [58]

To summarize our argument thus far: Derzhavin as a figure was too close to mythical space (History), and the declaiming of the poem too close to public ritual (possible "ordination"), for Pushkin, with his ambition and youthful ardor, not to want to leap at the opportunity. Having done so, however, the poet also quickly learned that there were forces beyond his control (e.g., Alexander's actions) that could change the meaning of his words and challenge the purity of his motives *after the fact*. All this made Pushkin's subsequent references to Derzhavin problematic and taut with contradictory meaning. Before

---

metier. He had forced me to write my 'Recollections at Tsarskoe Selo' for the 1814 examination" (*Pss*, VIII:31). The word may be a humorous overstatement elicited by the pleasant chance meeting with his old teacher, or, again, it may be revealing of the mature writer's urge to distance himself retrospectively from the powerful undercurrents of this beginning (i.e., the poem belongs more to the occasion of Galich's assignment than to Pushkin's free imagination). Galich certainly was responsible for the assignment, but it is unlikely, given Pushkin's character and the relations of students to faculty at the Lyceum, that the teacher could have *forced* him to write the poem he did.

57. *Pss*, I:412, 434–35. See also Vatsuro, in *SII*, 548–50.

58. *Pss*, II:246: *Sluzhen'e muz ne terpit suety.*

turning to those later examples, I would like to pause for a moment on another work contemporaneous with "Recollections" that also engages Derzhavin, but in a lighter key. "Fonvizin's Shade" (Ten' Fon-Vizina, 1815) is in every way a fascinating counterexample to "Recollections": maximally private (the work is imputed to Pushkin and since 1935 has been included in his works, but it does not exist in an authorized copy and was never published by the poet in his lifetime), playfully irreverent, strictly literary and metaliterary as opposed to historical and patriotic. It is written by a version of the "Voltairean" Pushkin who challenged church authority and conventional morality more out of insouciance and because "it was there" than conviction,[59] and who authored "The Monk" (Monakh, 1813), the pornographic "Barkov's Shade" (Ten' Barkova, 1814–15), and eventually *The Gabrieliad* (Gavriiliada, 1821).[60] Much of the humor in Pushkin's poems of the period derives from the use of inverted "classical" magniloquence and travestied liturgical language (the Lyceum students were learning the Arzamasians' chief strategic weapon of turning, through grotesque contextualization, the archserious diction of the church service against its protectors, the Shishkovites). Pushkin's and Delvig's letters to each other, for example, were even into the late 1820s saturated with the Arzamas-period semantics of the pseudobiblical or pseudo–high style/"classical."[61]

The story of how a famous eighteenth-century man of letters, now deceased, returns from the underworld to view the current state of Russian literature, "Fonvizin's Shade" has, since its discovery, primarily been mined for the insights it offers into Arzamas-Beseda polemics and contemporary literary politics as Pushkin understood them.[62] However, thanks to its essen-

---

59. See, e.g., Khodasevich's argument on Pushkin's motivation for writing *The Gabrieliad* in his "O Gavriiliade," *Stat'i o russkoi poezii* (Petersburg: Epokha, 1922), 99–105.

60. To be sure, "Barkov's Shade," whose attribution to Pushkin is contested by some scholars to this day, cannot be called "Voltairean" in the way the more mildly scabrous "The Monk" can. If indeed the former work does belong to Pushkin's pen, it is plainly more "pornographic" than anything else he wrote; the tasteful and measured Voltaire presumably would not have indulged in the off-color "priapic" extravaganza of "Barkov's Shade." At the same time, the challenge to conventional morality implicit in all these works, despite their formal differences, owes a significant debt to Voltaire's anticlericalism.

61. See, e.g., Delvig's letter to Pushkin of February 1828 in *Druz'ia*, I:202; it ends with a mock request, full of liturgical phrases, for "Saint Aleksandr's" blessing of *Northern Flowers*.

62. The theme of an underworld confrontation (i.e., the settling of scores from a "higher," or here "lower," vantage), replete with mythological figures (Mercury, etc.)

tially private nature and history of nonpublication, the poem also provides a rare glimpse of how the young poet perceived Derzhavin on his own (Pushkin's) terms, with, so to speak, "the gloves off." Tsyavlovsky has shown that in all probability the work was written in November–December 1815, that is, almost exactly a year after "Recollections."[63] The poem's thematics dovetail neatly with those of "The Little Town" (Gorodok, 1815), with its comparison of the poet's library to a cemetery, on the one hand, and with those of a more purely Anacreontic character, such as "To Batyushkov" (Batiushkovu, 1815), "My Legacy. To Friends" (Moe zaveshchanie. Druz'iam, 1815), and "The Tomb of Anacreon" (Grob Anakreona, 1815), on the other: the death of the poet, one's artistic legacy, the grave, this world versus the under-/otherworld, etc. But these poems proceed from a stylized *pagan* point of view—one not pre-Christian but playfully post-Christian and Voltairean—that was deliberately intended to raise Shishkovite hackles.[64] (Recall that Derzhavin's Anacreontic streak and celebration of the physical world coexisted simply and organically with his religious sensibility; indeed, Derzhavin was so incensed by Batyushkov's irreverence in "Vision on the Banks of the Lethe," Pushkin's principal model in his pastiche, that he threatened to "take up arms even more."[65])

---

representing different points of view in the Shishkovite-Karamzinian debates, was prominent in works of the preceding decade (1800s): N. P. Brusilov's "Socrates' Conversation with a Fop [Petit-Maître] of the Present Age in the Kingdom of the Dead" (1803), Semen Bobrov's "Happening in the Kingdom of Shades, or The Fate of the Russian Language" (wr. 1805, not pub. but well known in the literary community), and of course Batyushkov's response to Bobrov, "Vision on the Banks of the Lethe" (wr. 1809), which was Pushkin's immediate model in "Fonvizin's Shade." For useful background to this period and to the nature of its intertwined political and linguistic polemics, see Uspenskii, "Spory o iazyke," 347–54 (see n. 14, above). It is interesting in this context that Uspensky mentions that Bobrov's criticism of Derzhavin was intended to shock his fellow writers, since "without doubt it was the law of those years for critics of all stripes to respond in print [only] positively about Derzhavin." On the other hand, one could find "significantly cooler evaluations among contemporaries in oral reactions and in correspondence" (354). Pushkin's position toward Derzhavin in "Fonvizin's Shade" falls clearly into this second, "sub rosa" category.

63. See Vatsuro, in *Sll*, 579, for information on the poem's publication history and for the internal evidence scholars have used to attempt to date its composition.

64. "The depiction of Shishkov and his followers as adherents of an exclusively Church-Slavonic literature [*tserkovno-slavianskaia literatura*] was a topos in Arzamasian and Arzamasian-affiliated satires" (Vatsuro, in *Sll*, 582).

65. *Bolee eshche vooruzhitsia* (cited K. N. Batiushkov, *Polnoe sobranie stikhotvorenii* [Moscow-Leningrad: Sovetskii pisatel', 1964], 274).

Thus, in "Fonvizin's Shade," we have a demonstrably pagan underworld, with references to Acheron, Apollo, Pluto, Charon, etc., just as in "The Little Town" we have a playful allusion to *velikii chetvertok*,[66] the "Maundy Thursday" of Passion Week.

The passage immediately concerning us occurs when Fonvizin's spirit, weary of the banal efforts of Khvostov, Shalikov, Shirinsky-Shikhmatov, and other figures satirized by the Arzamasians,[67] asks his guide to show him the "singer of Catherine" (*pevets Ekateriny*). Mercury grudgingly consents. Derzhavin is pleased with the unannounced visit from the otherworld and forthwith launches into a parodic rendition of his "Lyro-epic Hymn on the Expulsion of the French from the Fatherland" (Gimn liroepicheskii na prognanie frantsuzov iz otechestva, 1813). These ten lines turn out to be significant for several reasons: (1) they are a sizable enough insertion to function in this setting as a text-within-a-text; (2) they are the only opportunity the reader has of actually witnessing the "banalities," saturated in Church Slavonic diction, of the Shishkovites (Pushkin has singled out Derzhavin in this regard); (3) they are taken virtually verbatim from lines scattered throughout the original, so that the force of the parody comes exclusively from its comic placement, and not from any deliberate tampering with Derzhavin's words; and (4) the thematics of the excerpt—the expulsion of the French, but with an allegorical framing that is *explicitly* biblical/apocalyptic (Lucifer emerging from the abyss, Napoleon, Paris as Babylon, the meek white-fleeced lamb, Gog, etc.)— is otherwise close to the subject of "Recollections." Fonvizin's reaction to Derzhavin's humorously recontextualized allegory is to claim that the old man has possibly lost his mind and to misquote perhaps his most famous line, from the ode to God ("You are God, you are a worm, you are the light, you are the night" [*Ty bog—ty cherv', ty svet—ty noch'*]), while Mercury/Hermes concludes, presumably voicing the otherwise publicly concealed sentiments of his author, "Denis! He [Derzhavin] will forever be famous / But why oh why must one live so long?"[68] Vatsuro has advanced the thesis that the presence of this

66. The diminutive ("chetver*ok*") is humorously irreverent (*Pss*, I:83).

67. Again, Batyushkov in the first instance. In "Vision on the Banks of the Lethe," Batyushkov makes fun of Bobrov, D. Yazykov (who refused to use orthographic hard signs), Shirinsky-Shikhmatov, Anna Bunina, etc., but he also takes shots at the epigones of Karamzin, e.g., Prince P. I. Shalikov. Pushkin may have gotten the idea to parody Derzhavin's style in "Fonvizin's Shade" from the way Batyushkov "sends up" Bobrov's heavily "Slavonicized" idiom in his poem.

68. *Pss*, I:144–45: «Денис! он вечно будет славен, / Но, ах, почто так долго жить?»

parody in the poem, following as it does directly on the public reading and early fame of "Recollections," is probably the single most compelling reason why Pushkin hid his authorship of "Fonvizin's Shade" and scratched out his first and last name in the manuscript copy.[69]

I propose to push this notion of creative anxiety, of the exhilarating friction within the fiction, a little farther, however. Pushkin, who had a superb memory and keen sense of composition as symmetrical thrust and counterthrust (the notion of expanded or ontological rhyme pair), could not be "simply" or "innocently" playing in these lines. (After all, his model, Batyushkov, "wisely" avoided engaging Derzhavin altogether—a move, to repeat, that didn't keep the old poet from being offended.) Pushkin is using, in an elaborate sidestepping gesture ("parody"), Derzhavin's own language to bury the older poet in order to make room for himself to be born. Likewise, he could not have uttered, in "The Little Town," a line such as "Not all of me is given over to decay," [70] into a void. Not only did the line resonate with Derzhavin's expression of confidence in his immortality in his famous "Monument" (Pamiatnik, 1/95)—"So! All of me won't die" (Tak!—ves' ia ne umru)[71]—it would enter into the limbo of Pushkin's memory until that later moment, in his "Exegi monumentum," when he would reinvoke it in much altered, and now utterly serious, circumstances. The young poet, psychically constructed the way he was, could not hide from this challenge. At the same time, as I suggested in the first part of this study, the profoundly *superstitious* Pushkin understood that his challenge had consequences and that it entered into a mysterious otherworldly economy, particularly in view of Derzhavin's *death* a few months later (July 1816), that would, like Don Guan's invitation to the statue of the jealous husband, come back to haunt him. Recall in this context our earlier point that Don Guan goes to the rendezvous with Donna Anna *after* the statue has nodded to him. Just as the prayer for cuckolds (rogonostsy) in The Gabrieliad would be a tossing down of the gauntlet to the other world that could not go unanswered, so too does the schoolboy Pushkin now initiate an ontological rhyme that, because of its setting, i.e., the mocking of what is most sacred, is bound at some point to elicit a fatal partner. In 1815 Pushkin manipulates

69. In *Sll*, 583.

70. *Pss*, I:89: *Ne ves' ia predan tlen'iu.*

71. Derzhavin also writes a very similar line in his 1788 poem on the death of Countess Rumyantseva: "And/but I am a poet and shall not die" (*A ia piit—i ne umru*), in *Stikhotvoreniia*, 121.

a *chuzhoe slovo*, "another's word" (Derzhavin's), as an expression of youthful pride and independence: the source is mocked, while the framing intelligence ("But why oh why must one live so long?") is celebrated; in 1826, in "The Prophet" (Prorok), and in 1836, in the Stone Island cycle, Pushkin will use other *chuzhie slova* (Isaiah, St. Ephraem's prayer, etc.), but there the source, biblical rather than pagan, will chasten its poetic framer, bringing about an act of spiritual askesis. Thus virtually from the beginning Pushkin seemed to realize that his acts of daring could not come for free; they had to cost something. It was a cost, however, that was worth it.

⚞ 1825–1826

Pushkin's subsequent "encounters" with Derzhavin, now no longer in the flesh, fall neatly into three temporal clusters, each one important for his development as writer and thinker: 1825–26, 1830–31, and 1836. The first of these clusters, played out against the background of the poet's northern exile and the Decembrist uprising, is associated with Delvig and Küchelbecker; the second with Pushkin's turn to prose on the eve of his marriage; and the third with his 1830s friendship with Nashchokin and with his final attempts to understand the mysteries of biography, or what I call the role of the "poet in history." From 1825 until well into the 1830s Pushkin is in the middle phase of the process of self-definition vis-à-vis the precursor: his statements about Derzhavin are in every instance complicated by irony and by ambivalent feelings toward the power of the originary myth. This is the phase where Pushkin has already lived a substantial portion of his creative life, knows of Derzhavin's human foibles (the man versus the myth), and sees his turning from Derzhavin—to artistic prose for example—as a range of options. But those options are not unlimited—the roles of Man of History, poet-statesman and poet-warrior, advisor to tsars (even though Pushkin tries this, after his fashion[72]) and beneficiary of patronage are closed to him. Here is the focal point of the irony, for in these subsequent encounters with Derzhavin's "shade" Pushkin, while exercising his protean gifts, understands precisely where he is not free and where he must *pay.* Pushkin's final meeting with Derzhavin comes in 1836, several months before his death, in the writing of the Stone Island cycle and in the publication of two works, *The Captain's Daughter* (Kapitanskaia dochka) and "My Hero's Genealogy" (Rodoslovnaia moego geroia), which the poet has been working on since the early 1830s but which now, in their appearance, become part of his "final word" on the issue of Derzhavin and biography. These texts, particularly "Exegi monumentum" and *The Captain's Daughter,* show Pushkin coming full circle on his own beginning and using a different sort of

72. In, e.g., "Stansy," the controversial 1826 poem addressed to the new tsar Nicholas.

irony, one tinged with cosmic wisdom and humility, and hence one less "anxious" and "territorial" than that displayed in earlier encounters.

Two of Pushkin's most explicit statements about Derzhavin came in letters, both written at the same time: the first to Bestuzhev (of late May/early June 1825), the second to Delvig (between 1 and 8 June 1825). The letter to Bestuzhev has more of a coolly cordial or "professional" tone; in it, Pushkin responds to Bestuzhev's article "Glance at Russian Literature in the Course of 1824 and at the Beginning of 1825,"[73] which argued the case that the first age of a literature has always been that of geniuses. Pushkin disputes this contention, using several traditions, including Latin, Italian, English, and Russian, to foreground certain inconsistencies in Bestuzhev's thinking. Assertions or criticisms on Bestuzhev's part such as "We [Russians] have criticism, but we do not have literature," "Why have we no geniuses and so few men of talent?" or "We have no literary encouragement — and thank God!" are, point by point, turned on their heads and shown in reality to be the opposite. Derzhavin is a leading figure in Pushkin's rebuttal: if his "idol, ¼ gold and ¾ lead, has not yet been assayed," it is the fault of the critics (or the lack thereof), not of Derzhavin's genius. At the same time, the fact that the poet uses the sculptural image of the idol (*kumir*), now partially undermined because of the alleged proportions of the metals (Derzhavin refers to his immortal likeness as being "harder than metals" in his "Monument"), already suggests how Pushkin's thinking has changed and become a complex amalgam of the positive (gold) and the negative (lead). In the second half of Pushkin's career *kumir* will come more and more to represent something *pejoratively* pagan, something potentially "un-Christian" in its insistence on three-dimensional reification. He then goes on to mention those works of Derzhavin — "Felitsa," "The Grandee" (Vel'mozha), "God," "On the Death of Meshchersky," "On the Return of Count Zubov from Persia" — that remain to be properly presented to the public. He retorts that Russia *does* have geniuses, beginning with Derzhavin and Krylov, and that its leading men of literature, again including Derzhavin, have received support and patronage. (The important exceptions mentioned here are Baratynsky and Pushkin himself.) Indeed, Derzhavin was "encouraged" not by one but by three rulers.[74]

73. Published in the almanac *The Polar Star for 1825*.

74. The encouragement given Derzhavin was, to be sure, by no means unanimous or unproblematic. Pushkin may be simplifying here a bit for effect. What is less disputable is the fact that Derzhavin was substantially enriched by his service to state and tsar and ended his life a man of considerable wealth. In financial terms, there can be no comparison between Derzhavin's life in a system of patronage and Pushkin's life, continually

Finally, the distinguishing trait of the Russian literary tradition so far has been its proud independence and refusal to curry favor in any way that could be construed as compromising: even Derzhavin, with whom "the voice of flattery fell silent," did not praise his monarch (or so Pushkin implies) in the interest of momentary gain but for the sake of "virtue" (here he quotes a line from the Zubov ode). It is the independence of the poet, his combination of "aristocratic pride" (*aristokraticheskaia gordost'*) and "authorial self-esteem" (*avtorskoe samoliubie*), that makes the Russian context different and may explain the chasm between "genius" and its public reception through "criticism." Pushkin then ends this section of the letter on a personal note: *he* does not want "the protection of equals," of a "scoundrel" (*podlets*) like Vorontsov, who though wealthy and powerful is not inherently, i.e., through his lineage, more *noble* than Pushkin, and yet who treats the poet as an inferior: "He imagines that a Russian poet will come to his antechamber with a dedication or an ode, but instead the poet comes with a demand for esteem, as a noble of six hundred years standing—a devil of a difference." The reader notes how Pushkin's statements about Derzhavin, delivered here to a colleague with whom he has more professional than friendly relations and with whom consequently he cannot fully open up, become personalized and potentially "hotter" as he moves from reflections on a previous era to his own situation.

The letter to Delvig should be read in tandem with the letter to Bestuzhev. The relevant passage, preceded and followed by typical Pushkin-Delvig banter and by literary and personal news, is striking for both its length and its intensity:

> After your departure I reread all of Derzhavin, and here is my final opinion. That strange man knew neither the Russian ABC's nor the spirit of the Russian language (and that is why he is below Lomonosov). He had no understanding of either style or harmony—or even of the rules of versification. That is why he must infuriate every fastidious ear. He not only does

---

complicated by debts and concerns about book sales, in the new world of the literary marketplace. It is this contrast that generates the "heat" in Pushkin's move from Derzhavin's "acceptable" flattery to his own untenable situation with Vorontsov mentioned near the end of the letter. Pushkin probably had Derzhavin's "three rulers" in mind when he later complained wryly to his wife about his inability to get along with three tsars (Pavel [whom he encountered only as a toddler and who ordered his nurse to remove the boy's cap—the poet's first "insubordination"], Alexander, and Nicholas) and then expressed the hope that his own son (Sasha) would not follow in his footsteps, i.e., would "not write verse and quarrel with tsars." Letter of 20–22 April 1834 in *Pss*, X:370.

not sustain an *ode,* but he cannot sustain even a stanza (with the exception of you know which ones). Here is what is in him: *thoughts, pictures, and movements which are truly poetic;* in reading him you seem to be reading a bad, free translation of some marvelous original. Really and truly, his genius thought in Tatar—and he did not know the Russian ABC's from lack of leisure.[75] Derzhavin, when he has in due course been translated, will amaze Europe, and because of national pride we shall not say what we know about him (to say nothing of his ministry). Some eight odes and several fragments of Derzhavin's must be preserved, but burn up the rest. His genius can be compared to Suvorov's genius—it's too bad that our poet too often crowed like a rooster.[76]

How are we to understand these two in many ways contradictory letters? Does the letter to Delvig really, in Gaevsky's formulation, "more than all others introduce us into Pushkin's sincere [*zadushevnye*] literary convictions"? Is it a genuine declaration of independence, "remarkable for its bold and accurate characterization of Derzhavin," indicating that "in the space of ten years a complete turnabout had transpired in the literary convictions of Pushkin, who at the Lyceum examination in 1815 had still revered Derzhavin"?[77] What aspects of the immediate context of the letters need to be taken into account in order to understand their meaning? As always with Pushkin, there is no *recorded* privacy or inner space that does not take account of its addressee. In the letter to Bestuzhev, the reader must be aware of Pushkin's relations with his correspondent, warm but by no means intimate, in order to place the statements about Derzhavin in their proper context. Because of his sense of honor and self-esteem, Pushkin would never openly criticize or mock Derzhavin to a third party, even a literary colleague like Bestuzhev, for fear that he might appear to be "tipping the scales" of literary justice for personal gain.[78] Such

75. The expression "did not know the ABC's from lack of leisure" is taken from I. I. Dmitriev's epitaph "Passer-by, Halt!" (1805) (*Pis'ma,* I:453; *Letters,* 286).

76. *Pss,* X:116; *Letters,* 224–25.

77. *Vestnik Evropy* (January 1881): 9; cited Modzalevskii in *Pis'ma,* I:453.

78. What Pushkin would allow to be said in public about Derzhavin under his name is clear from a letter (of 2 March 1827) sent by Pogodin to V. F. Odoevsky about the latter's participation in the journal *The Moscow Messenger* (Moskovskii vestnik): "Your critique of 'The Monument of Muses' [section] has been reduced on the insistent demand of Pushkin. Here follow his words, which I repeat with diplomatic accuracy: 'There is a lot here that is intelligent and fair, but the author does not know propriety: can one say about Derzhavin and Karamzin that their names arouse pleasant memories, and that it is with

behavior would be dishonorable, *podlo*. Thus, while Pushkin is being as honest and impartial as he can in explaining the history of the Russian situation and in correcting Bestuzhev's errors and misjudgments, he is constrained by the interlocutory rules of this exchange, rules that are for him always precisely calibrated. The ardor that enters into the description of why a *Russian* writer like himself cannot tolerate the arrogance of a Vorontsov is there precisely because Pushkin understands that his situation has become radically different from Derzhavin's, but that, in this forum, the difference cannot be explicitly spoken about.

The letter to Delvig is also both honest (Pushkin is saying exactly what he feels at the moment) and heated (his assessment of Derzhavin cannot be separated from his situation of exile at Mikhailovskoe), but within the voice zone of a much different addressee. Delvig is the closest thing to "family" in Pushkin's life, more of an equal than Pushkin's younger sibling Lev, and much closer than the poet's own parents.[79] Pushkin recognizes Derzhavin's shaggy ("Tatar") genius, but at the same time he maximally demythologizes the older poet and thus maximally asserts his independence from the myth, which cast such an imposing shadow on his official debut as poet. Yet the myth, even here, cannot be fully exorcised from Pushkin's creative consciousness (and the life he has still to live), for the reason that it is intimately implicated in the "family romance" of Tsarskoe Selo, and of Delvig in particular. Mikhailovskoe was in many ways the most lonely and vulnerable period of Pushkin's life. It was, as we have suggested, the period when the poet might feel his fate was most unlike that of Derzhavin. But the storm clouds of banishment had their occasional silver linings—the company of the Osipova-Vulf family at nearby Trigorskoe, the solicitude of Pushkin's nanny, Arina Rodionovna, and especially the visits of close friends from the Lyceum days. On 11 January 1825 Ivan Pushchin appeared unexpectedly at the doorstep of his former neighbor at

---

sorrow that we find schoolboy errors in Derzhavin. After all, Derzhavin is Derzhavin. His name is dear to us. . . . I have connections. People might consider me to be in agreement with the opinion of the reviewer. And in general, one shouldn't speak about Derzhavin in the same tone as one speaks about N. N. or G. G.' " (Modzalevskii in *Pis'ma*, II:225).

79. Recall that Pushkin's relations with his father, Sergei Lvovich, were particularly strained at this time following an "explosion" in the early months (i.e., fall 1824) of exile to Mikhailovskoe: Sergei Lvovich, anxious over his son's political reputation, had been asked by the police to open his mail and, in effect, to function as a spy for the government. For Pushkin, this was the epitome of baseness. See his letter to Zhukovsky of 31 October 1824 (*Pss*, X:83–84; *Letters*, 185–86).

Tsarskoe Selo. And it was in late April 1825, just a few weeks before this letter was written, that Delvig, after various delays, made the by no means routine journey to Mikhailovskoe, an event that reconfirmed, after years of exile, the friends' special Lyceum bond. Delvig arrived on the eighteenth or nineteenth and, after games at billiards, dinners prepared by Arina Rodionovna, visits to the ladies at Trigorskoe, and, most important, long private chats, departed on the twenty-sixth.[80]

The contents of the second letter are given a fuller illumination if we juxtapose the dating of Pushkin's vacillations about the inclusion of "Recollections" in the *Verse* of 1826 with the visit of Delvig. On 27 March 1825 Pushkin writes his brother Lev and, following various requests and instructions, asks the question, "Oughtn't 'Recollections at Tsarskoe Selo' be printed at the end [of the *Verse* of 1826] with the *Note* that it was written by me at 14, and with an excerpt from my Memoirs (about Derzhavin), eh?"[81] But then this sentence is crossed out of the letter, with the note "No" written in above it.[82] In April Delvig arrives, and in the first half of May, that is, immediately after his departure, Pushkin changes his mind again, and tells his brother: "Print 'Tsarskoe Selo' and the Note belonging to it."[83] In late May and/or early June the poet writes his two letters to Bestuzhev and Delvig, which appear to be, despite the framing camouflage (typical of Pushkin), his attempt to think his way through the problem of "Recollections" and its place in his biography. The letter to Delvig in particular would seem to indicate that, vis-à-vis Derzhavin, Pushkin can at last act as a free agent (again, within the appropriate context): he is telling his best friend and the keeper of Derzhavin's flame that the rules of the initial encounter, the mythical aura and the reverence before the older poet, no longer need apply to him. According to this logic, "Recollections" can be included in the collection as a record of the times and of a Pushkin (note the stress on *age 14*) who no longer exists.

One might even speculate at this point that Pushkin changes his mind after Delvig's visit because the friend, thinking the best and in any event probably pleased with Derzhavin's role in Pushkin's debut (i.e., the poem is not necessarily "contaminated"), urges that "Recollections" be republished.[84] To which

---

80. *Druz'ia*, I:183.
81. *Pss*, X:106; *Letters*, 212.
82. Vatsuro in *Sll*, 550.
83. *Pss*, X:113; *Letters*, 220.
84. Alekseev writes: "Pushkin's argument with Delvig over the significance of Der-

realm, then, Pushkin might reason, does "Recollections" belong; the realm of friendship with Delvig, chaste service to the muse, and the noble beginnings at the Lyceum, or the realm of public *slava* (glory, fame) associated with Derzhavin, adjustments to the text made for ideological and personal reasons, and the potential response of a meddling censorship?[85] Is it "private" or "public" property? Whatever the case, in September 1825, when the manuscript of the *Verse* had passed the censorship and Pletnev was able to send the author the final table of contents for approval, Pushkin still made no move to exclude the poem. Quite the contrary: he seemed to accede to the prominent placement of "Recollections" as initial item in the section entitled "Various Poems." But he did not send the Note (the "private" editing of the "public" poem).[86] Pushkin's last act in this private drama was to reconsider yet again and to remove the poem, suddenly and for no explicit reason, not only from the *Verse* of 1826 but from all subsequent editions of his poetry published in his lifetime. Thus, while the good Delvig's presence probably played a not insignificant role in Pushkin's thinking (otherwise, why did he reread all of Derzhavin right after Delvig's departure?), misgivings about his having consciously manipulated the older poet's mythical status to initiate his own career must have continued to haunt Pushkin. He was not free after all.

There are two more elements to Pushkin's 1825 revisiting of the Derzhavin

---

zhavin in the history of Russian poetry — an argument that took place in Mikhailovskoe and then was continued in letters — was in all likelihood connected with these [Lyceum-period] recollections, thoughts, and conversations about the personal creative paths of poet-friends. Rereading at this time 'all' of Derzhavin, Pushkin naturally focused particular attention on those verses of Derzhavin in which the latter defines his civic and literary merits" (Alekseev, "Stikhotvorenie Pushkina," 201 [see n. 23, above]). My objection to Alekseev's otherwise superb commentary is that it inevitably sees Pushkin's interactions with the "shade of Derzhavin" as warm, uplifting, and neatly coterminous with the positive semantic field of Lyceum friendships.

85. Tomashevsky has hypothesized that Pushkin ultimately excluded "Recollections" from the *Verse* of 1826 because the changes in his description of the tsar (Alexander) made in a later (1819) copy would have appeared provocative to the censorship (Tomashevskii, *Kniga pervaia*, 63 [see n. 43, above]).

86. This is assuming, as does Tomashevsky (*Pss*, VIII:369), that the late 1835 piece ("Derzhavin") in "Table Talk" is an excerpt or reconstruction from the earlier "Notes" (Zapiski) that Pushkin destroyed in the aftermath of the Decembrist uprising. I. Feinberg (*Nezavershennye raboty Pushkina*, 7th ed. [Moscow: Khudozhestvennaia literatura, 1979], 314–16) considers the *zapiska* to have survived intact, while Modzalevsky (*Pis'ma*, I:423) believes it to have been reconstituted from memory.

myth through his friendship with Delvig that deserve some scrutiny: his shifting understanding of the role of "inspiration" (*vdokhnovenie*) in poetic creation and genre classification, and the linking of the ode, Derzhavin's special province in the eyes of Pushkin's generation, with the theme of "acts of civic valor" (*grazhdanskie doblesti*). In a rough draft summary[87] of ideas prompted by two 1824 articles by Küchelbecker on the current state of Russian poetry,[88] Pushkin wrote down his well-known postromantic definition of inspiration.[89] These drafts date to 1825–26, that is, to a time close to or even possibly intersecting with Pushkin's "argument" with Delvig over Derzhavin and his "final word" after rereading the older poet. Traditionally it is assumed that Pushkin has only Küchelbecker in mind when he objects to the latter's privileging of the odic sentiment and of *vostorg* (ecstasy) in works of genuine poetry, beginning with the odes of Derzhavin. Küchelbecker finds that contemporary lyric poetry lacks strong, "sublime" feeling and is too often susceptible to the "chewing over" of stylish "lyrical" *toska* (ennui).[90] True poetry, argues Küchelbecker, should possess "power, freedom, and inspiration" (*sila, svoboda i vdokhnovenie*). Pushkin's anti-Küchelbeckerian definition of *vdokhnovenie* and his reservations about *vostorg* are what, in this context, most concern us: *vdokhnovenie* is, for Pushkin (to repeat), "the disposition/orientation of the soul to the most vivid reception of impressions, and consequently, to the rapid grasp of ideas, which aids in the explanation of the former";[91] and "*ecstasy* [*vostorg*] excludes *calmness,* which is a necessary condition for the *beautiful.* Ecstasy does not presuppose the power of mind, which arranges the parts in their relation to the whole. Ecstasy is short-lived, inconstant, and hence not capable of producing a truly great perfection (without which there is no lyric

87. The piece was not published during Pushkin's lifetime.

88. "On the Direction of Our Poetry, Especially Lyric [Poetry], over the Past Ten Years" (O napravlenii nashei poezii, osobenno liricheskoi, v poslednee desiatiletie, June 1824 in the almanac *Mnemozina*) and "Conversation with Bulgarin" (Razgovor s Bulgarinym, October 1824 in *Mnemozina*).

89. *Pss,* VII:29–30, 461–62.

90. «До бесконечности жуем и пережевываем эту тоску и наперерыв щеголяем своим малодушием в периодических изданиях» (cited *Pss,* VII:461).

91. «Расположение души к живейшему принятию впечатлений, след[ственно] к быстрому соображению понятий, что способствует объяснению оных» (*Pss,* VII:29). Cf. this definition and the nearly identical description of Charsky's feelings as he composes verse in the unfinished *Egyptian Nights* (Egipetskie nochi, 1835), in *Pss,* VI:245–46; *CPF,* 250.

poetry). Ecstasy is the intense condition of a single imagination. There can be inspiration without ecstasy, but ecstasy without inspiration does not exist."[92]

Pushkin's addressee in these remarks is not, it seems, only Küchelbecker. As early as 1814, in his poem "To the Poet-Mathematician" (K poetu-matematiku), Delvig too was a strong proponent of Derzhavinian *vostorg*. In that work he argues about the incompatibility of logic or ratiocination, which is necessary in algebra and geometry, with the sublime *vostorg* of the poet in his relations with the muse.[93] Ultimately, the speaker enjoins his poet-mathematician friend to make up his mind, to choose between the "owls" of precise calculation and the "Pegasus" of poetic flight.[94] Delvig's point of departure, as Alekseev has suggested, was an article on inspiration and ecstasy published by Derzhavin in 1811, where the young man's idol had written:

In direct inspiration there is neither [logical] connection nor cold reasoning. Inspiration even avoids them and in its lofty flight seeks only vivid, exceptional, absorbing ideas. *Inspiration* is nothing other than a living sensation, a gift of the heavens, a ray of divinity. The poet, in the complete rapture of his feelings, becoming inflamed with this fire from on high or, more precisely, with imagination, enters the state of ecstasy [*vostorg*], reaches for his lyre, and sings what his heart commands. If one doesn't feel oneself thus enflamed or enraptured, one should not take up the lyre.[95]

92. «*Восторг* исключает *спокойствие*, необходимое условие *прекрасного*. Восторг не предполагает силы ума, располагающей части в их отношении к целому. Восторг непродолжителен, непостоянен, следственно, не в силе произвесть истинное великое совершенство (без которого нет лирической поэзии). Восторг есть напряженное состояние единого воображения. Вдохновение может быть без восторга, а восторг без вдохновения не существует» (*Pss*, VII:30).

93. E.g., "In ecstasy does the poet speak, / Explaining his love to Alina" (В восторге говорит поэт, / Любовь Алине изъясняя) (Del'vig, "K poetu matematiku," *Polnoe sobranie stikhotvorenii*, 228–34 [see n. 28, above]).

94. Del'vig, *Polnoe sobranie stikhotvorenii*, 234.

95. «В прямом вдохновении нет ни связи, ни холодного рассуждения; оно даже их убегает и в высоком парении своем ищет только живых, чрезвычайных, занимательных представлений. *Вдохновение* не что иное есть, как живое ощущение, дар неба, луч божества. Поэт, в полном упоении чувств своих разгораяся свышним оным пламенем или, простее сказать, воображением, приходит в восторг, схватывает лиру и поет, что ему велит его сердце. Не разгорячась и не чувствуя себя восхищенным, и приниматься он за лиру не должен» (G.R. Derzhavin, *Sochineniia*, ed. Ia. K. Grot, 9 vols. [St. Petersburg: Izd. Imperatorskoi Akademii Nauk, 1864–83],

Pushkin's ruminations of 1825–26 read like a systematic undoing of these earlier comments.[96] In the concluding stanzas of Delvig's poem, the youthful speaker invokes Derzhavin in lofty terms as the Russian bard who has defeated Pindar and Horace and who has dared to hurl thunderbolts at the powerful and to sing of virtue. In other words, Pushkin's closest friend, together with Küchelbecker, another fondly recalled Lyceum comrade, is subtly implicated in the 1825–26 break with Derzhavinian *vostorg.*

Two additional clues give these notes away as a polemical return to Lyceum-period semantics: first, Pushkin says at the end of *his* definition of a cooler, more lucid *vdokhnovenie* that "inspiration is as necessary in poetry as it is in geometry,"[97] which is probably a direct allusion to and reworking of Delvig's "To the Poet-Mathematician";[98] and then, in his final comparison of works of

---

VII:523). The article was originally read at an 1811 meeting of the Beseda group. See discussion in Alekseev, *Pushkin,* 16–17 (see n. 29, above).

96. For additional discussion of the differences between Derzhavin's and Pushkin's understandings of poetic inspiration, see Gorodetskii, *Lirika,* 45–53; and Zapadov, *Masterstvo,* 247–48 (see n. 23, above). Pushkin's obvious reservations about the use of *vostorg* (with all its attendant connotations) does not mean that the word falls out of his poetic lexicon after a certain point. What does happen, however, is that *vostorg* can no longer be invoked in a serious context without summoning up certain eighteenth-century "odic" expectations — expectations that may appear ambiguously anachronistic and "stylized" in the cynical world of Nicholaevan Russia. When, for example, the speaker in Pushkin's controversial anti-Polish (and anti-European, especially anti-French) poems of 1831 appeals to the shade of the hero of the Napoleonic wars (Kutuzov) to instill a collective Russian "voice" (the biblical *glas*) with *vostorg,* he has clearly reentered the semantic field of Derzhavin's famous odes to Catherine's favorite generals. (See, "Before the sacred tomb" [Pered grobnitseiu sviatoi], "To the Slanderers of Russia" [Klevetnikam Rossii], and "The Anniversary of Borodino" [Borodinskaia godovshchina], in *Pss,* III:208–13.) But there are differences. First, at the end of "Before the sacred tomb" the martial spirit of Kutuzov does not awake, but sleeps soundly, because his successor *has not been found.* And second, now the addressee for these poems is "Europe" as much as Russia, and so the poet can be seen to be "closing ranks" with is countrymen as France, not understanding this "family squabble" and still bearing a grudge over the "barbarians' " defeat of Napoleon, enters the fray on the side of Poland. Thus, it is still difficult to imagine Pushkin penning a civic ode *addressed exclusively or primarily to his Russian readers* after 1825 that deploys the semantic field of *vostorg* in a concrete fashion and "on the level." My thanks to Megan Dixon for alerting me to this "odic" application of *vostorg* in Pushkin's anti-Polish poems of 1831.

97. *Pss,* VII:29.

98. See Alekseev, *Pushkin,* 26.

inspired genius with those created out of *vostorg,* he cites the lack of a guiding *plan* — of the ability to contemplate, to "get outside of" feeling, and to see the relation of "parts to whole" — in the "Olympian" odes of Pindar or in Derzhavin's "The Waterfall." Thus, by 1825, as he tries his hand at more varied genres (e.g., "Shakespearean" drama) and as he gravitates in these experiments closer to historical reality, Pushkin rejects something else about Derzhavin — that state of Pythic utterance qua *self-oblivion* made famous in the odes. But again, this decision is not at all simple, straightforward, or disinterested, as much Soviet scholarship is wont to imply; rather it is deeply personal and "hot" with its own twistings and turnings, going as it does back along that same Derzhavin-Delvig axis to the — as Pushkin now sees it — inauthentic "odic" state out of which his first "Recollections" was written. These musings, moreover, are considerably complicated and made to appear hauntingly prescient if set in their proper context: in the years and months leading up to December 1825, colleagues such as Küchelbecker and Ryleev could be seen to be practicing a virtual cult of the "misplaced sublime" — a cult that centered squarely on the *vostorzhennyi* odist and public-spirited Derzhavin, whose deeds continued to speak as loud as, if not louder than, his words.

But — and this is my final point in this section — Pushkin's ambivalent feelings about "Recollections" and about the "Derzhavin-Petrov" odic voice zone in that work that was not in a sense sufficiently "his" to be included in the 1826 *Verse* have an even more specific poetic referent in the months leading up to and then following the December 1825 debacle. To get to this referent, however, we have, as always with Pushkin, to do some rather precise detective work. Küchelbecker had, from the early 1820s, been coming at the phenomenon of European romanticism through the lens of Derzhavinian "odic" civic-mindedness, which required that he not only be a "prophet," but that he outwardly declare, in no uncertain terms, his allegiances. Prophets, so to speak, must *prophesy* something. Thus in 1821–22, when he, like Pushkin, was in the south, he wrote several works that made their way to his now famous classmate via manuscript copies and that boldly announced his current biases: among these were "To Ermolov" (Ermolovu, 1821) and "Prophecy" (Prorochestvo, 1822). In the first he declares that it is the fervent wish of all genuine poets, i.e., those with "proud, flaming hearts," to sing the exploits of great civic heroes, as Homer once sang Achilles, as *Derzhavin sang Suvorov,* and now as he wishes to sing Ermolov, one of the heroes of the Napoleonic wars, the current commander of Russian forces in the Caucasus, and a figure much admired by the Decembrists.[99] And in "Prophecy," whose first line reads "And the word of God came to me" (*Glagol gospoden' byl ko mne*), the "exiled" speaker has an Old Testament vision, or "Jeremiad," of the liberation of Greece wherein the unrighteous oppressor (the British-supported Turks) is to be smitten by the fierce right hand (*desnitsa*) of the Lord of Hosts (*Savaof*) amid much grinding of bones and wailing. This angry God, in a manner unmistakably reminiscent of Derzhavin's outspoken transposition of Psalm 81 in "To Rulers and Judges" (Vlastiteliam i sudiiam, 1780?), "shakes and smashes thrones" because "He is the shield for the righteous, for the free."[100] When Pushkin read these poems, composed in a context of self-conscious "exile" that Küchelbecker likened to Pushkin's own "wilderness," he wrote to his brother Lev, in a letter of 4 September 1822, "I have been reading the verse and prose of Küchelbecker—what a strange bird! Only into his mind could enter the Jewish [*zhidovskaia*] idea to sing Greece, magnificent, classical, poetic Greece, the Greece where everything breathes mythology and heroism, in Slavono-Russian verses taken entirely from Jeremiah. What would Homer and Pindar say? . . . The 'Ode to Ermolov' is better, but the verse 'Thus did Derzhavin sing, having fallen in love with Suvorov' [a line from 'To Ermolov'] is already too Greek."[101] Here the attentive reader notices that Pushkin associates the odic tone not only with a biblical text (indeed, many of Küchelbecker's images in "Prophecy" come right out of Jeremiah) in a manner that recalls Derzhavin's free use of the Psalm 81 format, but also with a *Slavono-Russian* verse base that is clearly, to Pushkin at least, awkwardly "archaic" (translate "Derzhavinian") in the early 1820s. This may be one reason why the Derzhavin-Suvorov link, i.e., *their* odic connection, leaps to the poet's mind as something potentially risible in this context—a love that seems too "Greek."[102] The ending of "Prophecy" is, in this context, so "un-Pushkinian" in its thundering explicitness (i.e., in its telling *what* the prophet will do, *whose* side he is on, etc.) that one imagines Pushkin remembering it as a way *not* to include the odic voice in his own verse:

> And I, both in exile and in dungeon,
> will proclaim God's word:

99. V. K. Kiukhel'beker, *Izbrannye proizvedeniia v dvukh tomakh* (Moscow-Leningrad: Sovetskii pisatel', 1967), I:150–51.

100. Kiukhel'beker, *Izbrannye proizvedeniia*, I:159.

101. *Pss*, X:37.

102. The mention of Homer and Pindar is also, for Pushkin, implicitly "Derzhavinian," as we recall from his response to Küchelbecker's articles in *Mnemozina*.

O God, I am in your right hand!
I will not allow Your words to be suppressed!
As the tempest rushes across the field,
so too will my voice ring out
and the Powerful will hear its echo:
each hair on my head is counted by You![103]

It was this series of associations — Küchelbecker having turned on his Lyceum comrades and gone over to the "archaists"/Derzhavin in a manner
dangerously explicit — that surfaced in Pushkin's 1825 revisiting of the Derzhavin myth himself. In other words, Küchelbecker was trying to say what, in
the context of the final years of Alexander's reign, could not be said, something Pushkin knew instinctively from his experience with odic "misprision"
in "Recollections." In this same 1825, for example, Küchelbecker writes in
Son of the Fatherland: "As when speaking of Lomonosov's successors, has he
[i.e., a certain German critic Küchelbecker is discussing] forgotten Derzhavin, the first Russian lyric poet, a genius whom alone we can boldly compare
to lyric poets of all times and peoples?" What is needed, as Küchelbecker
continues in the same review, is an odic *vostorg* going back to Derzhavin
and Petrov (Pushkin's points of departure in "Recollections"!) that is great
for the un-self-conscious intensity of its feeling and despite (because of?) the
formal blemishes (*nedostatki*) it grandly disregards. Our poets, insists Küchelbecker, should not "decorate/embellish [*ukrashat'*] their feelings," should
not place them in the "smoothed-out" (*vyglazhennyi*) forms of elegiac/Gallo-
Russian speech, but allow those feelings to be "*ripped from* [*vyrvutsia*, cf.
istorgat'/vostorgat'] the soul as powerful, tender, alive, and flaming as they
were sometimes ripped from the rich soul of Derzhavin."[104] Likewise, it was
in March of 1825, that is, virtually contemporaneously with Delvig's visit and
with Pushkin's plan to reread all of Derzhavin, that Pushkin wrote the *mock
ode* "To Count D. I. Khvostov": with its thickened odic register now made to
look ridiculous, its pedantically "scholarly" footnotes, its invocation of "fa-

---

103. Kiukhel'beker, *Izbrannye proizvedeniia*, I:160–61: «А я — и в ссылке, и в тем-
нице / Глагол господень возвещу: / О боже, я в твоей деснице! / Я слов твоих не
умолчу! — / Как буря по полю несется, / Так в мир мой раздастся глас / И в слухе
Сильных отозвется: / Тобой сочтен мой каждый влас!»

104. "Razbor fon der Borgovykh perevodov Russkikh stikhotvorenii," in *Syn otechestva* 17 (1825): 80; cited Iu. Tynianov, *Arkhaisty i novatory* (Leningrad: Priboi, 1929),
186–87.

mous shades" and mythological gods from antiquity, its mention of the now deceased Byron in his incarnation as Greek freedom fighter, its reference to the speaker as "an unknown poet [the archaic *piit*] / who will sing *in a new state of rapture* [*v vostorge*]" of heroic deeds, etc. — all clearly having as their target not Khvostov (here the "screen"), but, as Tynianov first suggested, Küchelbecker's Jeremiad on the "blood of Hellas" in "Prophecy."[105]

I cite these details not merely to implicate Küchelbecker (and Delvig) in Pushkin's ruminations on Derzhavin and the latter's odic voice in the important year of 1825, a fact that is both indisputable but also, so far at least, more or less academic. After December 1825, with the fate of that very same Küchelbecker (and others close to the poet) hanging (literally) in the balance, the issue of which voice to use when speaking about the sacred role of the poet was no longer academic. This brings us to my final speculation about the *poetic* residue of this period — Pushkin's "Prophet." When in September 1826, immediately before his famous and in other ways determinative meeting with the new tsar Nicholas, Pushkin allegorized for his post-Decembrist time-space the sixth chapter of Isaiah,[106] he undoubtedly had Küchelbecker's "Prophecy" in mind. That Pushkin uses images from a sacred text, here the Bible, is not new; after all, he did essentially the same thing, even working with a number of the same images (the prophet in the desert, the moment of divine revelation, etc.), when he reset Islamic holy scripture in "Imitations of the Koran" earlier in his Mikhailovskoe exile. However, something has changed here in the great poem and poetic/biographical turning point "The Prophet." If Derzhavin and his faithful follower Küchelbecker use sacred texts, Psalm 81 and Jeremiah respectively, to transpose the tradition of devotional verse (*dukhovnye stikhi*)[107] into

---

105. *Pss*, II:223–24. See discussion in Tynianov, *Arkhaisty i novatory*, 206–23.

106. See the superbly contextualized analysis in Stennik, *Pushkin*, 163–92 (see n. 23, above). Another source I don't discuss here is F. N. Glinka's "The Calling of Isaiah" (Prizvanie Isaii, 1822), which in the spirit of Küchelbecker demands that the prophet "go to the people" and "loudly expose vice" (mentioned Stennik, *Pushkin*, 183). Pushkin's own lexical and temperamental development from "Imitations of the Koran" to "The Prophet" is treated with characteristic subtlety in V. E. Vatsuro, "Prorok," *Zapiski kommentatora* (St. Peterburg: Akademicheskii proekt, 1994), 7–16. At the end of his article, first published in 1980, Vatsuro also provides a useful synopsis of the secondary literature on the Isaiah source in "The Prophet."

107. See Stennik's discussion of Pushkin's perceived preference for a "Lomonosovian" as opposed to "Derzhavinian" approach to the sacred text in the tradition of eighteenth-century *dukhovnye stikhi*: the former stressed fidelity to the letter and spirit of the original, while the latter was much freer and more openly topical. Stennik, *Pushkin*, 170–84.

a blunt instrument (and freewheeling allegory) with which to lambast specific abuses of power, then this newly chastened Pushkin, who can no longer *mock* his friends who are paying dearly for their explicitness, must place his poetry at the service of an energy force that to him is both real and nonspecific — it doesn't belong to the tsars, just as it doesn't belong to the Decembrists, no matter how Pushkin may feel for the latter as friends. This makes Pushkin's "The Prophet" one of those mysterious poems in his oeuvre — others include "Arion" and "The Upas Tree" — that don't take sides and that only he could write. "Freedom" and "authority" don't exist in pure form, but as motile extensions of one another. The closer the post-1825 Pushkin gets to the sacred space of myth or religious sensibility, the less apt he is to use that "access" for any ulterior purpose.[108] And in this respect, the ending of "The Prophet" is one that is as "un-Derzhavinian" and "un-Küchelbeckerian" as that of "Prophecy" was, then in 1822 and now even more so in 1826, "un-Pushkinian":

> "Arise, prophet, and see, and harken,
> be filled with my will,
> and, traversing seas and lands,
> burn peoples' hearts with my word."[109]

Using the *Slavono-Russian* lexicon (the archaic Church Slavic *vizhd'* and *vnemli*) parodied in the "Khvostov" ode; citing an imaginary biblical direct address (the *Vosstan', prorok* that is very close to Küchelbecker's *Vosstan', pevets, prorok Svobody*); developing the same notion of *glagol* as the word of God; seeing his role as to traverse the world the way his friend moves about like a tempest in the field, etc. — all these are Pushkin's utterly serious, but also supremely conscious, reactions to the sacred space of *chuzhoe slovo* (another's word). The poetic word as *vdokhovenie* (the awareness of what is happening to him as he speaks) turns and encompasses the poetic word as *vostorg*. Isaiah is the sacred word no longer to be mocked, just as Küchelbecker and the others may indeed be secular martyrs whose "archaic" ways reaped for them the whirlwind, but Pushkin will not say for whom, politically, ideologically, that poetic word is uttered.[110] It burns the hearts of its listeners, whoever they may

---

108. See notes 173 and 174 of the first part of this study.

109. *Pss*, II:304: «Восстань, пророк, и виждь, и внемли, / Исполнись волею моей, / И, обходя моря и земли, / Глаголом жги сердца людей.» The last line seems to echo, but now in a "sacred" register, a refrain from Derzhavin's 1805 poem "Gypsy Dance" (Tsyganskaia pliaska): «*Жги* души, огнь бросай в *сердца* / От смуглого лица.»

110. As Vatsuro writes, "About what it is precisely he [the prophet] speaks we don't

be, because its judgment is in the first instance of itself (of its unworthy human receptacle that nonetheless must accept its painful gift), and only from that follows its importance as the truth. Küchelbecker's outer, upper-case political freedom ("prophet of Freedom") has become inner, spiritual — the "stand-in-relation-to" of the burning words themselves.

---

ever find out. It may appear strange, but this poem about the prophet breaks off exactly at the moment when its hero becomes the Prophet" ("Prorok," 16).

The Boldino autumn of 1830 marks the next important encounter with the ghost of Derzhavin. These weeks of unprecedented creative activity were for Pushkin deeply and eerily *transitional:* preoccupied by, among other things, his "descent to prose," the poet was pursued by anxieties about his coming marriage, fearful for the safety of his fiancée (the epidemic of "cholera morbus"[111]), and increasingly desperate at her inaccessibility (the fourteen layers of quarantine). Many of the works of this remarkable autumn, as scholars have long recognized, are dominated by the thematic nexus of the "fatally erotic," or, to use the symbolic emblem of *The Tales of Belkin,* the Derzhavin-inspired "Cupid with an overturned torch."[112] Once again, however, this return involves both Derzhavin as precursor and Delvig as intermediary: Delvig, significantly, had used references to an "extinguished torch" (*fakel pogasshii*) and to a forgotten "Amour" in the opening lines of his "On the Death of Derzhavin" (Na smert' Derzhavina, 1816), a poem that made Pushkin its primary addressee and that in its conclusion called on him to take up the lyre abandoned by his great predecessor.[113] Not only had Delvig been the one to discover Pushkin, he in effect, in this poem, officially passed the torch of Russian poetry from Derzhavin to his friend.[114]

Pushkin's thoughts during this time returned repeatedly to his beginning, to premonitions of death, and especially to Derzhavin: in D. A. Ostafev's

111. For the record, Pushkin mistakenly identified the first European invasion of Asiatic cholera as the more familiar "cholera morbus."

112. Derzhavin, for example, commissioned engravings of cupids with inverted torches for the edition of his complete works. See Davydov, "Pushkin's Merry Undertaking," 33 and illustrations (see n. 23, above).

113. Del'vig, *Polnoe sobranie stikhotvorenii,* 253–54 (see n. 28, above); cited Davydov, "Pushkin's Merry Undertaking," 43.

114. Pushkin, for his part, returned to the theme of his early friendship with Delvig in the shadow of "Derzhavin's coffin" in the 1830 (Boldino autumn) poem "We were born, my sworn brother" (My rozhdeny, moi brat nazvanyi) (*Pss,* III:185). Cited Davydov, "Pushkin's Merry Undertaking," 44.

album, for example, he inscribed, on 26 November 1830, Derzhavin's famous last verses about the river of time and the maw of oblivion awaiting everyone ("Reka vremen . . .").[115] And in the notes he made for an autobiography, which are usually dated by scholars to this same Boldino autumn, we find under the year 1814 the intriguing telegraphic phrase "Examination, Galich, Derzhavin — poetry writing — death."[116] Here the associations with beginnings and endings are clear (note the dashes as opposed to commas following "Derzhavin"), yet the chronology is wrong: "1814," which was not the year of Derzhavin's death, as presumably Pushkin knew well, is "infected," as it were, by the atmosphere of "1830." Pushkin understands that he too could be a victim of the plague,[117] and so he puts his old artistic house in order and his earlier incarnations behind him as he prepares to become, not the romantic poet and Byronic apprentice, but "A.P.," *editor* of the tales of the *late* Ivan Petrovich Belkin.

As Sergei Davydov and I have demonstrated elsewhere, these tales must be read at an elaborately camouflaged metaliterary level in order to be properly understood.[118] Central to their design is the seemingly anomalous tale "The Coffinmaker," a story of the misadventures of a ridiculously sullen artisan who is moving shop. Offended by his treatment at the German Schultz's wedding anniversary — "Come, old man," jokes one of the guests, "drink to the health of your corpses!" — the hero secretly decides to snub the "furriners" in his plans for a housewarming party and to take instead an opposite course: "Why

115. M. Tsiavlovskii et al., *Rukoiu Pushkina* (Moscow-Leningrad: Academia, 1936), 667–68.

116. *Pss,* VIII:55.

117. "The cholera morbus is about me. Do you know what kind of wild beast it is? The first thing you know it will swoop down on Boldino, too, and it will bite us all — the first thing you know I shall set off to Uncle Vasily's [Pushkin's uncle Vasily Lvovich died on 20 August 1830], and then you will be writing my biography" (letter of 9 September 1830 to Pletnev; *Pis'ma,* II:106; *Letters,* 429).

118. See "Pushkin's Saturnine Cupid: The Poetics of Parody in *The Tales of Belkin,*" *PMLA* 96.1 (January 1981): 8–21. Wolf Schmid has recently suggested that, given the compositional histories of the stories, it is unlikely that Pushkin could have had his entire metaliterary plan for the cycle (see below) in mind as he wrote "The Coffinmaker," the first of the works to be completed. See his *Proza Pushkina v poeticheskom prochtenii: "Povesti Belkina"* (St. Petersburg: Izd. S.-Peterburgskogo universiteta, 1996), 263–65; original pub. in German as *Puškins Prosa in poetischer Lektüre: Die Erzählungen Belkins* (Munich, 1991). Schmid's caution is well taken, although that there is an intricate metaliterary dialogue going on in the *Tales* and that it involves both the poet's and contemporary Russian literature's "descent to prose" appear at this point beyond dispute.

do these heathens [*basurmane*] laugh? . . . I wanted to invite them to my new house and give them a feast, but now I'll do nothing of the kind. Instead I'll invite those for whom I work: the Orthodox dead [*pravoslavnye mertvetsy*]." What Pushkin is doing here is returning to the thematics of his earliest verse (e.g., the notion of precursors as *mertvetsy* in "Fonvizin's Shade"), but with a humorously encoded private semantics that is as far as possible from the public authorship of the initial "Recollections."[119] Thus, in metaliterary terms, the artisan Adrian Prokhorov[120] possesses the "editor's" initials, has been, like Pushkin himself, plying his trade (involving *proizvedeniia*, "works" both artistic and artifactual) for some eighteen years but is now moving shop, and so on.[121] And over his place of business hangs a sign displaying "a plump Amour with an inverted torch" and bearing the inscription "Plain and colored coffins sold and upholstered; coffins also let out for hire."[122] This latter is a playfully encoded reference to Pushkin's use of parodic plot structure and elusive metaliterary logic in the tales to "bury" powerful precursors (up to this point

119. Davydov shows convincingly how Arzamasian semantics and mock rituals figure prominently in the metaliterary parody at the center of "The Coffinmaker," especially with regard to the interlocking themes of "burial" (the fate of the Shishkovite) and "house-warming" (the goal of the new Arzamas member): "the main occupation of this . . . society . . . was the arrangement of funerals and wakes. Like new members of the more respectable 'Académie Française,' each new member of 'Arzamas' had to read an obituary of his deceased predecessor [i.e., the 'corpse' of a Shishkovite]. . . . During these Arzamasian invocations, the 'Beseda corpses' rose from their graves, in a manner reminiscent of 'The Coffinmaker' " ("Pushkin's Merry Undertaking," 40).

120. As always with Pushkin, however, there is a very tight bond between the literal and the figurative. In fact, there was an actual Adrian Prokhorov, who did run such a shop and did live virtually next door to the Goncharovs in Moscow. Pushkin mentions him in a letter, of 4 November 1830, while writing to his fiancée from Boldino: "Aren't you ashamed to have remained on Nikitskaya [i.e., in town] during the plague? It's all right for your neighbor Adrian, who has profitable deals to make" (*Letters*, 436; *Pss*, X:244; orig. in French). See also *1799–1837: Pushkin i ego vremia*, comp. S. G. Blinov et al. (Moscow: Terra, 1997), 273; originally pub. in Kharbin in 1938.

121. "The idea of changing domain is an important one in the four longer tales: Silvio's house after the first duel is changed to the count's house after the second duel; Marya Gavrilovna's house (close to Vladimir) before the blizzard is changed to the new house (close to Burmin) after the blizzard; and Vyrin's stationhouse is changed to Dunya's new house in Petersburg. In 'The Lady Peasant' there is no change of domain, but after all masks are dropped in the final *cognitio*, the hostile houses are unified in marriage" (Bethea and Davydov, "Pushkin's Saturnine Cupid," 20n34).

122. See n. 96, Part I.

Russians had been too willing simply to imitate western prose models) and at the same time to "marry" the foreign and the domestic in a Russian prose worthy of the name.[123]

The humorous or irreverent aspect of Pushkin's encounter with Derzhavin in this instance is seen in the interaction between epigraph and storyline in "The Coffinmaker." The epigraph comes from "The Waterfall," one of Pushkin's favorite Derzhavin texts: "Do we not see every day coffins, / The gray hairs of an aging universe?" (*Ne zrim li kazhdyi den' grobov, / Sedin driakhleiushchei vselennoi*).[124] But in their high seriousness and metaphysical generality these words are grotesquely at odds with the description of Prokhorov's "housewarming." In the story's central passage, the Orthodox dead do appear to arise at the invitation to visit Prokhorov's (and his creator's) new home. During the phantasmagorical gathering, a "little skeleton . . . [whose] skull smiled affably at the coffinmaker" makes its way through the crowd and extends its arms in a "bony embrace." It was to this skeleton that Prokhorov "had sold his first coffin," in 1799 (the year of Pushkin's birth), "*[passing off] a deal one for an oaken one to boot.*" Here, deeply hidden in the "ghoulish little *entr'acte*,"[125] the author has again "edited" the story of his relations with Derzhavin — in the embrace from beyond the grave, in the reference to a "first coffin" (note the "cheaper construction" of "Recollections"), and in the rejection of the skeleton's gesture of intimacy (Prokhorov shouts and pushes his well-wisher away, at which point the latter falls to the ground and breaks to pieces). As if to confirm the connection, the spokesman for the Orthodox dead is a "brigadier," a reference to Fonvizin, author of a play by the same name, source for the lead epigraph to the *Tales*, and the "jolly corpse" (*veselyi mertvets*) we recall from "Fonvizin's Shade."

The Orthodox dead raise a hue and cry, as indignant at Adrian's treatment

---

123. "But Pushkin, a literary coffin maker, not only buries the dead in his parodies. More important, he gives them new life. As Schultz says punningly, 'the dead cannot live without coffins.' It is at this level of meaning that the sign over Prokhorov's shop is finally decoded and the larger design of the *Tales* comes clear. At once both saturnine coffin maker and puckish god of love, A.P. weds his fortunate couples over the graves of stock heroes and weds Russian prose to a western European tradition over the graves of domestic poets" (Bethea and Davydov, "Pushkin's Saturnine Cupid," 18).

124. Pushkin slightly misquotes the original: not *kazhdyi den'*, but *vsiakoi den'*.

125. Richard Gregg, "A Scapegoat for All Seasons: The Unity and the Shape of *The Tales of Belkin*," *Slavic Review* 30.4 (1971): 760.

of one of their own as Adrian was offended by the joke of Schultz's guest. They angrily surround Prokhorov, and he, overcome and losing his nerve (*poterial prisutstvie dukha*), falls on the bones of the skeleton, that is, *back* into its embrace, and loses consciousness. In making fun of the dead, not only is Pushkin here having his little joke, he is treading close to that superstitious boundary where by mocking the potency of an otherworldly power (Derzhavin's authority), he is calling that power to come for him (Don Guan's invitation to the statue, uttered during this same Boldino autumn). After all, the Pushkin who is "descending to prose" and placing his great benefactor in a cheap coffin is also *betraying* that benefactor's and his own first calling—*that of poet*. By saying it was he ("A.P.") who sold the skeleton his first coffin, when on a meta-literary level (or rather in actual fact) it was *Derzhavin* who showed the eager and all too willingly "odic" schoolboy a kindness, he is distorting the truth and, for all the fun, acting in a way that is not "poetically" generous or noble. He is getting in the last word against an interlocutor who cannot answer back. And "A.P." knows it. For the truth of the matter is there is nothing stylistically "coffin-like" (i.e., parodic) or legitimately "Pushkinian" (i.e., the mature use of tradition) about "Recollections," despite its splendid display of language. This is precisely the challenging, willfully *reductive* meaning concealed in the little skeleton's name: "Kurilkin" comes from *kurilka*, the "splinter" used to start fires (a deflation of the torch motif) and the source of the "Kurilka is alive!" (*Zhiv Kurilka!*) saying, which is uttered in the presence of someone who is thought to have long disappeared.[126] This "whittling down" of Derzhavin is a much greater risk in the context of the first Boldino autumn than in the youth and obscurity of "Fonvizin's Shade." Indeed, against the background of Pushkin's upcoming marriage and his shift in "métier" (to prose writer, historian, journalist), it is a truly awesome and doubt-filled turning away from everything "the poet" has stood for in his life up to that point. For that reason, we should not be misled when the strange housewarming turns out, in rather typical Pushkin fashion, to be nothing but a comic bad dream. If Pushkin had died in the fall of 1830 having left as his legacy, among other things, the *Tales of Belkin*, Russian prose would still have its "primer," its blueprint for future

---

126. Davydov, "Pushkin's Merry Undertaking," 45–46 (see n. 23, above). Here Davydov also makes the ingenious connection between "Kurilka is alive," on the one hand, and Derzhavin's famous "I am not dead!" and Pushkin's "But why oh why must one live so long" ("Fonvizin's Shade"), on the other.

possibilities. And at the center of the *Tales,* both physically and conceptually, would stand "The Coffinmaker"—the bizarre and in its way haunted "Exegi monumentum" of that cycle.

The premonitions regarding Cupid's overturned torch did come true in Pushkin's life immediately following the first Boldino autumn, only the death was not his own but that of his best friend: on 14 January 1831 Delvig died of "putrid fever" (probably a form of typhus), and on 18 February the marriage with Natalia Goncharova took place. From this point on, Pushkin's return to Derzhavin would proceed under a different constellation of concerns and interests: his life as family man, his growing interest in history and historiography (but of a *nonromantic,* nonmythological sort), and his close friendship with another man, Pavel Nashchokin.[127] Curiously, Nashchokin is mentioned in the same letter to Pletnev (of 21 January 1831) in which Pushkin speaks tersely yet movingly about the depth of his sadness over the loss of Delvig: "Yesterday I spent the day with Nashchokin, who has been hard hit by his [Delvig's] death—we spoke of him, calling him the deceased Delvig, and this epithet was just as strange as it was terrible. Let us consent to it. So be it. Baratynsky is ill with grief. It is not that easy to knock me off my feet. Stay well—and let's try to stay alive."[128] There is something peculiarly right about the fact that Pushkin was discussing Delvig with the person who would be his closest friend in the 1830s, that, even in his grief, he was touching the reality of that death, putting his finger, so to speak, to the wound even as it hurt ("Let us consent to it"), and that, in Nashchokin's presence, he was turning back to life and the living ("let's try to stay alive").

It would be difficult to overestimate the significance of Pavel Nashchokin's friendship with Pushkin in the 1830s, particularly now in the absence of Delvig. (See illustration 10.) Indeed, in terms of kindness, nobility of spirit, subtle taste, forbearance, and a goodwill that knew no bounds or accountability, Nashchokin came in his own way to fill the role in Pushkin's life earlier occupied by Delvig.[129] Yet there were important differences in the two friends;

---

127. Interestingly enough, however, the thematic nexus joining Derzhavin, Delvig, and death in Pushkin's mind remained strong: when inquiring about Pletnev's silence in a letter of 11 April 1831, and humorously suspecting death, Pushkin writes, "If you are no longer in this world, then beloved shade, greet Derzhavin for me and embrace my Delvig" (*Pss,* X:269; *Letters,* 484).

128. *Pss,* X:261; *Letters,* 455.

129. See discussion in M. Gershenzon, "Drug Pushkina Nashchokin," *Mudrost' Push-kina* (Moscow: tip. Knigoizdatel'stvo Pisatelei v Moskve, 1919), 216–17. Bartenev speaks of

Nashchokin offered Pushkin an altogether new and quite un-Delvig-like biography. It was, first of all, a life *not* lived through literature: Nashchokin provided a haven for all manner of "artists" and bohemian hangers-on — indeed his home was both a museum featuring the works of those he patronized and a kind of living theater and continually revolving stage where various levels of Moscow society passed through — but he himself did not have the discipline or the focus to be a writer. He touchingly asks Pushkin, for example, not to correct the spelling errors and grammatical solecisms in his letters.[130] In short, as opposed to Delvig, with whom Pushkin shared countless *literary* memories and battles (and in the letters to whom there is always the palpable scent of Arzamasian semantics, totally absent, for example, in communications with Nashchokin), in "Voinich" Pushkin found a friend who *lived* in a vivid or "poetic" way, but was himself not a man of letters. This was a crucial distinction as Pushkin moved from the 1820s to the 1830s. Nashchokin possessed a "wide" Russian nature of legendary proportions; he had a troublesome gypsy mistress (Olga Andreevna), gambled out of a love for "powerful sensations" (*sil'nye oshchushcheniia*), was an avid collector of ancient coins and weapons, gave sumptuous parties while teetering on the brink of bankruptcy, went through fortunes (as many as ten) and acquired new ones with an uncanny alacrity that seemed tailor-made for a literary plot. In fact, as scholars have long speculated,[131] it was probably Nashchokin and the countless stories relating to his life or told by him that lie behind a number of Pushkin's 1830s plots, including those of *The Little House in Kolomna*, *Ezersky*, *Dubrovsky*, and *A Russian Pelham*. According to one legend, for instance, it was Nashchokin's passion for the actress Asenkova that caused him to dress up in a maid's attire and secretly spend a month in his new love's employ, a story that his friend then made droll use of in *Little House*. If Delvig was forever associated with the mythical time of Pushkin's poetic infancy, then Nash-

---

Pushkin's love of Nashchokin's "unique mind" and "talented, broad nature and superior heart," and Gershenzon cites his "remarkable generosity and intelligent, patient indulgence" (216).

130. *Druz'ia*, II:337.

131. The biography and personality of Nashchokin became better known in modern times when Tsyavlovsky published Bartenev's renderings of Nashchokin's "stories about Pushkin" in 1925 (*Rasskazy o Pushkine, zapisannye so slov ego druzei P. I. Bartenevym* [Leningrad: Izd. M. i S. Sabashnikovykh, 1925]). The best single work on Nashchokin is still Gershenzon's 1904 article (cited above) "Drug Pushkina Nashchokin," reprinted in *Mudrost' Pushkina* (1919).

chokin was associated with the writer's maturity, with the "living down" of public myth, and with a spontaneous life force[132] and an ever-changing biography that possessed remarkable plot-generating potential in the "real world," in history. Things, as it were, *happened* to Nashchokin in a way that Pushkin found endearing and fascinating. Finally, despite his amazing contretemps, more than any other friend Nashchokin could speak to Pushkin about family rhythms, confinements, births and christenings (the friends were godparents to each other's children).[133] There was something "authentic" and "eighteenth-century" about the open, good-natured Nashchokin that was bound to appeal to the salon-weary and, especially by the mid-1830s, socially trapped Pushkin. And it is in this aspect of Nashchokin's biography that we must dig for clues to the Derzhavin connection.

Several details in Nashchokin's memoirs, which Pushkin urged his friend to write and which he apparently helped to edit, are striking in the context of Pushkin's works and thinking of the 1830s. First, the theme of personal independence and dignity — *no matter what* — was sounded with particular force in Nashchokin's recollections of his father, General Voin Vasilevich Nashchokin. This man had been audacious enough, in the son's retelling, to slap Suvorov — the same Suvorov whose name and martial exploits would be immediately linked in Pushkin's mind with Derzhavin and the latter's various poems in praise of the generalissimo[134] — when Suvorov had bragged that he had been hunting glory on the field of battle while Nashchokin senior had been hunting rabbits. When Suvorov complained to the Empress Catherine herself, she advised him to let the matter drop; but Suvorov sought his revenge by having a medal sent to his adversary anyway, with the note that it was being awarded at the personal intercession of Suvorov. Again, Nashchokin's father responded in

132. "Vous êtes éminemment un homme de passion," writes Pushkin in a letter of 24 November 1833 (*Pss*, X:356).

133. Pushkin spent eighteen days at the now married Nashchokin's Moscow home in May 1836. He wrote his wife on 14 and 16 May that he was mostly sitting at home, *en famille*, with the Nashchokins and that his life in Moscow was "staid and decent/orderly" (*stepennaia i poriadochnaia*). It seemed only Nashchokin understood, apparently instinctively, Pushkin's needs at this time (cf. "Liubit menia odin Nashchokin") (*Pss*, X:452). Considering the difficulties of this particular year in Pushkin's life, V. V. Kunina has termed this final stay with Nashchokin the "poet's last respite" (*posledniaia peredyshka dlia poeta*) (*Druz'ia*, II:327).

134. Perhaps the most famous was the lament at Suvorov's passing: "The Bullfinch" (Snegir', 1800).

a manner that was certain to draw a smile from the fiercely independent Push-kin: "My father did not accept the medal, saying that he would not be obliged to anyone except himself."[135] What is more, Potemkin's anecdote about General Nashchokin's pride — "He responded to God with respect, but also as if to one lower in rank: since he was a major general, he looked on God as a brigadier"[136] — sounds suspiciously like Pushkin's angry diary entry of 10 May 1834 when he learned that his letters to his wife were being opened at the Moscow post-office and shown to the tsar: "The Emperor was displeased that I spoke of my position as *kameriunker* without tenderness and gratitude. But I can be a subject, even a slave [*rab*], but what I won't be, even before the Lord God, is a lackey [*kholop*] and jester."[137] In sum, everything about the colorful figure of Nashchokin's quintessential eighteenth-century father would have appealed immensely to the Pushkin of the 1830s, especially the author of *The Captain's Daughter*: from his abrupt response to the new emperor Pavel ("You're hot-tempered, I'm hot-tempered, hence we'll not be able to get on together"[138]), to his eccentric entourage, including a female blackamoor (*arapka*) valet and an impudent jester, to his marriage in one day to Nashchokin's mother and his training of the latter to a military life by making her sit on a cannon and firing it from under her! This man, whose very name means "warrior" (*voin*), seems a potential model for Grinev père, the patriarch qua stern military type in *The Captain's Daughter*. Even the younger Nashchokin's humorous experience with his tutors, one described as French and the other described as being unceremoniously dismissed because he had been the cause of the boy's first bout with drunkenness, sounds very close both to Fonvizin's world and, more important, to the world presented in the opening pages of Pushkin's historical novel.[139]

135. *Druz'ia*, II:333. Cf. Pushkin's well-known "letter of advice" to his brother Lev writ ten between 4 September and 6 October 1822: "Never accept favors. A favor, most of the time, is an act of treachery. Avoid patronage completely, because it enslaves and degrades" (original in French; *Pss*, X:40; *Letters*, 103).

136. *Druz'ia*, II:333.

137. "Large 'Academy,'" XII:329. Pushkin is also echoing here another respected eighteenth-century figure, Lomonosov, who made similar remarks (i.e., about self-respect and the refusal to be a lackey before the highborn) in a famous 19 January 1761 letter to I. I. Shuvalov.

138. *Druz'ia*, II:333.

139. *Druz'ia*, II:335–36.

All this background information about Nashchokin is given by way of preface to his one major "retelling" of Pushkin's attitude toward Derzhavin:

> Pushkin did not like the poet Derzhavin as a person. . . . Pushkin told how the famous poet acted basely [*spodlichal*] during the Pugachev Rebellion, how he showed cowardice [*strusil*] and handed over to be sacrificed the commandant of a fortress, the same commandant who is depicted under the name of Mironov in *The Captain's Daughter*. It goes without saying, [however,] that Pushkin had a high opinion of Derzhavin's [literary] talent.[140]

Providing of course that Nashchokin is reporting his recollections accurately — and it is hard to believe he could be wrong about something of this magnitude and vividness — this is certainly the most puzzling and provocative statement ever made by Pushkin about his benefactor and rival. Given the history of previous "encounters," these words can least of all be taken at face value, as a simple expression of fact. They need to be placed in their immediate context of the 1830s, especially Pushkin's work on *The Captain's Daughter* and *The History of Pugachev*, and they need to be themselves resisted, wrestled with, and understood from multiple perspectives. For these words are damning — nothing is higher in Pushkin's scale of values than one's honor — and they are *personal*, that is, they are spoken not about Derzhavin "the singer of Felitsa" but about Derzhavin the man. It is not fortuitous that Pushkin chose Nashchokin as the one addressee for this other final word.

140. Tsiavlovskii, *Rasskazy o Pushkine*, 48, 123.

✺ 1836

In the last part of this study, I will compare three works of 1836 in the context of Nashchokin's recollection: "My Hero's Genealogy" (Rodoslovnaia moego geroia, pub. 1836), *The Captain's Daughter* (Kapitanskaia dochka, wr. 1832–36, pub. 1836); and "Exegi monumentum" (wr. 1836).[141] The compositional history of these works and others closely related to them stretches back over the 1830s and incorporates the thematic concerns of these years, but the fact that each was either completed or published in 1836, the last year of Pushkin's life, and, moreover, that each is tightly bound up with a final return to Derzhavin, is extremely striking and thus potentially significant.[142]

Pushkin published "My Hero's Genealogy" in *The Contemporary* in 1836. The poem is a good starting point for understanding Pushkin's final return to Derzhavin for several reasons: (1) it is one of the last poems Pushkin published and, despite its tone (jaunty with a polemical edge), it fits into the frame of mind that authored the Stone Island cycle; (2) it is directly concerned with the issue of biography and particularly with what, under current circumstances, passes for legitimate or plot-worthy "facts" when speaking of a life; (3) it conceals, through its connections with "My Genealogy," a powerful *autobiographical* dimension; and (4) it appears to be intertextually engaged, through its reworking of certain themes and formal structures of "My Genealogy," with a Derzhavin poem ("An Order to My Gatekeeper" [Prikaz moemu privratniku, wr. 1808]) that Pushkin sought to publish for the first time in *The Contemporary*, also in 1836. Let us first look at the transition from autobiography to biography in "My Genealogy" and "My Hero's Genealogy," and then

141. There are other Pushkin works of the 1830s that engage Derzhavin, in particular "Autumn" (Osen', 1833), but in the interest of space and because their thematic concerns intersect largely with those of the works discussed below, they will not be treated in detail here. See, e.g., G. P. Makogonenko, "Anakreontika Derzhavina i ee mesto v poezii XIX veka," *Izbrannye raboty* (Leningrad: Khudozhestvennaia literatura, 1987), 224–27; and "Pushkin i Derzhavin," 121–23 (see n. 23, above).

142. Other works important for this last section of our study are: "My Genealogy" (Moia rodoslovnaia, wr. 1830), *Ezersky* (wr. 1832–33), and *The History of Pugachev* (Istoriia Pugacheva, wr. 1833–34, pub. 1834).

turn briefly to Derzhavin's "An Order to My Gatekeeper," which Pushkin, as I will speculate, could not have considered publishing without thinking of his own poetic statements on the same topic.

"My Genealogy" is permeated with the literary polemics of the late 1820s and 1830s and with Pushkin's concerns about the fast-approaching eclipse of his noble class (the *stolbovoe dvorianstvo*). Writing at the end of the first Boldino autumn, Pushkin is more personal and autobiographical in this poem than anywhere else in his entire oeuvre. He takes on Russia's current great and powerful by assaulting their ancestors (Menshikov, Kutaisov, Razumovsky, etc.) and repeating stories about their devious routes to fame and riches, and he asserts the proud, bellicose, and ancient roots of his own people. But most of all, Pushkin's irony and vitriol in this case are directed against the underhanded tactics of Faddei Bulgarin ("Figlyarin"), the man who epitomizes the "new" in Russian literary politics. This is the same Bulgarin of murky background who seemed to take pleasure precisely in not being a gentleman,[143] who could not be reached by any appeal to "honor," who spread scurrilous rumors about Pushkin's relatives (the story about Pushkin's black great-grandfather Gannibal being purchased by Peter the Great for a bottle of rum), and who in general was very adept at using the new "no-holds-barred" rules of the literary marketplace to steal the initiative (if not actual plots) from the "aristocrats" (Pushkin, Delvig). Pushkin of course could not play by these rules, hence his anger. One reason why this poem could never be published was that it was, above all, *too personal*. Pushkin's pained reaction at the demise of the old aristocracy and the rise of the new post-Petrine "meritorious" aristocracy is covered over by a kind of brittle sarcasm—"no, despite my ancient lineage, I am now a bourgeois [*meshchanin*], I have to *earn* my way as a writer, and am proud of it"—which was inappropriate for the creation of anything "Pushkinian." Pushkin is too close here to *justifying himself*, to showing his grievance both before the *novaia znat'* (the new aristocrats) and before the literary *raznochinstvo* (the Bulgarins), something impossible for his amour propre. He could not, that is, get to the issue of what constituted an authentic biography for his time by revealing this much of himself in this way.

As we know, Pushkin continued this theme of the decline of his class and

---

143. To the "Pushkin party" at least. Strictly speaking, Bulgarin was a gentleman, of Polish descent, whose family, while not wealthy, had roots in the *szlachta* (Polish gentry class). But provoked by Bulgarin and his turncoat ways, Pushkin and his friends were not trying to be "fair."

the necessity of imagining a different type of biography in *Ezersky*, but he eventually abandoned that project and transposed its initial conception to one of his greatest creations, *The Bronze Horseman* (Mednyi vsadnik, wr. 1833). However, for our purposes it is interesting to note that themes and phrases from "My Genealogy" are repeated virtually verbatim in the similarly entitled "My Hero's Genealogy": the speaker as ironic *meshchanin* (bourgeois), the importance of origins and family history, the thinly veiled disappointment at the culture's loss of historical consciousness, the nostalgia for *gramoty* (authentic "documents") and for one's *gerb* (coat of arms) as attestation of lineage, the irritating presence of Figlyarin, and many more. The difference of course is that now Pushkin is speaking not only about himself, but about his hero Ezersky, with the result that his speaker's voice loses some of the sharper aspects of personal animus and begins to approximate the sound of the narrator in *Eugene Onegin*, especially the way his thoughts are controlled and distanced by the structure of the Onegin stanza. Curiously enough, the eleventh stanza of *Ezersky*, which is also the first stanza following the end of "My Hero's Genealogy" (the published poem was based on a rearranged version of the central stanzas of the planned larger work), invokes Derzhavin. It is here, and in the next stanza, that Pushkin's speaker asks why he does not have the right to sing the story of Ezersky, the scion of a once powerful and aristocratic family who now lives on his public servant's salary:

> Upsetting the muse with interrogation,
> My critic would say with a smile,
> "What sort of enviable hero
> Have you chosen! Who is your hero?"
> "And what of it? He's a collegiate registrar,
> But what a severe man of letters you are!
> I sing him—and why not?
> He's my friend and neighbor.
> Derzhavin sang his two neighbors
> As well as Meshchersky's death;
> The singer of Felitsa could also be
> The singer of their weddings, their dinners,
> And the funerals following on their feasts,
> Though the world did not seem to mind at all."
>
> But I will be reminded that there's quite a difference
> Between Derzhavin and myself,

That beauty and ugliness
Are separated by one line,
That Prince Meshchersky was a senator,
And not a collegiate registrar,
And that it would be better if a poet
Chose a lofty subject. . . .[144]

Although these lines were not published in "My Hero's Genealogy," they were, as it were, lurking right below the surface of Pushkin's consciousness. It was a question of "tone," of what Pushkin could say about his hero without intruding too much of himself into the argument, a dilemma he apparently resolved to his satisfaction in the more thoroughly "masked" *The Bronze Horseman*. Still, in thinking of the fate of a friend such as Nashchokin (or indeed of his own), Pushkin was immediately drawn to the options for biography, for making sense and "shape" of a life, open to Derzhavin. The preromantic Derzhavin could either sing of Meshchersky or Catherine (the "odic" Derzhavin) or make fun of pompous "neighbors" (M. A. Garnovsky) attempting

144. «Допросом музу беспокоя, / С усмешкой скажет критик мой: / "Куда завидного героя / Избрали вы! Кто ваш герой?" / — "А что? Коллежский регистратор, / Какой вы строгий литератор! / Его пою — зачем же нет? / Он мой приятель и сосед. / Державин двух своих соседов / И смерть Мещерского воспел; / Певец Фелицы быть умел / Певцом их свадеб, их обедов / И похорон, сменивших пир, / Хоть этим не смущался мир". // Заметят мне, что есть же разность / Между Державиным и мной, / Что красота и безобразность / Разделены чертой одной, / Что князь Мещерский был сенатор, / А не коллежский регистратор — / Что лучше, ежели поэт / Возьмет возвышенный предмет . . .» (*Pss*, IV:249).

In the second chapter of the unfinished *Egyptian Nights* (Egipetskie nochi, wr. 1835), Pushkin took as epigraph Derzhavin's most famous line from "God" (Bog, 1784), "I am a tsar, I am a slave, I am a worm, I am a god," which he had treated parodically earlier in his career in "Fonvizin's Shade" (wr. 1815). Then during the Italian's improvisation, which is placed in the prose narrative as poetic text and is on the theme of inspiration, we find lines (uttered by a passerby from the "crowd") that resonate unmistakably with the just cited stanza 12 of *Ezersky:* "A genuine poet is obliged / for his inspired songs / to choose a lofty subject" (*Obiazan istinnyi poet / Dlia vdokhnovennykh pesnopenii / Izbrat' vozvyshennyi predmet*) (*Pss*, VI:250). In other words, the implication is that Derzhavin had the freedom as poet to seek out radically different incarnations (tsar, slave, etc.), but that the poet of today, in a later nonheroic time, is constrained by obsolete convention (the logic of which the "crowd" is still governed by) to sing what is "lofty." That Pushkin is playing off the difference between poetic and prosaic expectations, but under the sign, so to speak, of Derzhavin, suggests that he is searching for inspiration (i.e., the unpredictable) in a world that is fast becoming "postpoetic."

to upstage him with their grander homes (the "satiric" Derzhavin) or celebrate weddings, feasts, and funerals (the "Anacreontic" Derzhavin of the early
1800s).[145] But the postromantic Pushkin could not. The "rules" had changed.
Why, reasons the ironic speaker, should I not have similar freedom with regard
to telling a life? If the rules of the literary marketplace have changed, so too,
goes this logic, must the rules for imagining a hero and his life. "Be proud,"
concludes the speaker in the next stanza, "you, poet, are such [i.e., no 'laws'
are written for you], / And for you there are no conditions/conventions."[146]

The links joining "My Genealogy," "My Hero's Genealogy," and these
stanzas from *Ezersky* would be enough to establish a powerful undercurrent
of Derzhavin-inspired musings converging on the year 1836. However, this
undercurrent becomes even more striking when we take into account Pushkin's intention to publish Derzhavin's poem "An Order to My Gatekeeper"
in *The Contemporary*. This poem had been circulating, apparently widely, in
various copies since Derzhavin first penned it in 1808.[147] But it had never
been published, presumably because of its personal and polemical nature.
The poem is something of an elaborate joke, which nonetheless managed to
raise the ire of its principal addressee: Derzhavin is giving instructions to his
privratnik (the one guarding his gate) and through him to the postman to
avoid delivering to his home the mail of another St. Petersburg "Derzhavin,"
a churchman, who lives close by.[148] What is immediately noticeable about the
work is its tone (humorous, confident, if not brash) and its elaborate emphasis on the *authenticity*, in all respects, of *this* Derzhavin.[149] In every point of
comparison (the poet is explaining why there should be no confusion in the
future with regard to who lives where), Derzhavin insists that his biography

145. Pushkin may be concealing here a return to the "cupid with the overturned torch"
motif in his interlocking reference to weddings and funerals.

146. "Gordis': takov i ty, poet, / I dlia tebia uslovii net" (*Pss*, IV:250). This response
also anticipates the theme of the poet's independence sounded in "Exegi monumentum."
See below.

147. A number of minor discrepancies exist between Pushkin's copy of the poem and
the copy published by Grot in Derzhavin, *Sochineniia*, III:420-24 (see n. 95, above).

148. The "other" Derzhavin is the Chief Priest (*ober-sviashchennik*) Ivan (Ioann)
Semenovich Derzhavin, who himself was a rather distinguished churchman in St. Petersburg. His long reply in verse ("An Order to My Secretary" [Prikaz moemu sekretariu])
was probably authored not by him but by a certain Father Gavriil Abramovich Pakatsky,
another priest with writerly ambitions. See Derzhavin, *Sochineniia*, III:424-29.

149. "I'm the real thing, he is my copy" (*Ia podlinnik, on spisok moi*) (Tsiavlovskii,
Rukoiu Pushkina, 581 [see n. 115, above]).

is real while his namesake's is a bland imitation: this Derzhavin wears a short tailcoat that has difficulty covering his bulk, while that Derzhavin wears a long and flowing cassock; this Derzhavin sang Mars, while that Derzhavin sings prayers; this Derzhavin was a "ruler of the people" (*narodnyi pravitel'*), while that Derzhavin is a retiring spiritual father; this Derzhavin leans forward to kiss ladies' hands with pleasure, while that Derzhavin extends his hand to his lady parishioners; this Derzhavin conceals the secrets of the heart (i.e., his romantic attachments), while that Derzhavin urges the confession of such secrets; and so on. One of the final comparisons, significantly, involves the poet's coat of arms, "a star held up [*derzhima*] by a hand," which is humorously contrasted with the churchman holding his walking stick.[150]

We don't know when Pushkin first read the poem or when the copy he intended to publish came into his possession.[151] However, based on both formal and thematic considerations, one could speculate that Pushkin had some version of this poem in mind when he wrote "My Genealogy" in 1830. The two poems have the same meter (iambic tetrameter), the same stanza length (8-line), and nearly identical rhyme schemes: *AbAbCCdd* in Derzhavin versus *AbAbCdCd* in Pushkin. Moreover, the distinctly *satiric-cum-autobiographical* thrust of the two poems, where the background and current status of the poet are being compared with those of a less "genuine" other (Derzhavin's comic alter ego versus Pushkin's bête noire Bulgarin), seemed to require this more direct form. (The Onegin stanza, for example, which Pushkin turned to in *Ezersky,* would have been too involved and "ingenious" a vehicle for conveying his blunt sarcasm.) Thus, what is important in this juxtaposition, if the assumption is correct, is the *difference* in tone between the Derzhavin and the Pushkin poems. Let us conclude this part of the discussion by comparing, for the sake of experiment, a stanza from each of the poems. First, Derzhavin:

> And neither is he like me in his word,
> Nor in his appearance, nor size, nor face;
> He may be noble in his soul
> But he is not a Derzhavin in his coat-of-arms.
> In mine there is a Star held up by an arm,
> While a walking stick or cane is borne by him.

150. Tsiavlovskii, *Rukoiu Pushkina,* 581–83.

151. The poem's publication in *The Contemporary* was refused by the censors. It first appeared in print only in 1859 in *Bibliograficheskie zapiski* (Bibliographical Notes).

He might be able to get a rosary [prayer] in print,
But I am able to shine with my golden lyre.[152]

Then Pushkin:

Beneath the seal of my coat of arms
I have kept/buried a stack of old documents
And I don't gad about with the new aristocracy,
And I have becalmed the haughtiness in my blood,
I'm a literate chap and a versifier,
I'm Pushkin simply, not Musin[-Pushkin],
I'm not a wealthy man, nor am I a courtier,
I'm a big shot by myself; I'm a bourgeois.[153]

Both passages are alike in their swagger, yet different. Note, for example, that each speaker tells his story by also telling who he is not (e.g., the importance of negative constructions in the various comparisons), that each mentions a coat of arms as a sign of authenticity, that each is known for being a poet. But the authorizing voice narrating this version of Derzhavin's life is completely inappropriate for Pushkin and his age. The coat of arms that Derzhavin so boasts about has been reduced to the function of a paperweight. Pushkin has neither Derzhavin's connections at court, nor his wealth, nor his status as statesman and courtier. All that remains of a former "haughtiness" (spes'), which captures perfectly the tone of Derzhavin's strutting as well, is Pushkin's *personal* sense of honor and his pride, here ironically deflected (note the descent from Derzhavin's "lyre" to Pushkin's "versifier"), in his craft. Indeed, the "I'm a big shot" (Ia sam bol'shoi) is probably yet another Derzhavinian intertextual reminiscence: in Onegin's journey, the speaker describes his new (postromantic) ideal as having a wife (khoziaika) and his fondest desires as "pokoi, / Da shchei gorshok, da sam bol'shoi" (peace, / And cabbage soup, and *myself in charge*),[154] which popular saying in the form of patriarchal

152. «И словом он со мной несходен / Ни видом, ростом, ни лицом; / Душой быть может благороден / Но Гербом не Державин он. / В моем: Звезда рукой держима; / А им клюка иль трость носима. / Он может четки внесть в печать, / Я— лирою златой блистать» (Tsiavlovskii, *Rukoiu Pushkina*, 583).

153. «Под гербовой моей печатью / Я кипу грамот схоронил, / И не якшаюсь с новой знатью, / И крови спесь угомонил. / Я грамотей и стихотворец, / Я Пушкин просто, не Мусин, / Я не богач, не царедворец, / Я сам большой: я мещанин» (*Pss*, III:198).

154. *Pss*, V:174.

triad (wife/home/mastery) goes back first to Kantemir's fifth satire (1762),[155] and then to Derzhavin's poem "Praise of Village Life" (Pokhvala sel'skoi zhizni, 1798).[156] But this use of an earlier century's bragging rights has now become edged with a penetrating *self-irony* (i.e., the valorized "I'm a big shot" + the despised "I'm a bourgeois") completely alien to Derzhavin. These words are Pushkin's, not Derzhavin's, because they present, once again, an expanded verbal awareness of what, on the existential plane, is a lack of options. Both genre consciousness (how Derzhavin is able to pass freely among his various speakerly roles, "odic," "Anacreontic," and otherwise—all still poetic) and social or class consciousness (how Derzhavin is able to rise out of his modest gentry background and make a name for himself not only as warrior and statesman but as first poet of the realm—this latter *his* creation by the way) come together athwart Pushkin's path. And they are the figurative and literal reminder that in him, Pushkin, the poet has descended to prose. If Derzhavin made the poet into a kind of tsar, a court of one that made its own laws, then Pushkin, not only not heeded by his sovereign but dressed in a *kameriunker's* uniform, has brought the role of the poet perilously close to that of court jester. This is why Derzhavin is so often on Pushkin's mind in the 1830s. In sum, to repeat, the very least that can be said is that Pushkin could not have considered publishing "An Order to My Gatekeeper" in 1836 without thinking of "My Hero's Genealogy," published in the same year, and without recalling his earlier, and more unguardedly autobiographical, "My Genealogy." It remains to be shown, however, how this complex awareness of Derzhavin will be carried directly into *The Captain's Daughter* and ultimately "Exegi monumentum."

To return now to Nashchokin's recollection of Pushkin's verdict on Derzhavin the man and to the latter's behavior during the Pugachev Rebellion. Nashchokin's words make a direct link between the young Lieutenant (*poruchik*) Derzhavin, who was trying to lift himself out of obscurity during the *pugachevshchina*, and the theme of betrayal/loss of honor (Shvabrin) in The

155. Kantemir was the first to use the expression *Shchei gorshok, da sam bol'shoi, khoziain ia doma,* in line 719 of his fifth satire ("Na chelovecheskie zlonraviia voobshche" [On Human Depravities in General]). It is difficult to say, however, whether Derzhavin was actually citing Kantemir or simply using what by later in the century had become a popular saying.

156. «*Хозяйка* мила, домовита / Печется о его детях ... // *Горшок* горячих добрых щей, / Корченый окорок под дымом, / Обсаженный семьей моей, / *Средь коей сам я господином*» (Derzhavin, *Sochineniia,* II:104).

Captain's Daughter.[157] What are the "facts" here, what could Pushkin have known? *The History of Pugachev* cites Derzhavin's activities in several instances, mainly in chapters 5 and 8. The first episode of consequence involves Derzhavin's quelling of a riot in a village near Malykovka (Saratov *guberniia*). Having learned that a crowd of peasants was threatening to join Pugachev's forces, Derzhavin boldly entered the village with only two Cossacks, confronted the mob and demanded to know who was in charge, and then ordered that its two ringleaders be hanged, which they promptly were. He followed by ordering that the entire village be flogged. Apparently Derzhavin had been successful in convincing the rioters that there were three regiments waiting to enter the village behind him.[158] It was about this same episode that Dmitriev made his remark, certain to intrigue Pushkin, that Derzhavin hanged the malcontents "out of poetic curiosity" (*iz poeticheskogo liubopytstva*).[159] In a word, there was nothing about Derzhavin's behavior at this point to explain Nashchokin's recollection, in fact quite the opposite. Pushkin presumably would have been impressed by Derzhavin's courage and ingenuity under duress.

There is, however, another important episode in chapter 8 that is, from

157. Possible connections between the historical Derzhavin, on the one hand, and the fictional Grinev and Shvabrin, on the other hand, have been analyzed perceptively in Irina Reyfman, "Poetic Justice and Injustice: Autobiographical Echoes in Pushkin's *The Captain's Daughter*," *Slavic and East European Journal* 38.3 (1994): 463–78, esp. 465–71. This article has been useful to me in the following discussion. Where I differ somewhat from Reyfman is in her emphasis on Pushkin's exclusive admiration for Derzhavin's "boldness" and his apparent lack of judgment about the Boshnyak affair. It is my argument that Pushkin *did* judge Derzhavin for leaving his post during the imminent threat of enemy attack, because first of all he did not know why Derzhavin did this and suspected cowardice (i.e., Pushkin only had the Boshnyak-Panin version of events). See below. On Derzhavin as a possible model for Grinev in *The Captain's Daughter*, see also David Bethea, "Slavianskoe darenie, poet v istorii i *Kapitanskaia dochka* Pushkina," in *Avtor i tekst*, ed. V. M. Markovich and Wolf Schmid (St. Petersburg: Izd. S-Peterburgskogo Universiteta, 1996), 132–49; and David Bethea and Angela Brintlinger, "Derjavine et Khodassevitch," in *Derjavine: face au dialogue des cultures*, ed. A. Davidenkoff (Paris: Institut d'études slaves, 1994), 167–78. Independent of my own work on Pushkin and Derzhavin, Professor Samuel Schwarzband of the University of Jerusalem presented a paper at IRENISE (Derzhavin conference, Paris, October 1993) on Derzhavin and *The Captain's Daughter*, whose findings I would also like to gratefully acknowledge.

158. Details of this episode (the so-called "Senator Baranov" version) were repeated both in the text of the *History* and in the "Remarks on the Rebellion" (Zamechaniia o bunte) (*Pss*, VIII:150, 261).

159. *Pss*, VIII:252.

our perspective, revealing.[160] In July 1774 Derzhavin was in Saratov, which was under threat from the rebel forces and which Derzhavin felt it his duty to place in a condition of military preparedness. Derzhavin, it turns out, had been on a secret expedition, approved at the highest level (now, since his first protector Bibikov's demise, Major General Pavel Potemkin), to try to find out the whereabouts of Pugachev and to aid in his capture. It is unclear from Pushkin's *History* how much of the background of this secret expedition he was aware of. In any event, Derzhavin wrote in his *Notes* that he had been encouraged by Potemkin himself, who, while hinting at Catherine's largesse toward her loyal supporters, was "placing all his hope" on the young man.[161] Thus it was in a determined frame of mind that he set about to improve the situation in Saratov. Pushkin describes Derzhavin's sense of mission (recall that Derzhavin very much wanted and needed to make a name for himself) in the following terms: "At the end of July Derzhavin arrived in Saratov, where his rank of lieutenant in the Guards, his sharp mind, and his ardent character gave him significant influence on the general opinion."[162]

But in Saratov the hot-tempered and righteous Derzhavin immediately came into conflict with the commandant of the city's fortress, Colonel Boshnyak.[163] Derzhavin did not believe the city was properly fortified, but Boshnyak, for his part, was not going to have his authority undermined by this brash young intruder. Derzhavin played his trump card by writing Potemkin and receiving from the latter an order requiring Boshnyak, under threat of trial, to carry out the proper preparations.[164] Derzhavin went so far on his own that, when the local population began to "grumble" at the measures being forced on them, he gathered those of them that he could and made them sign statements saying they would be executed if they believed Pugachev was indeed Tsar Peter III and if they did not aid in every way in his capture. Pushkin even writes that, losing his temper, Derzhavin attempted at this point to have

160. Tsyavlovsky also makes the probable connection between Derzhavin's role in the fall of Saratov and Pushkin's comment to Nashchokin, but he does not expand further on it. See Tsiavlovskii, *Rasskazy o Pushkine*, 123 (see n. 131, above).

161. Derzhavin, *Sochineniia*, VI:493 (see n. 95, above).

162. *Pss*, VIII:182.

163. For a full overview of this conflict with Boshnyak and Derzhavin's behavior in Saratov, see Ia. K. Grot, *Materialy dlia biografii Derzhavina. 1773–1777. Deiatel'nost' i perepiska Derzhavina vo vremia pugachevskogo bunta* (St. Petersburg: v tipografii Imperatorskoi Akademii Nauk, 1861), 52–88. See also Derzhavin, *Sochineniia*, VIII:154–75.

164. Derzhavin, *Sochineniia*, VI:494.

Boshnyak arrested.[165] Then in early August, upon learning that Pugachev had left Penza and was en route to Petrovsk, Derzhavin asked for and was granted permission by the local authorities to mount a detachment of Cossacks to go to Petrovsk and save the weapons there from falling into his hands.[166] But the mission failed because the rebel forces had already taken Petrovsk; in fact, when they had the opportunity Derzhavin's Cossacks went over to Pugachev, and Derzhavin himself, with Pugachev hotly in pursuit, was barely able to make it back to Saratov.

It is here in Pushkin's *History* that we find the one sentence that is most likely the explanation to the Nashchokin recollection: "Derzhavin managed to get to Saratov, whence on the next day he left with Lodyzhinsky [a civilian 'brigadier' responsible for overseeing the welfare of the colonists],[167] leaving the defense of the city in charge of the Boshnyak he had reviled." The connection is then further strengthened by the account of how, once the rebels attacked, Boshnyak, like Mironov, fought bravely, though ineffectively, against the odds, and how as a last-ditch effort the commandant left the fortress with a handful of men and took the attack to Pugachev, fighting "for six hours straight . . . through countless throngs of bandits."[168] The difference between fact and fiction in this case is that Boshnyak somehow survived, whereas Mironov was quickly captured and hanged by Pugachev. The Boshnyak-Panin version of Derzhavin's conduct under fire was bound to be damning. In fact,

165. *Pss*, VIII:182.

166. A fascinating coincidence occurs at this point. On the eve of the Petrovsk expedition, Derzhavin had the following vision: "Standing in the middle of his room (in a peasant's hut) and conversing with Lodyzhinsky, Novosiltsov, and Sverbeev [local officials and military comrades], he looked by chance out the small side window and saw there the head of a skeleton, all white, as if it were composed out of mist. It seemed to him that it was opening wide its eyes and clanking its teeth. Even though, as Derzhavin says, it was difficult at that sight to ward off the feeling of superstitious fear, he still did not put off his journey, nor did he tell anyone about the vision, which any person would take to be a bad omen" (Derzhavin, *Sochineniia*, VIII:165–66; Grot, *Materialy*, 67). Recall in this context Pushkin's own superstitious feelings about the "shade of Derzhavin" and his pointed use of the image of a Derzhavinian skeleton-cum-military man (Sergeant-of-the-Guards Kurilkin) in "The Coffinmaker."

167. Lodyzhinsky was a Derzhavin ally. In terms of rank, he was technically superior to Boshnyak, but because of his lack of military experience, which he acknowledged, there continued to be confusion and acrimonious debate about who was actually in charge of the defense of Saratov.

168. *Pss*, VIII:183.

Count Panin,[169] the commander-in-chief, presumably through Boshnyak's testimony, became so skeptical of Derzhavin's role in the fall of Saratov that he demanded an official accounting and went so far as to threaten to hang Derzhavin as a traitor along with Pugachev. Thus, Derzhavin's military exploits during the *pugachevshchina* were cast under a shadow, and it took much effort on his part and on the part of his protectors to clear his name.

There is no historical evidence to confirm that Pushkin ever read Derzhavin's autobiographical *Notes* (Zapiski). Indeed, these *Notes* are believed to have existed in only one copy that remained with Derzhavin's widow until 1842, several years after Pushkin's death.[170] In addition, there is Pushkin's own statement in a footnote to the fifth chapter of the *History* that "Derzhavin has written his notes which, unfortunately, have not yet been published."[171] Here, ironically, the "unfortunately" (*k sozhaleniiu*) could mean one of two things: it is a shame that Pushkin has not had access to them or it is a shame that he cannot quote them because they are not yet published. Strong evidence exists, however, that Pushkin probably did not read the *Notes:* he leaves the impression in the *History* that Derzhavin departed Saratov abruptly and for no good reason (i.e., the "Boshnyak-Panin" version). But in his *Notes* Derzhavin makes it quite clear that he was determined on remaining in Saratov as the enemy approached ("Derzhavin, bearing the name of an officer, considered it unbecoming to remove himself from the path of danger"[172]), but then was called away by the news of the threat to the peasants at nearby Malykovka, where he had spent a good part of the campaign and had established loyal contacts. These approximately fifteen hundred peasants feared for their lives if they did not go over to Pugachev and requested that Derzhavin, if he was still alive, come to Malykovka and lead them to Saratov. Gerasimov, Derzhavin's factotum in Malykovka, wrote that the peasants there had been affected by the report of the Cossack about-face in Petrovsk, and in order to save the situation it was paramount for Derzhavin "to come himself as quickly as possible

169. As if to make matters more complicated, by this point in the campaign Panin had his own personal reasons for disliking the outspoken Derzhavin and thus for favoring the version of events offered by Boshnyak.

170. *Pss,* VIII:221. See Derzhavin, *Sochineniia,* VI:409: "The real *Notes* were kept as a secret [*khranilis' kak taina*]."

171. Grot states that Pushkin's request to Derzhavin's heirs for permission to see the poet's papers on the Pugachev Rebellion was denied (*Materialy,* 1). He also alludes to the unreliability of certain aspects of Pushkin's version of Derzhavin's activities.

172. Derzhavin, *Sochineniia,* VI:498.

and to encourage the accursed masses [*prokliataia chern'*] with his own person." [173] Thus, under such circumstances, it would have been equally "base" of Derzhavin if he had turned his back on these men. Derzhavin informed Lodyzhinsky of the situation and left a written explanation that is documented in the *Notes*.[174] It is difficult to believe, therefore, that Pushkin would have left the impression that he did in the *History* had he read Derzhavin's *Notes* and understood the complexities of his dilemma. This means, in effect, that Push-

173. Grot in Derzhavin, *Sochineniia*, VIII:170.

174. Derzhavin, *Sochineniia*, VI:499. This is the conscientious Grot's balanced (and wordy) assessment of the episode in *Materialy*, 69: "In his *Notes* Derzhavin attempts to justify his action [the decision to leave Saratov] primarily with the help of two circumstances: first, by citing the fact that several days before his mission to Petrovsk Boshnyak had given him an order from the Governor of Astrakhan that stated that, if Derzhavin was in charge of an armed unit, he was not to remain in Saratov but to go to Irgiz; and second, by citing the written notification received by Derzhavin from Gerasimov that the Malykovka peasants, who had been gathered at Derzhavin's order and who were approaching Saratov, had heard about the betrayal [to the Pugachev side] of the Cossacks at Petrovsk and did not want to go any further, demanding that Derzhavin, if he were still alive, come himself to them and lead them to the city. While neither of the two documents cited here is among Derzhavin's papers, we still do not doubt that that they existed, because in his justificatory report to Count P. I. Panin, who subsequently demanded from him an accounting as to why Saratov was left, they are shown to be among the appendices as Nos. 12 and 13. Against these justifications one may note only that we cannot find the two documents in the report to P. S. Potemkin written shortly after the event. But here one needs to bear in mind that by then Derzhavin had no need to justify himself: he asks simply that Potemkin not lay on him the charge of cowardice because he left Saratov. That he sent to the Malykovka peasants the order to hasten to the city is only confirmed by what is said in the *Notes* about the news received about them, although on the other hand it opens up the possibility that Derzhavin did not dare to go to meet them, about which he speaks in detail in the *Notes*." And then in Derzhavin, *Sochineniia*, VIII:169: "To such an extent did Derzhavin, with his insistent arguments, turn Boshnyak against him that the latter could announce, on the eve of the Petrovsk expedition, that by order of the Governor he [Derzhavin] must immediately remove himself to Irgiz as the place properly designated for his current billeting. And although after this Derzhavin was fully within his rights not to await Pugachev's attack on Saratov, even more so since he, having arrived temporarily with a distinct goal, and without military command, was in no way obligated to participate in the defense of Saratov according to a plan that he himself strenuously opposed, still, feeling his honor as a Russian officer, he decided to share the danger with the other inhabitants of the city: he requested from Major Semanzh a company that currently lacked an officer-in-charge, and he had already assumed command when an unexpected circumstance forced him to reject that plan, demanding [instead] his presence in another place."

kin wrote both the *History* and *The Captain's Daughter* believing that, with regard to the capture of Saratov, Derzhavin had acted as a coward.

Be all this as it may, there are so many parallels between Derzhavin's real life (details of which Pushkin must have known well) and Grinev's fictionalized life during the Pugachev rebellion that it seems more than likely that Pushkin had the older poet in mind, at least typologically, as he worked on his own maturing *nedorosl'* (minor). Add to this the fact that Pushkin himself, in his comments to Nashchokin, makes the connection between Derzhavin's behavior during the uprising and the fate of the endearing Mironov, and the case appears stronger still. Here, for example, are some of the possible parallels between Derzhavin's biography leading up to and during the *pugachevshchina* (gleaned from the *Notes*), on the one hand, and *The Captain's Daughter*, on the other: (1) Derzhavin and Petrusha Grinev come from provincial gentry backgrounds; (2) both are given rudimentary educations right out of Fonvizin's *Nedorosl'* (Derzhavin's emphasizes German, Grinev's French); (3) both have typical father-patriarchs who decide to enlist their sons in the tsarist military; (4) both learn about the life of a soldier "from the bottom up" (by the time of the *pugachevshchina* both are junior officers); (5) both go through a learning period where they gamble and make undesirable acquaintances (theme of cardsharping); (6) both try their hand at poetry as simple military men; (7) both come to understand that their future is tied to their activities during the Pugachev rebellion; (8) both meet people who bind their fates in seemingly mysterious ways to both Pugachev and Catherine (Serebryakov, Maksimov); (9) both actually come to fight together at one point (as Grot was the first to suggest, the Lieutenant Colonel Petr Grinev who was Derzhavin's comrade-in-arms in Samara became the hero of Pushkin's historical romance);[175] (10) both mount or try to mount various secret expeditions during the rebellion; (11) both come to defy the local bureaucracy in acts of insubordination; (12) both are nearly killed by Pugachev; (13) both face various legal problems after the revolt is quelled (both are denounced, through others, to the empress, so that their future remains for a time in doubt); (14) both see Pugachev himself

175. It is intriguing in this regard that Lieutenant Colonel Grinev's activities are described within paragraphs of the same chapter 5 of Pushkin's *History* where Derzhavin's already mentioned bravery in putting down a riot and hanging its instigators becomes a prominent theme (*Pss*, VIII:149–50). There was also another Grinev known to Pushkin, Second Lieutenant A. M., who like Derzhavin was charged with abetting Pugachev and who had to clear his name (cited Reyfman, "Autobiographical Echoes," 469 [see n. 157, above]). This of course only reinforces the Grinev-Derzhavin thematic nexus.

face-to-face in a *tulup* (hareskin or sheepskin coat);[176] and (15) both have their fortunes decided—though Grinev's, to be sure, is the more "novelistic"— through the direct intercession of Catherine herself.[177]

Having cited such parallels, however, we must not forget the essential difference: Pushkin believed Derzhavin was capable of baseness (*spodlichal*), while his hero Grinev never loses his *personal* honor.[178] How is this difference incorporated into the actual text of the novel? It is, I would suggest, smuggled into the work as a variant on the theme, already heavily mediated by Derzhavin, of inspiration. In this regard, not only does Pushkin "leave the hero his heart"[179] in his shift from the factual to the novelistic Pugachev, he apparently does the same for this novelized "Derzhavin." In Grinev, Pushkin creates a Derzhavin type who is stripped of his later glory and fame: this version is a Derzhavin who, true to himself, seeks nothing more than the ideals of "peace, cabbage soup, and myself as boss." And the key to Grinev's character is that Pushkin endows him with his, and not Derzhavin's, version of *chest'* (honor) and *vdokhnovenie* (inspiration). The better Grinev gets to know Pugachev, the more articulate and, as it were, *inspired* become his answers to the risk-laden questions put to him by this human embodiment of history's dark heart. Pushkin gives to Grinev, who is no poet in terms of artistic talent,[180] that very

176. In Derzhavin (*Zapiski*) a *zasalennyi* (soiled) *tulup*, in Pushkin-Dmitriev (*History*) a *belyi baranii* (sheepskin) *tulup*, and in *The Captain's Daughter* a *zaiachii* (hareskin) *tulup*.

177. Reyfman mentions some additional typological parallels between Derzhavin and the novelistic Grinev in "Autobiographical Echoes," 470.

178. One implication of this interpretation is that the base Shvabrin becomes a receptacle for traits and themes associated with the "Saratov" (Boshnyak-Panin) Derzhavin. This would explain, for example, the theme of poetry in the relations between Shvabrin and Grinev. Shvabrin's "teacher" is Trediakovsky: Derzhavin was one of the very few writers, and the only one of his status, who continued to claim Trediakovsky as a model well into the late eighteenth and early nineteenth centuries. See discussion in Reyfman, "Autobiographical Echoes," 465–67.

179. The difference between the "elevating deceit" (*vozvyshaiushchii obman*) and the "low truth" (*nizkaia istina*) in Pushkin's poem "The Hero" (Geroi, 1830), where one of the speakers (the "poet") urges the "friend" to "leave the hero his heart," has often been used by critics as a way of understanding the different "Pugachevs"—the factual one of the *History* versus the mythical one of *The Captain's Daughter*.

180. Pushkin is making fun not only of Grinev the aspiring poet when he has the simple Ivan Kuzmich tell his hero that all poets are "dissolute people and hopeless drunks" (*Pss*, VI:284) and urge him to give up writing verse. He is also, in his typical droll way, making fun of himself. As he wrote Vyazemsky on 3 August 1831 in the context—not unlike the *pugachevshchina*—of the cholera-inspired riots at the Novgorod and Staraya

quality of mind he felt the real Derzhavin lacked: the ability *not to lose one's head,* or as Pushkin had written earlier, that "rapid grasp of ideas" that went along with the "vivid reception of impressions." One reason we can be fairly certain that Pushkin had his earlier definition of inspiration in mind as he worked on *The Captain's Daughter* is that he returns to it, virtually verbatim, in the contemporaneous *Egyptian Nights* (wr. 1835),[181] and, what is more, he sets it off against the notion of *external volition* (i.e., the historical theme): "No one except the improvisatore himself [i.e., the 'poet'] can comprehend this alacrity of impressions, this close tie between one's own inspiration and another's external will."[182] Hence in *The Captain's Daughter* inspiration becomes an existential and historical category and not merely a "poetic" one. Now Pushkin is not only, or not even primarily, confronting his great precursor on artistic terms. Rather he wants to place a certain kind of consciousness, which he inevitably links with his own, as close as possible to genuine risk, real historical turmoil, imminent and violent death. Lest we forget, this is the same "test," now much more specific and historicized, that Pushkin has sought from his first steps as a poet, when he regretted in "Recollections" not being able to join his older colleagues in the battle against Napoleon.[183]

Not fortuitously, it is "poetic awe" (*piiticheskii uzhas*) that arouses Grinev when, on the day his friends have been executed and he himself nearly hanged,

---

Rus military settlements, "It's bad, Your Highness. When such tragedies are before your eyes, there is no time to think about the dog show [*sobach'ia komediia*] of our literature" (*Pss*, X:289; *Letters*, 520).

181. "[Charsky] was a poet nevertheless, and his passion for poetry was indomitable: when he felt this *nonsense* approach (that was what he called inspiration), he locked himself in his study and wrote from morning till late night. . . . One morning Charsky felt he was in that exuberant state of mind when fantasies arise before you in clear outline, when you find vivid, unexpected words in which to incarnate your visions, when verses readily flow from your pen, and when resonant rhymes run up to meet well-ordered thoughts" (*Pss*, VI:245–46; *CPF*, 250). As stated, there are aspects of this description that echo very closely (*raspolozhenie dushi* vs. *raspolozhenie dukha*) phrasing found in Pushkin's draft definition of *vdokhnovenie* written some ten years earlier.

182. *Pss*, VI:251; *CPF*, 255.

183. Reyfman ("Autobiographical Echoes," 472–73) provides useful background on Pushkin's ongoing interest in (or perhaps obsession with?) the issue of personal courage in a dangerous situation (cf. Pushkin's famous audience with Nicholas to explain his attitude toward the Decembrist uprising) and of "a poet's possible role and mode of behavior during times of social upheaval."

he listens to the rebels sing their folk song about the gallows awaiting them.[184] And when asked by Pugachev during one of their several tête-à-têtes, "Don't you believe that I am your Sovereign Majesty? Give me a straight answer," Grinev hesitates before this particular riddle of survival and then answers in a way that shows he has taken a position *on the outside* of the irreconcilable binaries (*muzhik/barin*) of his historical situation. He answers both directly, in that he answers sincerely, and indirectly, in that he does not respond with a "yes" or "no." His conduct here and elsewhere stuns the novelistic Pugachev (*Moia iskrennost' porazila Pugacheva*[185]). Like Ivan Kuzmich (Captain Mironov), the military man Grinev père would have said "You're not our sovereign, you, fellow, are an impostor and pretender," which is, from within that individual's system, undoubtedly correct.[186] But the son, moved to answer differently, has his own reasons for not embracing the strict judgmental code of the father. He *tells Pugachev the truth* ("Listen, let me tell you the honest truth"[187]) by telling him that "God only knows" who he is and that his game, regardless of who he is, is a dangerous one. At the same time, he keeps his honor by again making explicit his refusal to serve as one of Pugachev's officers, even adding that, if given his freedom, he cannot promise not to fight against his present benefactor. In other words, as Pushkin carefully presents it, this is a moment not to lose oneself (i.e., Derzhavinian *vostorg* or the "misplaced sublime") but to find oneself, to become not the Poet in History, but a good and honest man who also happens to be the *inspired consciousness* in, and of, history. The autobiographical "notes" (*zapiski*) of the novelistic character Grinev, whose father's intitials are *A*[ndrei] *P*[etrovich] and whose own are *P*[etr] *A*[ndreevich], become then, in this reading, the *Zapiski* of Derzhavin to which the historian Pushkin was denied access but which he now, as "publisher"/*izdatel'*, rewrites in his own fashion as *The Captain's Daughter*.

Before turning to Pushkin's last encounter with Derzhavin in "Exegi monumentum," it might be well to revisit one final time Nashchokin's recollection. Given the power of the Pushkin icon and especially the way this national poet has been "monumentalized" in Soviet times, there is a tendency to take him calmly at his word and above all to establish authority by determining what it was the poet said (the textological tradition) and where the source for that

184. *Pss*, VI:314.
185. *Pss*, VI:316.
186. *Pss*, VI:308; *CPF*, 311.
187. *Pss*, VI:315.

particular utterance may reside ("subtextual" or "intertextual" approach).[188] But Pushkin's consciousness is not only an "archive" of sources but a dynamic, aggressive, "stand-in-relation-to" psychology. By now this same personality had been wrestling with the "shade of Derzhavin" for some twenty years. Is it not appropriate then, without resorting to the more intrusive forms of psychoanalytic criticism, at least to question why this statement was made in the manner it was and to whom it was? I would argue in this connection that the summary boldness of Pushkin's condemnation — there is no room for any semantic ambiguity in the terms *spodlichat'* (to act basely) and *strusit'* (to act cowardly) — is strange in the context of Derzhavin's recorded courage in dispersing the mob as described earlier in Pushkin's *History*. How can Derzhavin enter a village with two Cossacks and turn back a potentially violent crowd in one instance and lose his head before Pugachev's attack on Saratov in another? So scrupulous with his sources elsewhere in the *History* and so intrigued with the eyewitness accounts of other poets and men of letters (e.g., Dmitriev, Krylov), could not Pushkin have found some additional information from those who knew Derzhavin and his version of the siege to support a less judgmental interpretation?

I would suggest, speculatively, that Pushkin was at some level not displeased with the Boshnyak-Panin version of events. That version left Pushkin the artist (as opposed to historian) something to work with, something that was his own, not Derzhavin's ("leave the hero his heart"). Furthermore, I would argue that the Grinev Pushkin inserts into the maelstrom of *pugachevshchina* is *his* (and his generation's) creation and comports himself in a way that, as Pushkin thought, Derzhavin had not done. The character traits that emerge as most salient in Grinev are (1) history *happens* to him with an amazing, almost prehensile force; and (2) regardless of the circumstances, he retains his honor and his openness to the wonder of events. It is not his *fame* as poet or statesman that counts, but precisely his commitment to keeping his word ("*Beregi chest' smolodu*," Protect your honor from an early age, his father tells

---

188. The Soviet textological approach (Oksman, Gillelson and Mushina, Petrunina, etc.) has meticulously gone through Pushkin's various "plans" for *The Captain's Daughter* and shown how the character of Grinev evolved from earlier versions (Shvanvich, Basharin, Valuev) and eventually split between the nobleman-cum-Pugachevian rebel (the final Shvabrin) and the nobleman who comes in contact with the "people's tsar," yet remains loyal (the final Grinev). My interest here is different: the psychology of creativity or "deep structure" underlying Pushkin's choice of Grinev as the noble (in both senses) youth who confronts Pugachev and passes the test Derzhavin failed. See below.

him), without which no other version of immortality is worthwhile. Although the biography is not his, I would argue that these traits, together with his vivid storytelling skills, belong to Pushkin's best friend and favorite interlocutor, Pavel Nashchokin. Here, for example, is how Gershenzon describes the Nashchokin underlying the contemporaneously composed but unfinished *Russian Pelham* hero: "everywhere he is able to find his footing quickly, everywhere he retains lucidity of thought and nobility of soul; it's as if he is inoculated against filth and lies, and in spite of all the pliability and instability in his character, he displays an amazing moral sturdiness."[189] Annenkov, likewise, suggests that in Nashchokin Pushkin had found his "man of experience [or yesteryear]" (*byvalyi chelovek*), who "personified the idea of an individual composed morally, so to speak, of pure gold, who never lost his value, no matter where he went or where he might turn up."[190] Left to sing in his "cruel century" (*zhestokii vek*), Pushkin responds by placing the "pure gold" of his generation back in a historical crisis situation where, apparently, Derzhavin failed. This was *his* word.

With its subject of the poet's legacy and its simultaneous adherence to and departure from Horatian and Derzhavinian subtexts about immortality, "I have erected for myself a monument not made by hand" has elicited a truly massive response in the secondary literature over the years. Some of the finest Pushkinists have tried to carve their initials on this monument, including such names as Gershenzon, Lednicki, and Alekseev. Because the lucid surface of Pushkin's words conceals fathomless, or what contemporary critics might call "abyssmal," depths of possible meaning, a strange (or possibly not so strange?) occurrence has taken place. The *slava* predicted in the poem has, in a significant way, obscured the contours of the original monument. Zhukovsky's well-meaning but ultimately crude emendations, inserted in order to make ideologically acceptable a work Pushkin presumably was not writing for publication in his lifetime, is the first such example of posthumous monumentalization. Another is the Soviet policy of orthographic atheism. With so many gardeners fastidiously tending the grounds around the monument's base, we have learned to approach the actual text only through a mesmerizing labyrinth of side arbors, self-enclosing hedgerows, and elaborately arranged flowerbeds in all their interpretive bloom. If not the *narodnaia tropa* (people's path) of the poem, then something else has grown up and around this most

189. Gershenzon, "Drug Pushkina," 221 (see n. 129, above).
190. Cited in Gershenzon, "Drug Pushkina," 221.

central of all Russian poetic monuments. Perhaps the most striking example of this phenomenon is M. P. Alekseev's 1967 study of the poem and its reception history. While it is certainly heroic in its willingess to gather all pertinent sources and to record how the poem has been read and misread over the past two centuries, the reader is left with a dizzying sense of not seeing the scholarly forest for the trees and with a powerful need for a simpler explanatory narrative. In this regard, it might be argued that an earlier-generation Pushkinist such as Gershenzon, who could not hope to compete with Alekseev in terms of sheer information and scholarly apparatus, is still somehow "closer" to Pushkin's monument.

I propose in this final section of my study to return to the three psychological traits of Pushkin's creative personality with which we began: his competitive urge and independence, his superstition, and his passion for formal symmetry or composition. By showing how these "dominanta" reengage Derzhavin one last time, I am not suggesting that this is the only explanatory narrative for the poem. As Pushkin turned to glance back over all his life and work up to August 1836, the possibilities for generating poetic narrative were close to infinite. Still, it will be my thesis that the return to Derzhavin in late 1836, under conditions of writing a poem about immortality and one's place in history, is certainly a potent and even crucial narrative.

First, the immediate biographical context, that not relating specifically to the words in the poem. Any understanding of "I have erected" would have to take as an implicit point of departure the major circumstances affecting Pushkin's mood during the last year of his life, including but not limited to a severe vulnerability with regard to questions of his wife's honor[191] and an eagerness, at the slightest pretext, to call a possible offender out to a duel (e.g., the Khliustin and Count Sollogub episodes); mounting debts (in the tens of thousands of rubles), together with waning popularity (only six hundred subscribers to *The Contemporary*); a social position that bordered on the untenable and dishonorable (the Moscow post office was still opening his personal mail); the death of his mother in March and the arrangement of his own burial plot next to hers at Sviatye gory (Mikhailovskoe), which was seen to at the time of her interment; and the coming twenty-fifth reunion of Lyceum comrades in October, which would inevitably elicit both warm memories and thoughts of those either dead (Delvig) or exiled (Pushchin, Küchelbecker).

191. Pushkin's letters to his wife over the last years are filled with anxious admonishments to monitor her behavior in a public setting and, if she must, to "play the coquette" (*koketnichat'*) in a seemly fashion.

Despite the original French enlightenment values, Pushkin was a remarkably *organic* personality. In a lyric poem, whose place was in a deeply personal cycle with a paschal message, these and other circumstances would have to serve as necessary orienting coordinates as one prepares to enter the poem.

"I have erected" is, as I have intimated, both a turning to Horace's ode "To Melpomene" ("Exegi monumentum") and Derzhavin's reworking of Horace in his "Pamiatnik," and a turning away from those sources.[192] Herein lies its essence as ultimate, final (re)turning. One recalls that by 1836 an entire pseudotradition of questionable imitations of Derzhavin's own imitation of Horace had grown up on Russian soil: not only was Pushkin aware of this development (and presumably to some degree scornful of it), he had been, in his own way, hovering at its edges since the early 1820s.[193] Yet Pushkin's "I have erected" is least of all a parody in the traditional sense, that is, its aim is not

192. I realize how my wording here (turning to + turning away) may sound, contra arguments elsewhere in this study, potentially "Bloomian." And this fact in turn creates, with its Freudian logic, its own version of anxiety of influence. To this I would respond by underscoring a point also made earlier in these pages: in the Russian context of the time, something else was at stake than merely "swerving" from Horace's and Derzhavin's *words*. In speaking the "truth" or vouching for "free speech" in a political system that was arbitrary and oppressive, poets could still compete with one another for priority in the tradition, but it is unlikely that that sort of rivalry was uppermost or determinative in their minds. The notion of another all-controlling father, beginning with the tsar, was just too close to the literal surface of things. To repeat, what Pushkin was denied access to by his belatedness was, in the first place, the older poet's *existential* options—his ability/chance to be "historical," his closeness (however complicated) to Catherine and those in power, what seemed to posterity as the very "office" of poet he created for himself, and the positive or "heroic" shape of his biography (from lowly gentry origins to great man rather than from ancient noble heritage to *kameriunker*—Pushkin's downward trajectory).

193. In 1821 N. Ostopolov published Horace's ode in the Latin original accompanied by Derzhavin's "imitation" and Vostokov's translation (cited Alekseev, "Stikhotvorenie Pushkina," 87n10 [see n. 23, above]). In 1823, while working on the closing stanzas (39–40) of the second chapter of *Eugene Onegin*, Pushkin was already thinking in terms of the Horatian-Derzhavinian texts as ways to encode his own right to immortality. To be sure, his tone there, in keeping with the time of composition and the intricate distancing of the Onegin stanza, is more playful. In one manuscript variant, for example, he considered two possible ways of ending stanza 39: *Vozdvignul pamiatnik [i] ia* (And I too have erected a monument) and *Exegi monumentum ia*. See discussion in Alekseev, "Stikhotvorenie Pushkina," 132–36. For the pseudotradition of homages to Derzhavin in the form of new imitations of his reworking of Horace, a practice that became particularly popular in the two decades following Derzhavin's death (1816), see Alekseev, "Stikhotvorenie Pushkina," 206–8.

to use the prior utterances of the great odists in order to mock them or defeat them on a poetic field of battle.[194] In every instance in Pushkin's poem where he cites and then slightly misquotes or distorts Derzhavin, the tone of that distortion does not come to rest on the pride of his, Pushkin's, earthly accomplishment. The secret of this "Exegi monumentum" is that it both records its legitimate right to *slava* and immortality and in the same breath turns away from that right. How does Pushkin manage this, and what does this mean in terms of the poem itself?

I would suggest that the poem needs to be read, first of all, from within several contexts simultaneously and that its stereoscopic splendor becomes apparent only when we as interpreters walk around it and gaze up at it from these various — but each crucially important — angles. The first such angle is the poem's placement in the Stone Island cycle,[195] which Pushkin composed in summer 1836: "Secular Power" (Mirskaia vlast', 5 July), "Imitation of the Italian" (Podrazhanie italiianskomu, 22 June), "From Pindemonte" (Iz Pindemonti, 5 July), "Hermit fathers and immaculate women" (Ottsy pustynniki i zheny neporochny, 22 July), "When I, pensive, roam beyond the city" (Kogda za gorodom, zadumchiv, ia brozhu, 14 August), and "I have erected" (21 August). As Sergei Davydov has persuasively demonstrated, this cycle is structured around the Easter Week calendar and the "ways of the cross."[196] Space does not permit a full exfoliation of Davydov's argument, but in essence he

194. Bondi, for example, who is correct to focus on the *departures* (*otstupleniia*) from Derzhavin in Pushkin's text, appears to link this fact too narrowly with the "worldly" strategies of satire and parody (*O Pushkine*, 446–467 passim, esp. 448). See as well the comparative analysis in Zapadov, *Masterstvo*, 252–55; and in Stennik, *Pushkin*, 316–21 (see n. 23, above).

195. N. V. Izmailov ("Stikhotvorenie Pushkina 'Mirskaia vlast' [Vnov' naidennyi avtograf]," *Izvestiia Akademii Nauk SSSR. Otdelenie literatury i iazyka* 13.6 [1954]: 555) first proposed that "I have erected" be included in the Stone Island cycle, but in initial position. Subsequently, scholars such as N. L. Stepanov (*Lirika Pushkina* [Moscow: Khudozhestvennaia literatura, 1959], 32) and especially Alekseev ("Stikhotvorenie Pushkina," 119–21) have disputed Izmailov's finding, primarily on formal grounds (i.e., the truncated fourth lines of each stanza of "I have erected" do not fit the metric profile of the rest of the cycle). Still, based on Davydov's (and also Stark's) evidence (see n. 2, above), it is difficult to suppose that this poem, with its dating and thematics, does not in a significant way "belong" to the indisputable Christian framework of the cycle — a framework which, for obvious ideological reasons, Soviet scholars have not been able to discuss until recently. The least that can be said is that "I have erected" shares in the tone of the cycle and at every level appears to be "infected" by it.

196. "Pushkin's Easter Triptych," 38–58 (see n. 2, above).

thinks through the emerging Christian thematics of these poems and comes to the conclusion that, despite their disputed numeration, they should be arranged in order to reflect the simultaneity in Pushkin's mind between poetic and Christian immortality (what Davydov calls "aesthetic theology"). Paramount in Davydov's reading is Pushkin's shift in the cycle, *which is also representative of a shift over the course of his life and career,* from pagan values (the plural "gods," *bogi,* of "From Pindemonte") to Christian ones (the central concerns of Christ's betrayal, crucifixion, and burial in "Imitation of the Italian," "Secular Power," and "When I, pensive, roam"). Also important is the evolution from pride (the supreme independence and self-sufficiency of the poet in "From Pindemonte") to Christian humility (the "To the will of God, O Muse, be obedient" of "I have erected"). Finally, Davydov shows how the Pushkin of late 1836 uses another's word (*chuzhoe slovo*) differently in these poems: in "Hermit fathers," for example, the poet cites virtually verbatim the prayer of St. Ephraem the Syrian in order not to mock (recall the use of Derzhavin's words in "Fonvizin's Shade") but to purge himself, in a Christian act of askesis, of the sin of "idle talk" (*prazdnoslovie*)—to tear out, in this last act of poetic self-mutilation and transcendance, the "sly and empty-talking tongue" of the sinner transformed into truth teller known to readers of the earlier "Prophet." Thus, as Davydov summarizes, "I have erected" should be read as the capstone of the cycle, "beautifully reflect[ing] [its] inner movement" and "point[ing] toward the day of Resurrection (Sunday)."[197] In its path from "No, all of me won't die" to "To the will of God, O Muse, be obedient" it retraces Pushkin's own final thoughts about the simultaneity (but not necessarily equality) of Christian resurrection and secular fame.

The most basic difference between the beginning Pushkin of "Recollections at Tsarskoe Selo" and the concluding Pushkin of "I have erected" is the presence of a *lived* biography. In this respect, Davydov's position (the structure of the cycle) can be usefully expanded upon. "I have erected" is a return to origins, above all to Tsarskoe Selo, but from the position of 1836 and from the now poetically *constructed* life implicated in that return. It forms, to a significant degree, the capstone of that "bio-aesthetic" cycle as well. All the life and art that have been lived and created between "Recollections" and "I have erected" are given their "final word" in these lines. There is nothing artificial or purely cerebral about this shaping process; quite the opposite in fact, since Pushkin is including those details that have become illuminated from within

197. "Pushkin's Easter Triptych," 57.

by his own values, friendships, personal triumphs and failures. Each word in "I have erected" has a literary and at the same time a private, hermetic meaning. Thus, at virtually every level of the poem, Pushkin is reinvoking in some important way the terms of his first confrontation with Derzhavin. Formally, for example, he is using a stanzaic pattern that, while differing from Horace and Derzhavin, occurs only one other time in his oeuvre: in the Lyceum period piece "Napoleon on Elba" (Napoleon na El'be, 1815).[198] Thematically, he is remembering and reincarnating many of the salient topoi of "Recollections": the contrast between Catherine's golden era and his own "cruel century," the shape of personal and national history, the desire for glory (the theme of martial conquest) and secular immortality (cf. the similar phrase in the earlier poem describing the coming fame of Catherine's gallant zemnye bogi [gods on earth], proidet molva iz roda v rod), the nobility of mercy (Alexander the victor carrying the olive branch into Paris), the central image of a monument (cf. the Chesma column and Kagula obelisk), and of course Derzhavin and the role of the poet in history.

I do not mean by this that Pushkin is somehow consciously parodying his former self or that "I have erected" is an inverted template of "Recollections." Pushkin's primary models are, to repeat, Horace and Derzhavin. Rather what I would like to suggest, following but also adjusting somewhat the focus of Alekseev and others, is that Pushkin was returning to the semantic and psychological fields of the Lyceum years through the prism of his capstone poem and that he could not do this without modifying that particular "ontological rhyme." Thus, the pagan, irreverent, Arzamasian references to jolly corpses and the underworld in a poem such as "Fonvizin's Shade" become, on the one hand, the torments of the damned (Judas) in a Christian hell in "Imitation of the Italian" (the sin of pride), and, on the other, the simple, Christian, prayer-like imitatio of "Hermit fathers" (the virtue of humility). So too do the youthful Anacreontic concerns of feasting, carpe diem, and a graveside humor projected exclusively from the vantage of this world become transmuted into the otherworldly ruminations and the deadly serious notion of the grave as final resting place in "When I, pensive, roam." Even a line so

---

198. Cited Alekseev, "Stikhotvorenie Pushkina," 118–19. Vickery (" 'Vospominaniia,' " 486–90 [see n. 23, above]) has also suggested there may be an "intonational" link between the penultimate and ultimate lines of the stanzas in "Recollections" and "Pamiatnik": i.e., a full 6-foot (alexandrine length) line followed syntactically in one breath by a concluding truncated (3- vs. 4-foot) line.

thoroughly embedded intertextually as "No, all of me won't die"[199] cannot be linked simply, as fact of literature *tout court*, to Derzhavin and Horace, but must be made to resonate, for certainly Pushkin's mind was not forgetting it, with the line in "The Little Town": "Not all of me shall be given over to decay" (*Ne ves' ia predan tlen'iu*). Here, then, I would like to make the point that in this final shaping of his biography Pushkin was *settling accounts*: he was, simultaneously, asserting a special brand of "nonanxious" independence, recognizing the cost of his past life (the merging of superstition with Christian askesis), and structuring this moment as a displaced symmetry or epistrophe.

With these preliminaries, we are now ready to analyze the final encounter with Derzhavin. Derzhavin begins his "Monument" with

> I have erected for myself a monument wondrous, eternal,
> it is firmer than metal and taller than the pyramids;
> neither whirlwind nor fleet-moving thunder can break it,
> and time's flight cannot destroy it.[200]

Pushkin begins his, following the Horatian epigraph ("Exegi monumentum"), with

> I have erected for myself a monument not made by hand,
> the people's path to it shall not be overgrown,
> its unsubmissive head has ascended higher
> than the Alexander [lit. "Alexandrine"] column.[201]

Two points can be made immediately about these similar but also quite different openings. First, Derzhavin published his in 1795, more than *twenty* years before his death, as a Lomonosov-inspired exercise to transpose Horace to his own situation. Indeed, Derzhavin made at least three attempts at erecting his monument for posterity: "My Statue" (Moi istukan, 1794), which served as a rehearsal for the present poem; "Monument," which was originally entitled

---

199. Curiously, halfway through his career Pushkin would have his condemned speaker utter, in "André Chénier" (Andrei Shen'e, 1825), "Soon all of me will die" (*Ia skoro ves' umru*) (*Pss*, II:233).

200. «Я памятник себе воздвиг чудесный, вечный, / Металлов тверже он и выше пирамид; / Ни вихрь его, ни гром не сломит быстротечный, / И времени полет его не сокрушит» (Derzhavin, *Stikhotvoreniia*, 233 [see n. 46, above]).

201. «Я памятник себе воздвиг нерукотворный, / К нему не зарастет народная тропа, / Вознесся выше он главою непокорной / Александрийского столпа» (*Pss*, III:340).

"To the Muse. An Imitation of Horace" (K Muze. Podrazhanie Goratsiiu); and "The Swan" (Lebed', 1804). Thus, in keeping with his position as court poet and public figure, Derzhavin was more concerned with the *official* lineaments of his monument and with how those features would be recorded and received by *the public* in the future. He did not need to see his life as completed in order to prepare his monument for display; in fact, he could put the finishing touches on his monument, not once but several times, and he could do so with a substantial portion of his life still before him ("The Swan" is significant here because it can be assumed that Derzhavin the public figure *is* complete at the time of its composition). Needless to say, Pushkin's attitude toward the erecting of his monument is totally different: this is, as we have said, his *final* word; his life is viewed as if not complete, then very close to being so; and the aspects of the monument that are open to public interpretation are, as we shall see, those that concern him least.

This last point leads directly into the second major difference in these openings: Derzhavin's tendency, given his time and place, to confident (i.e., unconscious) *literalization,* with regard both to the Horatian subtext[202] and to the notion of *pamiatnik* itself; Pushkin's tendency, given his coordinates, to the figurative, but the figurative that hides abysses of private, concrete meaning. Derzhavin's words are closer to the surface of *things;* there is no room in them for irony or ambiguity vis-à-vis predecessors. Horace and Lomonosov are simply the occasions legitimizing his monument. The first modifiers for his legacy are "wondrous, eternal": while abstract, they stress the monument's *outer* glory and imperviousness to the vagaries of time. Likewise, the other images in the stanza all have to do either with the monument's stout construction (firmer than *metal,* taller than *pyramids*) or with its permanence in the face of nature (*whirlwind, thunder*) or time. Derzhavin's words stand there, like a statue, prepared to withstand any external force outside them. They are *monumentalized.*

Pushkin's words are both permanent and shimmering with a multitude of inner meanings. His first departure from Horace and Derzhavin is the marked (i.e., final position) insertion of "not made by hand" (*nerukotvornyi*) for "wondrous, eternal." This word instantly moves the dialogue with Derzhavin *inward.* Pushkin cares not for the literalized monument, for the bust

---

202. Cf.: "Exegi monumentum aere perennius / Regalique situ pyramidum altius, / Quod non imber edax, non Aquilo impotens / Possit diruere aut innumerabilis / Annorum series et fuga temporum."

or the statue, but for the continuously released energy of the poetic word
and for the *miracle of personality*. This word *nerukotvornyi* looks in two directions simultaneously. First, given its placement in the Stone Island cycle,
it invokes the Christ who promises to destroy "this temple made by hand"
(*khram sei rukotvornyi*) and to erect in three days "another not made by hand"
(*drugoi nerukotvornyi*) (Mark 14:58). And second, it seems to Christianize
Derzhavin's pagan monument: hidden but not developed in the precursor's
"*chudnyi*" (*wondrous*) is the miracle of poetic speech, its "*chudo + tvornyi
genii*" (wonder-working genius). Not wanting to repeat Derzhavin, Pushkin
avoids the literalization of *chudo* but then draws the reader's attention to the
miracle of that which is real, though not made by hand. Christ's representative, the verbal miracle worker (*chudo + tvorets*), looks at his work, which is
miraculous (*neruko* [miracle] + *tvornyi* [made]).

But the problem of Derzhavin's literalization and Pushkin's mature reaction
to it goes even deeper than this.[203] Derzhavin's "Monument" was flanked by
both "My Statue" and "The Swan": both poems would have been not only
well known to Pushkin but immediately implicated, in a very personal way,
in his own poem. Derzhavin's penchant for literalization, which goes hand
in hand with his preromantic, undivided character, is particularly evident in
"My Statue," when he addresses an actual bust recently completed for him by
the sculptor Jean Dominique Rachette. In this work he carries on a dialogue
with himself about his claim to immortality, and at one point, convinced that
his greatest contribution was his usefulness to Catherine, he imagines his bust
being moved into the Colonnade (the so-called Cameron Gallery) inside the
old palace at Tsarskoe Selo, where the pedestaled likenesses of Russia's "im-

---

203. To be fair to Derzhavin, it should be noted that he was certainly not unaware of
the difference between verbal and physical, three-dimensional monuments. As he writes
at the end of "To My Second Neighbor" (K vtoromu sosedu, 1791), where he compares
the "monumental" home of a self-promoting neighbor (M. A. Garnovsky) with the edifice of his own deeds: "It is only glory and the love of fellow citizens / that erect for us
sturdy homes; / they, like the heavens, / stand [firm] and despise the thunderbolts" (*Liubov' grazhdan i slava nam / Lish' vozdvigaiut prochny domy; / Oni, podobno nebesam, /
Stoiat i preziraiut gromy*) (*Stikhotvoreniia*, 177). He tells the neighbor not to build something (Garnovsky's house is under construction) that will steal the light from his abode
(understood both literally and figuratively). Even so, Derzhavin's monologic view of his
place in history — the man, the deeds, and the poet were all one — constituted for Pushkin
something too fully "embodied," not sufficiently self-aware (i.e., *vostorzhennyi*), and in
this sense too given to the literal and to literalizing. That in some sense Pushkin *needed* to
see Derzhavin in these terms is itself doubtless significant.

mortals" were featured and where Catherine herself used to stroll and arrange balls. (See illustration 13.) As Derzhavin says in the explanatory note to his own works, "At Tsarskoe Selo there was a Colonnade, decorated either with half idols or with the busts of famous men, among whom was Lomonosov. The author thought that in time he too would have such a right."[204] While Derzhavin fears that he will be accused of flattering Catherine (in his case prophetic considering what happened to his monument in the post-Pushkin years) and in the end advises his wife to keep the bust at home next to that of Catherine, this very literalization of his fame (the posthumous placement of the poet as *kumir* [idol] at Tsarskoe Selo) was bound to be a factor in Puskin's deliteralizing of *slava* in his own "I have erected." Derzhavin's bust was too close to several things: the notion of fame as actual heroic deeds/*podvigi* (military, governmental),[205] the notion of tsar as wise patron, the notion of actual, physical pantheon, and finally the notion of Tsarskoe Selo as sacred territory.

Derzhavin's third attempt at immortalizing himself, this time in the flight of a Pindaric and Horatian swan, is, if it is possible, even more reconditely embedded in the deliteralizing layers of "I have erected." For it is here that the voice of Delvig enters, a final time, into the creative process. To get to Delvig, however, we must look first at the only mention of a literal monument in Pushkin's first stanza: the Alexandrine column erected in honor of the Emperor Diocletian in Alexandria in the fourth century, but which here is clearly a calque for the massive Alexander column, unveiled in 1834 on Palace Square in St. Petersburg in a ceremony demonstrably not attended by Pushkin. Rather than Derzhavin's Horatian and universalist pyramids, Pushkin has decided to include an allusion that penetrates deeply into his own personal mythology. For this newest and grandest of columns was raised to commemorate Alexander's and Russia's victory over Napoleon—reference to it, therefore, takes us silently back to the original setting of "Recollections." Recall, first, the literal monuments of "Recollections"—the Chesma column (also a *stolp*) and the Kagula obelisk. (See illustration 12.) These monuments, which are the tangible traces of public, military, and, by association, *Derzhavinian* glory (and

---

204. Cited Grot in Derzhavin, *Sochineniia*, I:616 (see n. 95, above).

205. As Derzhavin exclaims in the first stanza of the poem, "But what sort of honor is it for me to be flattered / By this immortal bust? / Without glorious deeds resounding in the world, / Even a tsar is nothing in the form of an idol" (*No mne kakoiu chest'iu l'stit'sia / V bessmertnom istukane sem? / Bez slavnykh del, gremiashchikh v mire, / Nichto i tsar' v svoem kumire*) (*Stikhotvoreniia*, 200).

which the schoolboy Pushkin could proudly link with his own family history), are found in a poem about recollections at *Tsarskoe Selo,* a poem that also happens to be Pushkin's official debut as a poet. They also occur in a poem whose current hero is Alexander I. The pride of the first stanza of "I have erected" is double-edged: genuine, in the sense that this "Alexander's" head is yet "unsubmissive" and extends higher than that "Alexander's" head (the angel with the cross in the likeness of the former tsar); and ironic, in the sense that among Pushkin's first words in print was a glowing, Derzhavinian eulogy of the tsar's nobility in the wake of the victory over Napoleon, a eulogy that would be subsequently retracted in later versions of the poem and then thoroughly inverted in epigrams, where Alexander is described as being a coward in battle and his *bust* that of a two-faced harlequin.[206] Pushkin concludes his first stanza with the attention squarely on a comparison (note the comparative degree in *vyshe*) of the two "Alexanders."

Concealed in this comparison is the voice of Delvig, who, as Alekseev has pointed out, encouraged Pushkin to continue with his poetry writing when Kachenovsky, the new editor at *The Messenger of Europe,* rejected without commentary several poems the young poet had sent to the journal in spring 1816.[207] Pushkin had written Delvig a verse epistle ("Happy is he who from youthful years" [Blazhen, kto s iunykh let]), an earlier version of what became "To Delvig" (Del'vigu, 1817), in which, demoralized and bereft of inspiration, he considered abandoning poetry altogether. This version ended with the lines: "Dread posterity will not recall me, / And the unfortunate's grave [lit. coffin], in the desert gloomy, wild, / Will become overgrown with the creeping dodder of oblivion."[208] Alekseev then astutely surmises that Delvig's encouragement of his friend, including his own writing of two epistles to Pushkin, helped the proud and sensitive young poet through his crisis. The epistle that addressed specifically the rejection by Kachenovsky was the 1816 "What? An inhabitant of the proud Alps" (Kak? Zhitel' gordykh Al'p), which remained long unpublished. But the epistle that both showed Delvig's encouragement (and prescience) and entered directly into Derzhavinian-Pushkinian mythical space was the 1815 "Who like the swan of flowering Ausonia [Italy]" (Kto, kak lebed' tsvetushchei Avzonii). Thus the heart of Alekseev's massively docu-

206. *Pss,* II:323, III:137.

207. Alekseev, "Stikhotvorenie Pushkina," 169–76 (see n. 23, above).

208. *Pss,* I:422: «Потомство грозное не вспомнит обо мне, / И гроб несчастного, в пустыне мрачной, дикой, / Забвенья порастет ползущей повиликой.»

mented argument is that, as Pushkin wrote his "I have erected" he thought
back on his early dejection and on the lines about an overgrown and forgotten
grave, as well as on the friend who first saw his gift and nourished it when
others would not. "I have erected," becomes, in this reading, an ultimate con-
firmation of the path toward which Delvig first pointed his friend.

But Alekseev's position is, I would submit, only half correct. It neglects one
important aspect of Pushkin's personality—the anxiety and the psychic cost of
creation. The other career that most appealed to the Lyceum-period Pushkin
was that of soldier. Many times, both in the Lyceum years and afterward, Pushkin hints that he is ready to quit the sweet yet confining "languor" (*nega*) of his
poet's "cell" for the trim riding breeches, epaulettes, and tent life of the military man.[209] In Delvig's first epistle, which *predates* the Kachenovsky episode
and was, importantly, the first time Pushkin's name was cited in print without
disguise after the appearance of "Recollections," the speaker opens with the
image of a Horatian swan[210] and then proceeds through the remainder of the
poem to announce what such a majestic verbal creature *does not do*. The swan
of poetry does not hang the standards of the vanquished on city walls, nor does
he decorate the columns of his capital with the bows of enemy ships. Rather
he, a private soul, learns to sing of the world's beauty and to pass the flame of
inspiration on to others. In the second stanza especially, Alekseev has shown
that, in an earlier version of the poem, the allusion to this man of public action
and spectacle was to none other than Alexander I: "This one does not wax
philosophical in congresses" (*Tot v kongressakh ne mudrstvuet*)[211] could refer
only to the Congress of Vienna of 1814–15 and to Alexander, its principal Russian participant.[212] In the poem's concluding lines the swan is finally named:

> Pushkin! He cannot hide even in the forests:
> His lyre will give him away with its loud singing,
> And from the mortals the immortal one will be carried off
> By a triumphant Apollo to Olympus.[213]

209. See Alekseev, "Stikhotvorenie Pushkina," 179–80.

210. Horace describes his transformation into a swan, the inspiration for Derzhavin's
poem, in one of his most famous *Carmina* (II, 20).

211. In later versions it is: "That one does not wax philosophical in councils [*v sove-
takh*]" (cited Alekseev, "Stikhotvorenie Pushkina," 175; see Del'vig, *Polnoe sobranie stikhotvorenii*, 191 [see n. 28, above]).

212. "Stikhotvorenie Pushkina," 186.

213. «Пушкин! Он и в лесах не укроется; / Лира выдаст его громким пением, /

In the "monument" to his own career, Pushkin is not, or at least not only, returning to thank Delvig for his schoolboy encouragement, even more so because this more important epistle has nothing to do with Kachenovsky and everything to do with Delvig's response to Pushkin's "Recollections at Tsarskoe Selo." The swan that opens the poem is a decoy; it is not, despite the cover of "flowering Ausonia," primarily Horatian. Instead, its most immediate incarnation for the young Delvig and Pushkin would be Derzhavin (*his* "Lebed' "). Delvig, the well-wisher and pure soul, is, before Pushkin's eyes, transforming the Derzhavinian swan into a Pushkinian one. We know this for two reasons. First, the copy of "Recollections" that Pushkin gave to Derzhavin was changed: the concluding allusion to Zhukovsky, the "scald" singing in the camp of Russian warriors, was removed, to be replaced by a phrase more flattering to Pushkin's doting benefactor and mythopoetic initiator: "Like the bard of ancient times, the swan of Hellas."[214] And second, in his poem on the death of Derzhavin, which he addresses to Pushkin as the rightful heir to the tradition (the myth *confirmed*), Delvig uses the same marked phrase about Apollo carrying off the sacred poet to the immortals on Olympus.[215] Thus, to return finally to "I have erected," Pushkin would not raise again the juxtaposition of the two "Alexanders" without thinking of Delvig's epistle (here Alekseev is certainly right) and Derzhavin's swan, that other image of immortality used by his friend to help launch his career "under the wing" of the older poet. That Derzhavin's swan was very much on Pushkin's mind in these last years may be confirmed by a final collateral textual detail: in "The Fairy Tale of the Golden Cockerel" (1834), the poet's most autobiographically freighted folk stylization,[216] the wise man-astrologer-castrate (*mudrets-zvezdochet-skopets*) who willingly advises Tsar Dadon with the help of his magic statuette is be-

---

И от смертных восхитит бессмертного / Аполлон на Олимп торжествующий» (Del'vig, *Polnoe sobranie stikhotvorenii*, 191).

214. Vatsuro in *Sll*, 549: «Как древних лет певец, как лебедь стран Эллины.» Note in this connection how in the eighth chapter of *Eugene Onegin* Pushkin's speaker links the start of his poetic career with the sound of the swans in the park at Tsarskoe Selo: "В те дни в таинственных долинах, / Весной, при кликах лебединых, / Близ вод, сиявших в тишине, / Являться муза стала мне" (It was in those days in secret vales, / During the spring, to the calls of the swans, / Nearby the water, shimmering in silence, / That the muse first made her appearance to me) (*Pss*, V:142).

215. Del'vig, *Polnoe sobranie stikhotvorenii*, 254.

216. See discussion on pp. 115–17 ("Jakobson: Why the Statue Won't Come to Life, or Will It?").

trayed by the ruler when he reappears to claim his one wish, the maiden (*devitsa*). This suspiciously familiar astrologer is presented as looking "all like a grizzled swan" (*ves' kak lebed' posedelyi*) [217] right before he is struck down by Dadon. But the *other* bird, the one that continues to function even after the death of its swanlike master and that embodies anagrammatically not Derzhavin but Pushkin ("*petushok*" = *Pushk*in), comes back to get the last word.

Pushkin's poem is saturated with the dual perspective, the simultaneity, of Delvig's wish that his friend be true to his inner calling and of Pushkin's own desires, ones which he battled his entire creative life, for public *slava*. Both perspectives, however, have Derzhavin as their point of origin. By the time he writes "I have erected," Pushkin has come to terms with his persistent urge, first expressed explicitly in "Recollections," to test himself and to win glory on the field of battle. He writes Davydov in 1836, for example, that "I have not managed, to the thunder of cannon / And in the fire [of battle] / to gallop after you on a furious steed"; instead, he has had to resign himself to being "a rider on meek Pegasus," who has "worn till it's gone out of style / The [dress] uniform of old Parnassus."[218] Yet this resignation is tempered by the knowledge that monuments to public glory cannot hold or sustain the elusive essence of personal nobility. The words of Pushkin's official "knighting" into a poetic calling in "Recollections" veered too close to the monumental. What he wrote about Alexander and what he was given in the mythopoetic potential of the moment by Derzhavin, not a light but a heavy gift in the final analysis, had to be altered by the movement of history. Those words had not yet the "moving stasis" of a genuine Pushkin and thus could not be included in the *Verse* of 1826. Not only Horace,[219] but ultimately Alexander and even, as Pushkin

---

217. *Pss*, IV:362.

218. «Не удалось мне за тобою / При громе пушечном, в огне / Скакать на бешеном коне. / Наездник смирного Пегаса, / Носил я старого Парнаса / Из моды вышедший мундир» (*Pss*, III:331).

One wonders in this connection how much "linguistic destiny" Pushkin, who was ever sensitive to this sort of wordplay, saw in his own surname (from *pushka*, "cannon"). For more on the martial theme in Pushkin's poetry, early and late, see pp. 74–88 ("Bloom: The Critic as Romantic Poet").

219. Pushkin calls Horace an "immortal coward" (*bessmertnyi trus*) in "To V. L. Pushkin" (V. L. Pushkinu, 1817) (*Pss*, I:222). He is referring to the story, confirmed by Horace himself, that the Roman poet was at one time a military tribune who, during a conflict with the Philippians, ran from the field of battle. Cited Alekseev, "Stikhotvorenie Pushkina," 180.

came to think, Derzhavin had all lost their heads in moments of crisis. This is the pride of Pushkin's ultimate epistrophe: the public man Alexander's column is huge but it is fixed, a monument not only to the dead but of the dead; the poet's alexandrines, however, are both fixed (their "prosodic foundation") and continuously moving, alive, capable of releasing energy.

Therefore, in conclusion, I would say that Pushkin's "I have erected" is not only about the movement within simultaneity of the paschal message (from pride to humility, from triumphant entrance to betrayal, despair, crucifixion, and resurrection); it is also, at its deepest level, about the long and arduous battle in Pushkin's soul between his good angel (Delvig) and his father-nemesis (Derzhavin). In this reading, virtually every departure from Derzhavin is made from the "good angel's" by now otherworldly perspective. Derzhavin's assertion "So! All of me won't die" becomes Pushkin's answering negation "No, all of me won't die" (stanza 2), the undivided confidence of "so" shifting subtly yet unmistakably to the difficult, all-seeing, *conscious* choice of "no." Derzhavin's glory will continue to grow as long as the universe esteems the Slavic peoples (the *public* consciousness); Pushkin's glory, on the other hand, will exist as long as there is one genuine poet in the world (the *private* consciousness) (stanza 2). The linguistic "imperialism" that joins poetic fame with the implicit conquering of peoples (the historical trajectory of Catherine's era) is also significantly eroded by Pushkin's irony and ambiguity, first noted by Soloviev; considering the careful "editing" of Derzhavin's text so far, Pushkin cannot take this role of national poet seriously (stanza 3). Yes, Pushkin understands that inevitably his monument will be used and seen this way in the future, but, as opposed to Derzhavin, he does not take pride in this fact. Derzhavin's *slukh* of "fame" becomes on Pushkin's lips the *slukh* of mere "rumor" or "gossip."

Furthermore, whereas Derzhavin sees his chief accomplishments as daring to praise Felitsa in a jocular style, speaking simply and honestly about God, and telling the truth to tsars with a smile, Pushkin underscores three quite different virtues: the awakening in his readers of *goodness, freedom,* and *mercy* (stanza 4). Once again, Derzhavin, despite his candor and many public contretemps, always worked within the system and saw virtue in bonding with his century and its secular structures; Pushkin insists on those values that transcend a given government and tsar. Indeed, one might make two hypotheses about this triad of virtues. First, Pushkin's decision to underscore in this valedictory not the "new sounds" (*zvuki novye*) of his poetry, as he first wrote, but the "good feelings" (*chuvstva dobrye*) of the final version is a reflection of that "gift for life" he admired so much in those such as Delvig and Nashchokin and believed was incarnated in his own better self. This particular simultaneity of the good and the beautiful could not be captured, the 1836 Pushkin reasoned, in the single reference to the "new sounds" of his poetry (i.e., its purely *aesthetic* quality). And second, the famous phrase "And I called for mercy toward the fallen ones" (*I milost' k padshim prizyval*) refers not only to Pushkin's poetically recorded concern for his Decembrist friends, but also to the implicit message of *The Captain's Daughter,* where Pushkin rewrites history—including Derzhavin's participation—in a way that uniquely stresses *milost'* (mercy) and allows peasant and nobleman, unofficially, *privately,* to break down the barriers that have heretofore made them into implacable enemies.

But, as one might expect, Pushkin saves his most eloquent departure from Derzhavin for last. Here, whatever anxiety still lurks in the proud testimony of the earlier stanzas ("I could not be this, and so I became that") is transcended as the poet turns away from the world and enters mythic space. Derzhavin's closing statements are everywhere full of the *proud* knowledge, following Horace, that he has deserved his version of the Delphic bays:

> O Muse! Take pride in worthy merit,
> and disdain those who disdain you;[220]
> with an unconstrained and unhurried hand
> crown your brow with the dawn of immortality.[221]

Pushkin's last words are couched in the tones of *humility:*

> To the will of God, O Muse, be obedient,
> not fearing insult, not demanding a crown;

220. Ironically, Derzhavin's only significant departure from Horace in this final stanza reveals his own Achilles heel: by saying "and disdain those who disdain you" (*I prezrit kto tebia, sama tekh prezirai*), the poet is attempting, it seems, to forestall those "enviers" who will accuse him of achieving his laurels through flattery. As we know from elsewhere in Derzhavin's work, this was perhaps his greatest fear, one that was, considering his future reception, not unfounded. Thus the fully confident, proud, Horatian tone of the final lines contains its worm of doubt. Horace's conclusion to "Exegi monumentum" reads simply: "Sume superbiam / Quaesitam meritis et mihi Delphica / Lauro cinge uolens, Melpomene, comam."

221. «О муза! Возгордись заслугой справедливой, / И презрит кто тебя, сама тех презирай; / Непринужденною рукой неторопливой / Чело твое зарей бессмертия венчай.» (Derzhavin, *Stikhotvoreniia,* 233 [see n. 46, above]).

praise and slander accept with equanimity,
and do not contradict the fool.[222]

At the risk of sounding banal, this is truly a remarkable way for a proud poet to end, as startling in its move inward as the *nerukotvornyi* departure of the first stanza. On the one hand, Pushkin "undoes" Derzhavin by turning his proud sentiments inside out. In terms of the challenge first put to Pushkin in "Recollections," this can be seen as a kind of ultimate upstaging. But the poet does not announce this victory in anticipation of secular laurels (note the rejected *venets*). He is not getting outside Derzhavin's language in order to make room for himself in the Russian pantheon ("Fonvizin's Shade"); nor is he sparring with Delvig about Derzhavin's legacy and its possible contamination of "Recollections." Least of all is he reducing the greatest Russian poet before his time to a smiling corpse as he turns to new genres within a still open biography. No, this last Pushkin rises above and turns away from what Derzhavin, in Pushkin's understanding, relentlessly strove for. There is strength and, strangely enough, even the hint of pride in the three imperatives of acceptance. But this is the pride, at the end, of having chosen Delvig's inner beauty, a pride that is, miraculously, indistinguishable from Christian humility. Perhaps the single most important change in the poem, from its rough to fair copy versions, is the replacement of "*To your own calling* [*Prizvan'iu svoemu*], O Muse, be obedient" to "*To the will of God* [*Velen'iu bozhiiu*], O Muse, be obedient."[223] The good angel has wrestled with its nemesis and emerged, after many dark nights of the soul, with its most cherished values intact.

This study has set out to prove what is certainly a truism, although a truism very difficult to demonstrate because of the subtlety of Pushkin's language and the rather hermetic quality of his biography: the creative personality seeks out challenge and confrontation and, in the case of a great poet, leaves the traces of that confrontation in verbal structures that continue to release enormous energy long after the historical personage is gone. Speaking of the "anxieties" that drove Pushkin gives us a psychological mechanism, even one that can be made quite subtle in its psychoanalytic variants and taxonomies, but unfortu-

222. «Веленью божию, о муза, будь послушна, / Обиды не страшась, не требуя венца; / Хвалу и клевету приемли равнодушно, / И не оспоривай глупца» (*Pss*, III:340)

223. "Large 'Academy,'" III:1034.

nately it asserts a homology (the principle of likeness) when what is needed is a mechanism to record *difference* and to register energy in motion. Or rather, the source of the energy can even be identified, but it cannot be felt from outside its linguistic environment. Which is to say, in the end, it is one thing to assert that an originary stone guest stands at the threshold of Pushkin's creative life and quite another to imagine the sparks that fly when, shod in each genre's version of poetic feet, it actually comes for the challenger. The secret of Pushkin's power on our imagination is that it can never be fixed, like the Proteus myth that naturally attached to him: the personality that came to write "I have erected" is above all one concerned with the simultaneity of good and beautiful, personal and impersonal, history and myth, poetry and prose, secular and Christian immortality. Pushkin is, at least soon after the penning of "Recollections," forever "both/and" and never "either/or." That is why that particular poem, in its context, had to cast such a large shadow on the created life that followed. Its muse was legally married to a still living *komandor* and was not yet willing to betray him to a murderous, sweet-talking Guan. One of the last statements Pushkin made about Derzhavin was in his review article "M. E. Lobanov's Opinion about the Spirit of Literature, both Foreign and Domestic," published (unsigned) in 1836 in *The Contemporary:* "The name of the great Derzhavin is always pronounced with a feeling of bias, even superstition." [224] Those words, so simple, severe, and seemingly straightforward, resonate far beyond their local meaning. They are, in this instance, a kind of ur-example for the critic and interpreter, both a place to stop and a place to start again in that endless search for the Pushkin who wrote the encouraging words to Ishimova on the day he was fatally shot.

224. *Pss,* VII:278.

INDEX

INDEX